FRENCH GRAMMAR

FRENCH GRAMMAR

Catherine Rita Martin, Ph. D.

ASSISTANT PROFESSOR OF FRENCH
FORDHAM UNIVERSITY

A COLLEGE COURSE GUIDE

Doubleday & Company, Inc.
GARDEN CITY, NEW YORK

TO

N. D.

Library of Congress Catalog Card Number 66-18065

Printed in the United States of America
First Edition

CONTENTS

Chapter Five

Chapter Six

Chapter Seven

CHAPTER EIGHT

CHAPTER NINE

CHAPTER TEN

CHAPTER ELEVEN

CHAPTER TWELVE

CHAPTER SIXTEEN

CHAPTER SEVENTEEN

Chapter Eighteen

Chapter Nineteen

Chapter Twenty

FRENCH PRONUNCIATION GUIDE

Final consonants in French are usually silent, with the exception of *c, r, f, l* (the consonants of the English word "careful").

The sound of *ay* (No. 8, below) and of *oh* (No. 24) must be made very staccato so as to avoid the vowel glide (ay-ee, etc.) of the English. Actually, the word "day" in English contains two vowel sounds, *ay* + *ee*; the word "go" contains *oh* + *oo*. We can notice this if we simply prolong the spoken words; we shall then find "day" gliding into the sound of *ee*, and "go" ending in *oo*. *This must not happen in the French sounds.* All we must hear are the first parts *ay* (no *ee*) and *oh* (no *oo*). The nasal sounds (Nos. 35–38) occur whenever {an, en, in, on, un / am, em, im, om, um} are followed by a consonant or are final. There is no nasal sound where the *n* or *m* is double or is followed by a vowel.

Each syllable of the French word is clearly pronounced; the final syllable gets the oral stress. In groups of words the last syllable of the word before the comma or semicolon rises in pitch and is stressed. The final word at the end of a declarative sentence falls.

No. of Sound	*Phonetic Symbol*	*French Spelling*	*English Approximation*	*Example French Word*
1.	[a]	a; à	a (imitate the sounds of a in madame)	madame [madam]; voilà [vwala]
2.	[ɑ]	â; -as	ah (father)	gâteau [gɑ̃to]; bas [bɑ̃]
3.	[b]	b, bb	b (bay)	bal [bal]; abbé [abe]
4.	[s]	c (before e, i); ss; ç	ss (guess)	ce [sə], ici [isi]; frisson [frisɔ̃]; garçon [garsɔ̃]
5.	[k]	c (before a, o, u); qu	k (kettle)	carte [kart], tricot [triko], cuve [kyv]; quelle [kɛl]
6.	[ʃ]	ch	sh (shine)	chat [ʃa]
7.	[d]	d	d (dog)	de [də]
8.	[e]	é; -ez; infinitive -er; -ai	ay (late)	chassé [ʃase]; chassez [ʃase]; chasser [ʃase]; chasserai [ʃasre]

9.	[ɛ]	è; ê; -ai-; -ei-; -ais	eh (elf)	lève [lɛv]; tête [tɛːt]; chaise [ʃɛːz]; treize [trɛːz]; chasserais [ʃasrɛ]
10.	[ə]	e	ʼ (silent); uh (the)	de la [dla]; le [lə]
11.	[ø]	-eu	(round lips as if to whistle; say "ay")	deux [dø]
12.	[œ]	-eu-; -œu-	(round lips as if to whistle; say "eh")	leur [lœːr]; sœur [sœːr]
13.	[f]	f, ff	f (fairy)	fête [fɛːt]; difficile [difisil]
14.	[ʒ]	g (before e, i); j	zh (treasure)	rouge [ruːʒ], régime [reʒim]; j'ai [ʒe]
15.	[g]	g (before a, o, u); gue; gui	g (game)	garçon [garsɔ̃], gomme [gɔm], aigu [egy]; guerre [gɛːr]; guide [gid]
16.	[ɲ]	gn	ny (canyon)	campagne [kɑ̃paɲ]
17.		h	(silent)	cathédrale [katedral]
18.	[i]	i; î; -y-	ee (seem)	il [il]; île [il]; Pyrénées [pirene]
19.	[l]	l	l (Ellen)	balle [bal]
20.	[j]	(i)*ll*; i + vowel	y (yet)	fille [fiːj]; étudier [etydje], nation [nasjɔ̃], reliure [rəljyːr]
21.	[m]	m, mm	m (meet)	mère [mɛːr]; femme [fam]
22.	[n]	n, nn	n (nine)	ne [nə]; mienne [mjɛn]
23.	[ɔ]	o	uh (rub)	robe [rɔb]
24.	[o]	ô; -os; au; eau	oh (rose)	hôte [oːt]; dos [do]; jaune [ʒoːn]; gâteau [gɑto]
25.	[wa]	oi	wah (want)	voilà [vwala]
26.	[u]	ou	oo (soon)	cou [ku]
27.	[w]	ou + vowel	w (was)	ouate [wat]; oui [wi]
28.	[p]	p, pp	p (pipe)	père [pɛːr]; appeler [aple]
29.	[r]	r, rr	r (vibration in throat as if to gargle)	rouge [ruːʒ]; terre [tɛːr]

30.	[z]	-s-; z	z (dozen)	rose [roːz]; douze [duz]
31.	[t]	t, tt	t (tip of tongue against back of upper teeth)	bête [bɛːt]; alouette [alwɛt]
32.	[y]	u	(round lips as if to whistle; say "ee")	rue [ry]
33.	[ɥ]	u + vowel	No. 32 shortened	cacahuète [kakaɥɛt]; huile [ɥil]
34.	[v]	v; w	v (avid)	vie [vi]; wagon [vagɔ̃]
35.	[ɑ̃]	an, am; en, em + consonant, or final	ah (nasalized)	enfant [ɑ̃fɑ̃]; ample [ɑ̃ːpl]; embêtant [ɑ̃bɛtɑ̃]
36.	[ɛ̃]	in, im; ain, aim; ein, eim; -ien + consonant, or final	eh (nasalized, with lips in position as if to smile)	cinq [sɛ̃k], important [ɛ̃portɑ̃]; nain [nɛ̃], faim [fɛ̃]; frein [frɛ̃]; essaim [ɛsɛ̃]; bien [bjɛ̃]
37.	[ɔ̃]	on, om + consonant, or final	oh (nasalized)	bonbon [bɔ̃bɔ̃]; bombe [bɔ̃ːb]
38.	[œ̃]	un, um + consonant, or final	the sound of u in "fur" nasalized	un [œ̃]; parfum [parfœ̃]

FRENCH GRAMMAR

CHAPTER ONE

The Definite Article: ***Forms of the Definite Article; Contractions of the Definite Article; Uses of the Definite Article; Omission of the Definite Article***
The Indefinite Article: ***Forms of the Indefinite Article; Uses of the Indefinite Article; Omission of the Indefinite Article***
Prepositions with Place Names: ***To, At, In, From***

LA VIE UNIVERSITAIRE

HENRI – Bonjour, Paul! Comment vont LES COURS?

PAUL – Pas trop mal, Henri. J'ai LA CLASSE tous les jours, sauf LE JEUDI.

HENRI – En quoi te spécialises-tu?

PAUL – EN FRANÇAIS.

HENRI – Naturellement, puisque tu parles FRANÇAIS depuis ta naissance.

PAUL – Et toi, Henri?

HENRI – EN MATHÉMATIQUES. Je veux être INGÉNIEUR.

PAUL – Qu'est-ce que tu as LE LUNDI? Voyons si nous avons les mêmes classes!

HENRI – Eh bien, j'ai LA GÉOMÉTRIE à dix heures . . .

PAUL – Non, Henri . . . Je pensais AUX COURS OBLIGATOIRES. Tu parles DES COURS FACULTATIFS.

UNIVERSITY LIFE

HENRY – Hello, Paul! How are the courses?

PAUL – Not so bad, Henry. I have class every day except Thursdays.

HENRY – What are you majoring in?

PAUL – In French.

HENRY – Naturally, since you speak French from birth.

PAUL – And you, Henry?

HENRY – In mathematics. I want to be an engineer.

PAUL – What do you have on Mondays? Let's see if we have the same classes!

HENRY – Well, I have geometry at ten o'clock . . .

PAUL – No, Henry . . . I was thinking of the required courses. You're talking about elective courses.

HENRI – Ah, oui. C'est juste! J'ai L'ANGLAIS à une heure avec LE PROFESSEUR BEDELL et L'HISTOIRE EUROPÉENNE à trois heures avec LE PROFESSEUR DUVAL.

HENRY – Oh yes. That's right! I have English at one with Professor Bedell and European history at three with Professor Duval.

PAUL – Voyons. Pour l'histoire nous serons ensemble, mais pour l'anglais, non. J'ai LE COURS de M. Mark, CHEF DU DÉPARTEMENT D'ANGLAIS.

PAUL – Let's see. We'll be together for history, but English, no. I have the course with Mr. Mark, the head of the English Department.

HENRI – Qu'est-ce que tu fais maintenant?

HENRY – What are you doing now?

PAUL – Je reviens DU BUREAU DU SECRÉTARIAT et je vais AU MAGASIN, ou plutôt À LA LIBRAIRIE me renseigner sur LES LIVRES qu'il faudra.

PAUL – I'm coming from the registrar's office and I'm going to the store, or rather to the bookstore to find out about the books I'll need.

HENRI – Je t'accompagne alors jusqu'à LA PAPETERIE. Il me faut DU PAPIER. J'ai L'INTENTION de taper mes notes ce semestre. C'est combien LA RAME? Tu as une idée?

HENRY – I'll go with you then to the stationery store. I need some paper. I intend to type my notes this term. How much a ream is it? Do you have any idea?

PAUL – Un dollar cinquante LA RAME, je crois.

PAUL – A dollar fifty a ream, I think.

HENRI – C'est bien. J'ai juste deux dollars dans LA POCHE.

HENRY – That's all right. I have just two dollars in my pocket.

PAUL – Est-ce que tu as remarqué L'ATMOSPHÈRE internationale DU TERRAIN UNIVERSITAIRE cette année?

PAUL – Have you noticed the international atmosphere of the campus this year?

HENRI – Bien sûr, Paul. Il y a dans ma CLASSE D'ALGÈBRE DES ÉTUDIANTS JAPONNAIS, ALLEMANDS, RUSSES et deux garçons DU MEXIQUE.

HENRY – Sure thing, Paul. In my algebra class there are Japanese, German, and Russian students and two boys from Mexico.

PAUL – Et LA FRANCE est très bien représentée dans LA CLASSE DE LITTÉRATURE. Qui sait? Peut-être que nous pourrons aller un jour EN FRANCE, EN ALLEMAGNE, ou même AU CANADA . . .

PAUL – And France is very well represented in the literature class. Who knows? Maybe someday we can go to France, Germany, or even Canada. . . .

HENRI – Ah, oui. Espérons! . . . Moi, j'ai faim. Si nous prenions UNE TASSE de café?

PAUL – C'est une bonne idée! Il paraît que LA VIE UNIVERSITAIRE va être tres agréable ce semestre, n'est-ce pas?

HENRY – Oh yes. Let's hope so . . . ! I'm hungry! Suppose we have a cup of coffee?

PAUL – That's a good idea! It seems that university life is going to be very pleasant this term, doesn't it?

I. THE DEFINITE ARTICLE

We must remember two things about nouns in French:

1. They are all either masculine or feminine (see Chapter II).
2. They are almost always preceded by an article:
   - the (definite article),
   - a or an (indefinite article), or
   - some or any (partitive article)

A. Forms of the Definite Article

BEFORE A MASCULINE SINGULAR NOUN	BEFORE A FEMININE SINGULAR NOUN	BEFORE ANY SINGULAR NOUN BEGINNING WITH A VOWEL OR "H" MUTE
LE	**LA**	**L'**

BEFORE ALL PLURAL NOUNS

LES

B. Contractions of the Definite Article

When we use the preposition *à* (*to, at,* and sometimes *in*) or *de* (*of, from*) before the definite article, care must be taken to make the following contractions:

à + le = au	**de + le = du**
à + les = aux	**de + les = des**

EXAMPLES:

au magasin	du bureau
aux magasins	des bureaux

However, the forms *à la, à l', de la, de l'* remain unchanged.

EXAMPLES:

à la librairie	de la librairie
à l'atmosphère	de l'atmosphère
à l'histoire	de l'histoire

Exercise 1

Fill in the proper contraction of the preposition *à* or *de* and the definite article.

1. (to the store) _____ magasin
2. (to the course) _____ cours
3. (at the bookstore) _____ librairie
4. (to the stationery) _____ papeterie
5. (to the engineer) _____ ingénieur
6. (to the history) _____ histoire
7. (to the boys) _____ garçons
8. (to the classes) _____ classes
9. (to the students) _____ étudiants
10. (to the campus) _____ terrain universitaire
11. (to the class) _____ classe
12. (at the office) _____ bureau
13. (of the professor or the professor's) _____ professeur
14. (from the office) _____ bureau
15. (from the stationery) _____ papeterie
16. (of the class) _____ classe
17. (of the student or the student's) _____ étudiant
18 (from the atmosphere) _____ atmosphère
19. (of the history) _____ histoire
20. (of the books) _____ livres
21. (of the classes) _____ classes
22. (of the students or the students') _____ étudiants
23. (from the store) _____ magasin
24. (from the life) _____ vie

C. Uses of the Definite Article

1. As in English, whenever the word "the" is used before a noun:

Je vais à *la* librairie. (I am going to the bookstore.)

2. Before anything that is named, unless "a" or "some" is expressed or understood:

J'ai *la géometrie* à dix heures, *le français* à une heure et *l'anglais* à trois heures. (I have geometry at ten o'clock, French at one, and English at three.)

3. Whenever a noun represents a classification (a usage that can always be recognized if the thought "in general" fits after the noun):

Il paraît que *la vie universitaire* va être très agréable. (It seems that college life is going to be very pleasant.)

4. Before days of the week, especially when the word "on" is expressed or understood ("on" is translated here by the definite article):

Qu'est-ce que tu as *le lundi*? (What do you have on Mondays?)

5. Before geographical names of countries, continents, rivers, mountains, oceans, etc. (unless as explained later under Sections IIIA, IIIB, below):

La France est très bien représentée. (France is very well represented.)

6. To translate the English "a" in expressing weights and measures:
   C'est combien *la rame*? (How much a ream is it?)
7. Before a title (such as Doctor, Captain, Professor, etc.) when we are talking *of* the person, never when we are talking *to* the person.
   J'ai l'anglais à dix heures avec *le professeur Duval.* (I have English at ten with Professor Duval.)

BUT: Not with the words Monsieur, Madame, Mademoiselle.

8. With parts of the body and articles of clothing where the English uses the possessive (my, his, her, your, our, their, etc.):
   Cet étudiant a toujours un livre à *la main.* (That student always has a book in his hand.)
   J'ai trois dollars dan *la poche.* (I have three dollars in my pocket.)

Use **LE, LA, L', LES** for:

1. "the"
2. names of things
3. classifications ("in general")
4. days of the week
5. geographical names
6. weights and measures
7. titles
8. parts of the body, articles of clothing

Exercise 2

Translate the English into French, supplying the proper definite article:

1. A quelle heure (at what time) avez-vous *French on Mondays*?
2. J'ai le français à une heure le lundi et à dix heures *on Thursdays,* avec *Professor Duval.*
3. Est-ce que *the course* est difficile?
4. Non, parce que (because) je me spécialise en français. Ce sont *the required courses,* comme (like) *history,* que je trouve difficiles.
5. *Elective courses* sont toujours faciles.
6. Avez-vous remarqué tous les étudiants étrangers (foreign) que nous avons cette année? Presque (almost) tous les pays sont représentés: *France, Germany, Canada . . .*

7. Voulez-vous m'accompagner jusqu' *to the stationery store*? Il me faut du papier.
8. C'est combien *a ream*?
9. Un dollar cinquante la rame, je crois. Si vous n'avez pas l'argent *in your pocket*, voici deux dollars.
10. Merci, j'ai l'argent. Allons d'abord (Let's go first) *to the bookstore.*

D. Omission of the Definite Article

1. After the prepositions *en* and *de*, referring to languages and in certain phrases when a noun serves as an adjective:

   En quoi te spécialises-tu? *En français.* (What are you majoring in? In French.)

   Il y a dans ma *classe de littérature* ... (There are in my literature class ...)

2. In parenthetical apposition:

   J'ai le cours de *M. Mark, chef* du département d'anglais. (I have the course with Mr. Mark, the head of the English Department.)

3. After the verb *parler* with a language:

   ... puisque *tu parles français* ... (... since you speak French ...)

BUT: The article is kept if another word comes in between *parler* and the language:

   Elle parle couramment le russe. (She speaks Russian fluently.)

4. In formal listings:

   Presque toutes les nationalités sont représentées: Français, Mexicains, Portugais, Japonais ... (Almost all nationalities are represented: French, Mexicans, Portuguese, Japanese ...)

> Omit **LE, LA, L', LES:**
> 1. after *de* ____, *en* ____ in certain phrases
> 2. in apposition
> 3. with a language after *parler*
> 4. in long lists

Exercise 3

Translate the English into French.

1. Vous vous spécialisez *in mathematics*, n'est-ce pas?
2. Moi, je me spécialise *in French.*

3. Mais vous parlez *French* comme un Français.
4. En bien, j'étudie *French* depuis cinq ans.
5. Nous avons *in class* des étudiants de tous les pays: *Germans, Italians, Spaniards . . .*

II. THE INDEFINITE ARTICLE

A. Forms of the Indefinite Article (*a, an*)

BEFORE A MASCULINE SINGULAR NOUN	BEFORE A FEMININE SINGULAR NOUN	BEFORE ALL PLURAL NOUNS
UN	**UNE**	**DES**

B. Uses of the Indefinite Article

The indefinite article is generally used as in English (with the exception of weights and measures, which take the definite article):

C'est un cours facultatif. (That is an elective course.)
Tu as une idée. (You have an idea.)
C'est combien la rame? (How much is it a ream?)

Des serves as the plural of *un* and *une.*

Il y a des étudiants portugais. (There are Portuguese students.)

C. Omission of the Indefinite Article

Un and *une* are omitted when the noun, after the verb *être* (to be), shows nationality, religion, profession (this noun usually will answer the question "what?"):

Je veux être ingénieur. (I want to be an engineer.)

BUT: If this noun is modified, *un* or *une* is not omitted:

M. Duval est un interprète très expérimenté. (Mr. Duval is a very experienced interpreter.)

Un and *une* are omitted before a noun in parenthetical apposition:

La phonétique, cours qui exige beaucoup de travail au laboratoire, est très populaire. (Phonetics, a course that demands a lot of work in the laboratory, is very popular.)

> Use: **UN** and **UNE** for English "a."
> Omit: 1. after *être*, before profession, nationality, religion
> 2. in apposition

Exercise 4

Translate the English into French, using or omitting the appropriate indefinite articles:

1. Est-ce que la géométrie est *a required course or an elective course*?
2. La géometrie est *an elective course* et l'algèbre aussi. La géométrie et l'algèbre sont *elective courses.*
3. Voulez-vous être *an engineer*? Oui, et Paul veut être *an interpreter*.
4. M. Dutour, *a professor in the French department,* est *an experienced interpreter*.
5. Est-ce qu'il est *a Frenchman*? Oui, c'est *a Frenchman who speaks Russian and German.*

III. PREPOSITIONS WITH PLACE NAMES

A. TO, AT, IN Are Translated by:

EN before *feminine* countries and continents
AU before *masculine* countries and continents
DANS before any modified country or continent
À before cities

EXAMPLES:

en France, *en* Espagne, *en* Irlande, *en* Asie, *en* Europe, *en* Afrique, *en* Chine
au Portugal, *au* Mexique, *au* Japon, *au* Canada, *au* Brésil, *aux* États-Unis (plural)
dans la France méridionale (Southern), *dans* l'Amerique du Sud
à Paris, *à* Marseille, *à* Londres, *à* Rome, *à* Berlin, *à* Moscou

B. FROM Is Translated by:

DE before *feminine* countries, continents, cities
DU before *masculine* countries
DES is plural

EXAMPLES:

de France, *d'*Espagne, *d'*Irlande, *de* Chine, *d'*Asie, *d'*Europe, *d'*Afrique, *de* Paris
du Portugal, *du* Mexique, *du* Japon, *du* Canada, *du* Brésil
des États-Unis

Exercise 5

Translate the English into French:

1. Nous espérons aller un jour *to France, to Spain, to Portugal,* and *to South America.*
2. Il y a tant de choses à voir *in France. In Paris* il y a la cathédrale de Notre-Dame et la Tour Eiffel; *in Southern France,* il y a les ruines romaines.
3. Ensuite (Then) *to Rome, Berlin, Moscow, London* et finalement de retour (back) *to the United States.*
4. Avez-vous jamais voyagé (Have you ever traveled) *in Asia*? Oui, j'ai voyagé *in Japan and China.*
5. Nous avons des étudiants *from Mexico, from Brazil, from Canada, and from England.*

Review Exercise

Words you will need in the translation of the sentences below:

ancient, *ancien, ancienne* (fem.)
author, *l'auteur*
about, *sur*
is writing, *écrit*
book, *le livre*
well known, *bien connu*
fascinating, *passionnant, fascinant*
quite a few, *pas mal de*
busy, *affairé, occupé*
people, *les gens*
I think, *je crois*
they intend to return, *ils ont l'intention de retourner*
this year, *cette année*
must be, *doivent être*

Translate:

1. University life is very pleasant this year.
2. I have five required courses and two elective courses: one is the European history class with Professor Roberts and the other is ancient history with Mr. Anderson.
3. I am majoring in history. We have English literature class on Tuesdays and Thursdays.
4. The professor, a well-known author, is writing a book about Shakespeare.
5. Professors are very busy people, I think.
6. Are you (fam.) majoring in English?
7. No, in mathematics. I want to be an engineer.
8. In our algebra class we have quite a few boys from France, Germany, and England, two from Japan, and one from South America.
9. Three are going to Canada this year. They intend to return to Europe.
10. Geometry and algebra must be difficult. No. They are fascinating.

CHAPTER TWO

The Noun: *Gender of Nouns; Plural of Nouns*

The Partitive: *The Full Partitive; The Partitive Expressed by DE; The Partitive Expressed by EN*

À LA LIBRAIRIE	AT THE BOOKSTORE
PAUL–Vous N'AVEZ PLUS D'EXEMPLAIRES neufs de cette anthologie?	PAUL – Don't you have any more new copies of this anthology?
LE LIBRAIRE – Non, je regrette, NOUS N'AVONS QUE DES EXEMPLAIRES d'occasion.	THE BOOKSELLER – No, I'm sorry, we have only used copies.
PAUL – Sont-ils en bonne condition? Combien EN avez-vous?	PAUL – Are they in good condition? How many do you have?
LE LIBRAIRE – Il nous EN reste deux . . . Les voici.	THE BOOKSELLER – We have two left . . . Here they are.
PAUL – Bon, je prends celui-ci. C'est combien?	PAUL – All right, I'll take this one. How much is it?
LE LIBRAIRE – Trois dollars cinquante. D'AUTRES LIVRES, monsieur?	THE BOOKSELLER – Three fifty. Any other books, sir?
PAUL – Non, merci, mais il me faut DU PAPIER CARBONE et UNE RAME DE PAPIER pour machine à écrire.	PAUL – No, thank you, but I need some carbon paper and a ream of typing paper.
LE LIBRAIRE – Nous avons DU TRÈS BON PAPIER à deux dollars la rame.	THE BOOKSELLER–We have some very good paper at two dollars a ream.
PAUL – Est-ce que vous EN avez de moins cher?	PAUL – Do you have any less expensive?
LE LIBRAIRE – EN voici à un dollar cinquante.	THE BOOKSELLER – Here is some at a dollar fifty.
PAUL – Ça fera l'affaire. Et avec ça, je voudrais avoir DES CHEMISES, DES TROMBONES et DE L'ENCRE.	PAUL – That will do. And with that, I'd like to get some folders, some paper clips, and some ink.
LE LIBRAIRE – COMBIEN DE CHEMISES, monsieur?	THE BOOKSELLER – How many folders, sir?

PAUL – Je crois que j'ai ASSEZ DE PAPIER CARBONE . . . Oh, pardon. UNE DOUZAINE DE CHEMISES, s'il vous plaît. Et c'est tout!

PAUL – I think I have enough carbon paper . . . Oh, I'm sorry. A dozen folders, please. And that's all!

I. THE NOUN

A. Gender of Nouns

Since every noun in French is either masculine or feminine, whether it stands for an animate or inanimate object, it is indispensable to learn the gender of each noun. Upon this knowledge will depend the use of the proper article and, as we shall see later, the agreement of adjectives and in many cases past participles.

Some very general suggestions to help in recognition of the gender of nouns are:

1. Words ending in a consonant are usually masculine; words ending in *e* or *é* are most often feminine. Although this is not intended as a rule, it will prove helpful.
2. Specific endings that do indicate gender are the following:

MASCULINE	FEMININE
-isme	*-tion*
-age	*-eur* (when ending an abstract noun)
-eau	

3. With regard to living beings, the gender usually associated with the being will often determine whether the noun is masculine or feminine: *le dentiste, la téléphoniste* (the telephone operator).
4. Compound nouns usually have the gender of the first noun: *le chou-fleur* (the cauliflower). Compound nouns made up of a verb and a noun are masculine: *le coupe-papier* (the paper cutter).

Exercise 1

Before each of the following nouns indicate the gender by giving the definite article; where the article is *l'*, add *m* or *f* after the noun:

1. _____ condition: condition
2. _____ étalage: display
3. _____ carnet: small notebook
4. _____ secrétaire: secretary
5. _____ gouvernement: government
6. _____ comptoir: counter
7. _____ grammaire: grammar
8. _____ crayon: pencil
9. _____ ruban: ribbon
10. _____ vitrine: show window
11. _____ journal: newspaper
12. _____ monnaie: change (money)
13. _____ argent: money
14. _____ craie: chalk
15. _____ chef-d'œuvre: masterpiece

16. _____ biographie: biography
17. _____ gomme: eraser
18. _____ employé: clerk
19. _____ reliure: binding
20. _____ roman: novel
21. _____ roman policier: detective story
22. _____ poésie: poetry
23. _____ cahier: notebook
24. _____ feuille: sheet
25. _____ taille-crayon: pencil sharpener (*taille*, a form of the verb *tailler*, to sharpen)
26. _____ revue: magazine
27. _____ écriteau: sign

B. Plural of Nouns

1. Generally, to form the plural of a noun, -*s* is added to the singular. If the singular already ends in -*s*, -*x*, or -*z*, the plural does not change:

l'anthologie, les anthologies
la fois (time), les fois
le choix (choice), les choix
le nez (nose), les nez

2. The following noun endings take a special plural:

(a) -*au* or -*eu* add -*x* in the plural:

l'écriteau (sign), les écriteaux
le feu (fire), les feux

Some nouns that end in -*ou* add -*x*: les bijoux (jewels), les joujoux, (toys), les choux (cabbages), les genoux (knees).

(b) -*al* becomes -*aux*:

le journal, les journaux

Some nouns that end in -*ail* also change to -*aux*:

le travail (work), les travaux
le vitrail (stained-glass window), les vitraux
le corail (coral), les coraux
l'émail (enamel), les émaux

3. Some nouns have completely irregular plurals:

l'œil (eye), les yeux
le ciel (sky), les cieux
monsieur, messieurs
madame, mesdames
mademoiselle, mesdemoiselles

4. Compound nouns must be analyzed because they pluralize according to the sense. A compound noun made up of:

(a) noun and noun, or noun and adjective—pluralizes in both

parts: les choux-fleurs (cauliflowers); les grands-pères (grandfathers)

(b) verb and noun — remains invariable: les coupe-papier (paper cutters)

(c) noun and prepositional phrase — pluralizes the first noun: les chefs-d'oeuvre (masterpieces); les timbres-poste (postage stamps), because "de la poste" is understood

Exercise 2

Give the plural of the following nouns:

1. le héros (hero)
2. le gaz (gas)
3. le hors-d'œuvre (the appetizer)
4. le coupe-papier (paper cutter)
5. le gâteau (cake)
6. le marteau (hammer)
7. le clou (nail)
8. le taille-crayon (pencil sharpener)
9. le chou-fleur (cauliflower)
10. le beau-père (father-in-law)
11. l'arc-en-ciel (rainbow)
12. l'œil (eye)

II. THE PARTITIVE

A. The Full Partitive

DU, DE LA, DE L', DES express "some" or "any" whether expressed or understood in English:

du papier carbone
de la craie
de l'encre
des chemises

If a noun in English indicates a whole classification ("all") or if the words "in general" can be understood after it, the definite article is used. If the words "some" or "any" can be understood before it, the partitive is used:

Les anthologies sont *des* livres utiles. (Anthologies are useful books.)
Here "anthologies" are taken "in general," but they are only "some" of the useful books.

Exercise 3

Express the idea of "some" or "any" before the following nouns:

1. carbon paper
2. poetry
3. novels
4. chalk
5. used copies
6. notebooks
7. money
8. change
9. expensive pens
10. interesting stories

Translate the following:

1. some folders
2. some paper clips
3. some typing paper
4. any copies
5. any ink
6. any prose
7. some blue ink
8. some paperbound books
9. some ribbon
10. some change

B. The Partitive Expressed by DE

The partitive expressed by only *de* is used as follows:

1. After a negation:

   Vous n'avez plus d'exemplaires neufs? (Don't you have any more new copies?)

   The full partitive is used after *ne . . . que,* which is not a negation but a limitation:

   Nous n'avons que des exemplaires neufs. (We have only new copies.)

   The full partitive is also used if the noun is not negated:

   Je ne recommande pas *des* anthologies pour que vous évitiez la lecture des textes originaux. (I don't recommend anthologies so that you may avoid reading the original texts.)

   Here the idea "anthologies" is not being negated, because the implication is that they are recommended. What is not recommended is the avoidance of reading the original texts.

2. Where an adjective precedes the noun, especially in the plural:

   D'autres livres?

BUT: du très bon papier

3. In the following expressions of quantity, plus a noun:

assez de (enough)	peu de (little)
beaucoup de (much, many)	tant de (as much, many)
	une douzaine de (a dozen)
combien de (how much, many)	une bouteille de (a bottle)
	pas mal de (quite a few, many)

EXAMPLES:

combien de chemises (how many folders)
assez de papier carbone (enough carbon paper)
une douzaine de chemises (a dozen folders)

BUT: Two expressions of quantity take the full partitive: *bien du (bien de la, bien de l', bien des* [a lot of]), *la plupart du (de la, de l', des* [most of]):

J'ai bien de la peine à trouver tous mes livres car la plupart des étudiants sont allés à la librairie avant moi. (I have a lot of trouble finding all my books, because most of the students have gone to the bookstore before me.)

4. Many idiomatic expressions of which the preposition *de* is a part do not require the full partitive:

   avoir besoin de
   avoir envie de

   Also, the words *quelquechose* (something), *rien* (nothing), *quelqu'un* (somebody) take *de* before an adjective:

   quelquechose de cher (expensive)
   rien de nouveau (new)
   quelqu'un d'important

EXERCISE 4

NOTE: Adjectives such as *beau* (beautiful, fine), *vieux* (old), *bon* (good), *grand* (big), *petit* (small), *long* (long), *jeune* (young) precede the noun. Adjectives pluralize the same as nouns.

How would you say?

1. no copies
2. no more carbon paper
3. a dozen folders
4. a lot of paper clips
5. some good pens
6. any old novels
7. (some) beautiful displays
8. enough change
9. some young clerks
10. most of the newspapers
11. many copies (translate two ways)
12. something good to read (*à lire*, to read)

C. The Partitive Expressed by EN

The pronoun EN is used whenever the noun is not expressed in the partitive construction. *En*, therefore, will mean "some, any, some of it, some of them, of it, of them, any of it, any of them." Care must be taken always to use *en* with the numbers and with such expressions as *beaucoup, peu*, and other expressions of quantity when the noun is not used:

Combien en avez-vous? (How much [How many] have you?)
Nous en avons deux. (We have two of them.)

NOTE: *En* can also be used adverbially to indicate "place from which," since it replaces the preposition *de* (which also means "from") plus a noun:

Êtes-vous allé à la librairie? (Did you go to the bookstore?)

Oui, j'*en* reviens. (I'm coming back *from it.*)

Exercise 5

Complete the following expressions with the use of *en*:

1. Avez-vous des chemises? Oui, j'_____ ai.
2. Avez vous assez de trombones? Oui, _____ assez.
3. Combien de pages ce livre a-t-il? Il _____ beaucoup.
4. Est-ce que nous avons besoin d'un bon vocabulaire? Oui, _____ besoin.
5. Est-ce que ce libraire vend (sells) des livres d'occasion? Non, il _____ pas.

Review Exercise

Complete the following sentences in French:

Le professeur m'a demandé (asked) aujourd'hui: "De quel genre [gender] sont les mots *journal, gâteau, taille-crayons, reliure* et *chef-d'œuvre,* et quel en est le pluriel?" J'ai répondu (answered) correctement à la question. J'ai dit (said): "_____ journal, _____ gâteau, _____ taille-crayons, _____ reliure et _____ chef-d'œuvre. Le pluriel de *journal* es _____, et les autres pluriels sont _____, _____, _____ et _____".

Après la classe de français, je suis allé (went) à la librairie. J'ai dit à mon ami: "*I need something important!*" Il me fallait (I needed) *typing paper, carbon paper, and folders*. En réalité, j'avais (I had) *enough carbon paper*. Je voulais acheter (I wanted to buy) *an anthology of French poetry* car j'aime (I like) beaucoup *poetry*. Le libraire n'avait que *used copies*. Il m'a dit que c'étaient *very fine books*. Le libraire m'a demandé: "*How much typing paper* désirez-vous?" J'ai répondu: "A *ream of paper*, s'il vous plaît!" Ensuite (then) j'ai acheté *some paperbound books, magazines* et *notebooks*. Je n'ai pas *any money* pour *expensive books*.

CHAPTER THREE

The Present Indicative: ***Formation of the Present Tense; Translation of the Present Tense***
The Negative
The Interrogative
The Negative Interrogative
The Imperative
The Present Tense of Orthographic-Changing Verbs of the First Conjugation
The Present Tense of Irregular Verbs

AU RESTAURANT	AT THE RESTAURANT
MME DULAC – Moi, JE PRENDS la bouillabaisse . . .	MRS. DULAC – I'll take the bouillabaisse . . .
MME LE BRUN – Et moi, JE CHOISIS la soupe à l'oignon.	MRS. LE BRUN – And I'll choose the onion soup.
MME DULAC – Bon, J'APPELLE le garçon . . . Garçon!	MRS. DULAC – All right, I'll call the waiter . . . Waiter!
LE GARÇON – Oui, mesdames, VOUS DÉSIREZ . . . ?	WAITER – Yes, ladies, you wish . . . ?
MME DULAC – APPORTEZ-NOUS la soupe à l'oignon et la bouillabaisse, s'il vous plaît.	MRS. DULAC – Bring us the onion soup and the bouillabaisse, please.
LE GARÇON – Et comme viande? JE VOUS RECOMMANDE le châteaubriant.	WAITER – And for meat? I recommend [to you] the steak.
MME DULAC – Très bien, JE LE PRENDS avec du chou-fleur et des épinards.	MRS. DULAC – Fine, I'll take it with some cauliflower and spinach.
MME LE BRUN – Moi, JE PRÉFÈRE les côtelettes d'agneau avec des haricots verts et des carottes.	MRS. LE BRUN – I prefer the lamb chops with string beans and carrots.
....	....
MME DULAC – ÇA FAIT dix minutes que NOUS ATTENDONS!	MRS. DULAC – We've been waiting for ten minutes!

MME LE BRUN – IL Y A tant de monde ici aujourd'hui . . . Ah! VOILÀ le garçon qui REVIENT.	MRS. LE BRUN – There are so many people here today . . . Ah! There's the waiter coming back.
LE GARÇON – Mes excuses, mesdames. VOULEZ-VOUS commander le dessert maintenant?	WAITER – My apologies, ladies. Do you wish to order dessert now?
MME DULAC – Non, merci, JE N'EN PRENDS PAS.	MRS. DULAC – Thank you, no, I won't take any.
MME LE BRUN – Comment ça SE FAIT-IL, Jeanne? Depuis quand ÊTES-VOUS au régime?	MRS. LE BRUN – How's that, Jeanne? How long have you been dieting?
MME DULAC – JE SUIS au régime depuis trois semaines, VOUS SAVEZ.	MRS. DULAC – I've been on a diet for three weeks, you know.
MME LE BRUN – En effet, VOUS MAIGRISSEZ! Mais c'est dommage parce que NOUS MANGEONS toujours bien dans ce petit restaurant. J'ADMIRE votre ténacité.	MRS. LE BRUN – You really are losing weight! But it's too bad because we always enjoy the food (eat well) in this little restaurant. I admire your tenacity.
MME DULAC – JE SUIS habituée maintenant au régime et JE ME PORTE à merveille! COMMENÇONS, voulez-vous?	MRS. DULAC – I'm accustomed to dieting now and I'm feeling great! Let's begin, shall we?
MME LE BRUN – Avec plaisir! Deux cafés noirs, garçon, et c'est tout.	MRS. LE BRUN – With pleasure! Two black coffees, waiter, and that's all.

I. THE PRESENT INDICATIVE

A. Formation of the Present Tense

The present tense is formed by removing the infinitive ending *-er*, *-ir*, *-re* of the first, second, and third conjugations respectively, and then by adding the personal endings given below:

Present Indicative of the Three Conjugations

	RECOMMANDER	CHOISIR	RÉPONDRE
je	recommandE	choisIS	répondS
tu	recommandES	choisIS	répondS
il / elle	recommandE	choisIT	répond__
nous	recommandONS	choisISSONS	répondONS
vous	recommandEZ	choisISSEZ	répondEZ
ils / elles	recommandENT	choisISSENT	répondENT

NOTE: The plural endings are identical in the three conjugations except that in the second conjugation *-iss* is inserted before the endings.

EXERCISE 1

Change the infinitive to the present tense of the verb. Other verbs that you will need are:

aimer, to like, to love
renverser, to upset, to turn over, to spill
finir, to finish
remplir, to fill
rougir, to blush
salir, to soil
entendre, to hear, to understand
perdre, to lose
rendre, to give back
vendre, to sell

1. Je (recommander) ____, je (choisir) ____, je (vendre) ____
2. Elle (apporter) ____, elle (maigrir) ____, elle (attendre) ____
3. Vous (désirer) ____, vous (remplir) ____, vous (perdre) ____
4. Ils (commander) ____, ils (salir) ____, ils (répondre) ____
5. Tu (renverser) ____, tu (rougir) ____, tu (entendre) ____
6. Nous (aimer) ____, nous (finir) ____, nous (rendre) ____
7. Le garçon (recommander) ____, . . . (remplir) ____, . . . (répondre) ____
8. Les deux messieurs (admirer) ____, . . . (choisir) ____, . . . (rendre) ____

EXERCISE 2

From the following set of endings, select the one that belongs with the subject: *-e, -is, -es, -it, -ent, -s, -___, -issons, -ez, -ons, -issent*

1. Nous command____
2. J'attend____
3. Il fin____
4. Vous aim____
5. Elles rempl____
6. Tu admir____
7. Le garçon désir____
8. Je chois____
9. Il recommand____
10. Ils perd____
11. Nous sal____
12. Elle rend____
13. Je renvers____
14. Les deux messieurs command____

B. Translation of the Present Tense

There are a number of ways the present indicative may be translated:

1. I wait:

   J'attends chaque fois que je viens dans ce restaurant. (I wait every time I come to this restaurant.)

2. I am waiting:

   J'attends le garçon. (I'm waiting for the waiter.)

3. I do wait:

   Vous n'attendez pas chaque fois! Si, j'attends! (You don't wait each time! Yes, I do wait!)

4. I have been waiting (and still am):

   J'attends depuis dix minutes. (I've been waiting for ten minutes.)

5. I'll wait (right now):

   Avez-vous le temps d'attendre? Oui j'attends. (Do you have the time to wait? Yes, I'll wait.)

Exercise 3

Translate:

1. I recommend
2. I do like
3. I am admiring
4. I have been admiring
5. We soil
6. He is giving back
7. You have been waiting for ten minutes
8. They order
9. We upset
10. You fill
11. She likes
12. He is getting thin
13. You (fam.) have been losing
14. You recommend
15. I am selling

II. THE NEGATIVE

The negative is expressed by placing the negative forms around the verb. The most common negatives are the following:

ne . . . pas (not):

   Je ne prends pas de dessert. (I don't take dessert.)

ne . . . jamais (never):

   Il ne finit jamais avant sept heures. (He never finishes before seven o'clock.)

ne . . . point (not at all):

   Je ne désire point de dessert. (I don't want any dessert at all.)

ne . . . plus (not any more, no longer):

   Nous n'aimons plus ce restaurant. (We don't like this restaurant any more.)

ne . . . guère (scarcely, hardly):

   Ils ne mangent guère les haricots verts. (They hardly eat the string beans.)

ne . . . personne (no one):

   Nous n'attendons personne. (We are waiting for no one.)

ne . . . rien (nothing, not anything):

Le garçon n'apporte rien. (The waiter is bringing nothing.)

Personne and *rien* can stand alone with the full negative force:

Qui désire du gâteau au chocolat? Personne. (Who wants chocolate cake? No one.)

Qu'est-ce que vous désirez comme hors-d'œuvre? Rien, merci. (What do you want as an appetizer? Nothing, thank you.)

Exercise 4

Translate the English into French:

1. *We don't like* la bouillabaisse.
2. *I never wait* plus de dix minutes.
3. *You aren't losing weight at all*, je vous assure.
4. Le monsieur *no longer likes* les desserts.
5. *They hardly finish* la viande quand *the waiter brings* le dessert.
6. *She scarcely answers.*
7. *I haven't been waiting* depuis longtemps.
8. *He never recommends* ce restaurant.
9. *We blush* quand *we upset* le verre de vin parce que *we soil* la nappe.
10. *She never takes* de pain parce qu'elle est au régime.

III. THE INTERROGATIVE

A question may be expressed in any of the following ways:

Est-ce que:

Est-ce que vous désirez châteaubriant? (Do you want the steak?)

Inversion:

Désirez-vous le châteaubriant? (Do you want the steak?)

The inverted form is usually avoided with *je* except in *ai-je* (have I), *suis-je* (am I), *puis-je* (may I, can I), *dois-je* (must I, ought I).

If there is a noun subject, it stands first in the inverted construction and the pronoun is repeated after the verb:

Ces messieurs désirent-ils le châteaubriant? (Do these men want the steak?)

In the case of the inversion of a reflexive verb, there is a pronoun on each side of the verb:

Comment ça se fait-il? (How's that?)

Rising intonation:

Vous désirez le châteaubriant? (You want the steak?)

Exercise 5

Translate the following forms using (1) est-ce que, (2) the inversion, (3) the rising intonation:

1. *Do you like* la soupe à l'oignon?
2. *Have those gentlemen been waiting* depuis longtemps?
3. *Are you ordering* le chou-fleur et les haricots verts?
4. *Is she getting thin*?
5. *Does he choose* toujours la tarte aux pommes?

IV. THE NEGATIVE INTERROGATIVE

The negative interrogative can be expressed in any of the following ways:

Est-ce que:

Est-ce que ce monsieur ne maigrit pas? (Isn't this man getting thin?)

Ne . . . pas around inverted verb and subject pronoun:

Ne maigrit-il pas? (Isn't he getting thin?)

If there is a noun subject, as in the case of the interrogative affirmative, the noun stands first, then the negative is placed around the inverted verb and pronoun:

Ce monsieur ne maigrit-il pas? (Isn't this man getting thin?)

Rising inflection:

Il ne maigrit pas?

Exercise 6

Translate the English into French:

1. *Don't you like* le flan comme dessert?
2. *Doesn't the waiter recommend* la tarte aux pommes?
3. *Aren't they filling* les verres?
4. *Doesn't she admire* votre ténacité?
5. *Don't I order* maintenant?

V. THE IMPERATIVE

Commands are expressed as follows:

Tu form of the verb with *tu* omitted (in the *-er* verbs, the *-s* is not used):

Apporte la viande. (Bring the meat.)
Choisis le dessert. (Choose the dessert.)
Réponds à la question. (Answer the question.)

Vous form of the verb with *vous* omitted:

Apportez la viande. (Bring the meat.)

Choisissez le dessert. (Choose the dessert.)
Répondez à la question. (Answer the question.)

Nous form of the verb (meaning "Let's") with *nous* omitted:

Apportons la viande. (Let's bring the meat.)
Choisissons le dessert. (Let's choose the dessert.)
Répondons à la question. (Let's answer the question.)

Exercise 7

Translate:

1. *Bring* le café.
2. *Order* la viande.
3. *Don't choose* la soupe à l'oignon.
4. *Answer* à ma question.
5. *Don't soil* la nappe.
6. *Let's wait for* le garçon.
7. *Let's fill* les verres.
8. *Let's not order* de gâteau.
9. *Let's finish* immédiatement.
10. *Let's sell* ce restaurant.
11. *Wait for* le garçon.
12. *Bring* le chou-fleur.
13. *Give back* le verre.
14. *Don't order* la glace.
15. *Finish* (fam.) ton diner.

VI. THE PRESENT TENSE OF ORTHOGRAPHIC-CHANGING VERBS OF THE FIRST CONJUGATION

A. After the infinitive ending *-er* has been removed, the final *-c*, or *-g* changes as follows before *-o*.

c becomes *ç* before *o*:	nous commençons
g becomes *ge* before *o*:	nous mangeons

B. The *-e* or *-é* becomes *-è* before a final *silent* syllable:

je préfère	nous préférons
tu préfères	vous préférez
il préfère	ils préfèrent

Some verbs double the final consonant under the same circumstances, instead of changing *-é* to *-è*:

j'appelle (from *appeler*, to call)
je jette (from *jeter*, to throw)

C. Verbs ending in *-yer* (such as *essayer*, to try; *nettoyer*, to clean; *essuyer*, to dry) change the *-y* to *-i* before a final silent syllable.

j'essaie, je nettoie, j'essuie
tu essaies, tu nettoies, tu essuies
il essaie, il nettoie, il essuie
nous essayons, nous nettoyons, nous essuyons

vous essayez, vous nettoyez, vous essuyez
ils essaient, ils nettoient, ils essuient

Verbs ending in *-ayer* (such as *essayer*) can also retain the *y* throughout all persons.

j'essaie, j'essaye	nous essayons
tu essaies, tu essayes	vous essayez
il essaie, il essaye	ils essaient, ils essayent

Exercise 8

Give the following forms:

1. I buy
2. We buy
3. Let's begin
4. We eat
5. They prefer
6. You (*vous*) prefer
7. She calls
8. We call
9. He throws
10. You (*vous*) throw
11. They begin
12. He eats
13. I try
14. We clean
15. They dry

VII. THE PRESENT TENSE OF IRREGULAR VERBS

Even irregular verbs follow a certain pattern. Note the following:

A. The endings are usually:

-S	-ONS
-S	-EZ
-T	-ENT

The verbs *vouloir* and *pouvoir* take *-x*, *-x*, *-t*.

The forms *vous êtes, vous dites, vous faites* are the only exceptions to the *-ez* ending for *vous*.

In reviewing the irregular verbs listed, particular attention should be given to the two verbs *avoir* and *être* (which serve as auxiliary verbs) as well as to the verb *aller*. These verbs do not conform to any pattern.

B. If the verb forms that accompany JE, NOUS, and ILS are learned, the other forms are automatically learned because they retain the stem:

JE VIENS	NOUS VENONS
tu viens	vous venez
il vient	ILS VIENNENT

Exercise 9

After having carefully consulted the Table of Irregular Verbs (see the Index) for the forms of the present indicative, fill in the blanks below:

	JE	NOUS	ELLE	VOUS	ILS
(aller)	______	______	______	______	______
(dormir)	______	______	______	______	______
(venir)	______	______	______	______	______
(connaître)	______	______	______	______	______
(vouloir)	______	______	______	______	______
(craindre)	______	______	______	______	______
(croire)	______	______	______	______	______
(dire)	______	______	______	______	______
(mettre)	______	______	______	______	______
(faire)	______	______	______	______	______
(écrire)	______	______	______	______	______
(lire)	______	______	______	______	______
(savoir)	______	______	______	______	______
(devoir)	______	______	______	______	______
(pouvoir)	______	______	______	______	______
(recevoir)	______	______	______	______	______
(voir)	______	______	______	______	______
(prendre)	______	______	______	______	______
(suivre)	______	______	______	______	______
(vivre)	______	______	______	______	______

Review Exercise

Translate:

1. Let's not wait any longer. I'll call the waiter.
2. Waiter, the menu, please. Let's order the bouillabaisse.
3. I'll take the steak. What are you ordering?
4. I'll choose the lamb chops, with carrots, spinach, and cauliflower.
5. Waiter, bring us the steak and the lamb chops, please.
6. Ah! The waiter is coming back. . . . Thank you. Let's begin, shall we? We always eat well in this little restaurant.
7. Don't you want any bread? No, thank you, I'm on a diet.
8. You're getting thin. How long have you been dieting?
9. I've been dieting for three weeks.
10. Do the ladies want to order dessert now? I recommend the apple pie or the custard.
11. Thank you, I don't want any dessert. Aren't you ordering any dessert, Jeanne?
12. No, I'll take coffee.

CHAPTER FOUR

The Conjunctive Pronouns: ***Position Before the Verb; The Reflexive Pronoun; Position After the Verb***
The Disjunctive Pronouns

À LA RECHERCHE D'UNE CHAMBRE

FRANÇOIS – Où est ce journal français? Ah, LE VOILÀ! . . . Voici l'annonce, Jacques.

JACQUES – LIS-LA-MOI, François, veux-tu?

FRANÇOIS – Grande chambre à deux personnes chez famille française . . .

JACQUES – Mais, qu'est-ce que nous attendons? RENDONS-NOUS-Y tout de suite!

....

FRANÇOIS – Bonjour, madame. Vous avez une chambre à deux personnes?

MME DUPONT – Oui, messieurs. C'est pour vous? Vous êtes étudiants, n'est-ce pas?

JACQUES – C'est juste, madame.

MME DUPONT – Très bien, messieurs. Venez AVEC MOI et JE VOUS LA FERAI VOIR.

FRANÇOIS–À quel étage SE TROUVE la chambre?

MME DUPONT – Au deuxième,* en arrière. Et vous avez la salle de bain à côté. Voici la chambre, messieurs.

JACQUES –C'est très tranquille, paraît-il. J'hésite à VOUS LE DEMANDER, madame, mais serait-il possible d'avoir une bibliothèque et une lampe?

LOOKING FOR A ROOM

FRANK – Where is that French newspaper? Ah, there it is! . . . Here's the ad, James.

JAMES – Read it to me, Frank, will you?

FRANK – Large double room with French family . . .

JAMES – Well, what are we waiting for? Let's get over there right away!

....

FRANK – Good afternoon. You have a double room?

MRS. DUPONT – Yes, gentlemen. Is it for you? You're students, aren't you?

JAMES – That's right, madame.

MRS. DUPONT – Very well, gentlemen. Come with me and I'll show it to you.

FRANK – What floor is the room on?

MRS. DUPONT – On the third, rear. And you have the bathroom right alongside. Here is the room, gentlemen!

JAMES – It's very quiet, it seems. I hesitate to ask you for it, but would it be possible to have a bookcase and a lamp?

* The first floor is called *le rez-de-chaussée*. Thus, the second floor is called *le premier étage*; the third is *le deuxième*; etc.

MME DUPONT – Ça pourrait S'ARRANGER, je crois.	MRS. DUPONT – That could be arranged, I think.
FRANÇOIS – Et MOI JE ME DEMANDAIS si nous pourrions avoir un bureau.	FRANK – And *I* was wondering if we could have a desk.
MME DUPONT – NE VOUS EN PRÉOCCUPEZ PAS, messieurs. Mon mari a tous ces meubles dans le grenier. Je n'ai qu'à LES LUI DEMANDER.	MRS. DUPONT – Don't worry about that, gentlemen. My husband has all those pieces of furniture in the attic. I have only to ask him for them.
JACQUES – C'est très gentil À VOUS, madame, et très gentil À LUI. Quel est le loyer?	JACQUES – That's very nice of you, madame, and very nice of him. What is the rent?
MME DUPONT – C'est quinze dollars par semaine. Ça VOUS CONVIENT?	MRS. DUPONT – Fifteen dollars a week. Is that agreeable to you?
FRANÇOIS ET JACQUES – Parfaitement, madame!	FRANK AND JAMES – Perfectly, madame!

I. THE CONJUNCTIVE PRONOUNS

The conjunctive pronouns are used as direct or indirect objects of the verb. It is extremely important to learn the meaning of each pronoun.

A. Position Before the Verb – in all cases except in the affirmative imperative.

ME (me, to me)	LE (him, it [m.])	LUI (to him, to her)	Y (there, in it, in them, to it, to them)	EN (some, some of it, some of them, from it, from them, any, any of it, any of them)
TE (you, to you)	LA (her, it [f.])	LEUR (to them)		
Se (himself, to himself; herself, to herself; themselves, to themselves)	LES (them)			
NOUS (us, to us)				
VOUS (you, to you)				

EXAMPLES:

Je vous la ferai voir. (I'll show it to you.)

J'hésite à vous le demander. (I hesitate to ask you for it.)
Ne vous en préoccupez pas. (Don't worry about that.)
Je n'ai qu'à les lui demander. (I have only to ask him for them.)
Nous allons nous y rendre. (We are going to get over there.)

EXERCISE 1

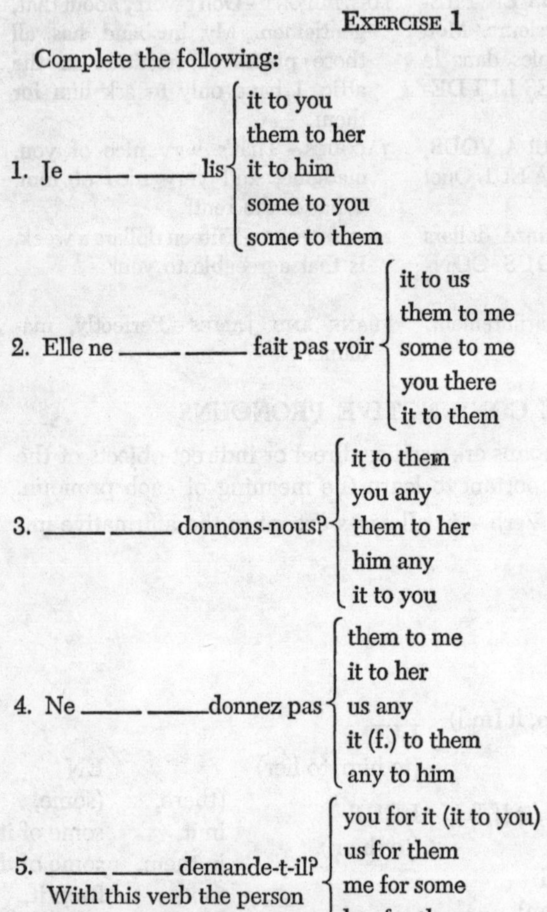

Complete the following:

1. Je _____ _____ lis { it to you / them to her / it to him / some to you / some to them }

2. Elle ne _____ _____ fait pas voir { it to us / them to me / some to me / you there / it to them }

3. _____ _____ donnons-nous? { it to them / you any / them to her / him any / it to you }

4. Ne _____ _____ donnez pas { them to me / it to her / us any / it (f.) to them / any to him }

5. _____ _____ demande-t-il? { you for it (it to you) / us for them / me for some / her for them / them for them }
With this verb the person is the indirect object; the thing is the direct object.

B. The Reflexive Pronoun

The pronouns *ME, TE, SE, NOUS, VOUS* – noted above under the conjunctive pronouns – serve also as reflexive pronouns. *As reflexive pronouns*, their meanings are: *ME* (myself, to myself), *TE* (yourself, to yourself), *SE* (see above), *NOUS* (ourselves, to ourselves), *VOUS* (yourself, yourselves, to yourself, to yourselves). Note that in the inverted form of the interrogation, a pronoun stands on each side of the verb.

Vous demandez-vous . . . ? (Are you wondering . . . ?)

Moi, je me demandais . . . (was wondering [literally: I was asking myself] . . .)

As *reciprocal pronouns, NOUS, VOUS,* and *SE* take on the meanings of "each other," "to each other," "one another," "to one another":

Nous nous parlons. (We speak to each other.)

Exercise 2

The following verbs will be needed for this exercise: *se lever* (to rise, to get up), *parler* (to speak), *raconter* (to tell, to relate), *se demander* (to wonder).

Translate the English into French:

1. *They tell each other* l'histoire.
2. *Don't get up!*
3. *We speak to each other* chaque jour au téléphone.
4. *I don't get up* à huit heures.
5. *Are you wondering?*

C. Position After the Verb (and attached by hyphens) in the affirmative imperative.

Here the order of pronouns is the same as in the English "Give it to me." The forms *ME* and *TE* are replaced by the stronger forms *MOI* and *TOI* when they stand last. If *EN* occurs, it is placed last in the construction.

EXAMPLES:

Rendons-nous-y. (Let's get over there.)
Lis-la-moi. (Read it to me.)
Donnez-nous-en. (Give us some.)

Exercise 3

Complete the following:

1. Donnez (*give*)

   -_____-_____ (them to me)
   -_____-_____ (it to her)
   -_____-_____ (some to us)
   -_____-_____ (it to us)
   -_____-_____ (them to him)

2. Lis (*read*)

   -_____-_____ (them to me)
   -_____-_____ (them to her)
   -_____-_____ (some to us)
   -_____-_____ (them to them)
   -_____-_____ (them to him)

II. THE DISJUNCTIVE PRONOUNS

The distinctive pronouns are *MOI* (I, me), *TOI* (you), *LUI* (he, him), *ELLE* (she, her), *NOUS* (we, us), *VOUS* (you), *EUX* (they, them [m.]), *ELLES* (they, them [f.]), *SOI* (oneself, themselves). Their uses are:

1. After a preposition: *Venez avec moi.* (Come with me.)
2. Standing alone: *Qui est là? Moi.* (Who is there? Me.)
3. Reinforcing a subject pronoun, especially in contrasts: *Et moi je me demandais...* (And I was wondering...)
4. Summing up a compound subject: *François et moi nous cherchons une chambre.* (Frank and I are looking for a room.)
5. For the indirect object when the direct object is a person other than *le, la, les: Présentez-vous à lui.* (Introduce yourself to him.)

Exercise 4

Complete the following:

1. Mon ami et *I* nous désirons une chambre.
2. La dame a une belle chambre *for them.*
3. Voilà la dame et son mari. *Introduce me to them.*
4. *I* demande une lampe tandis que *he* demande un bureau.
5. Qui est ce monsieur-là? Qui? *He*? C'est un locataire. *Introduce yourself to him.*

Review Exercise

Translate:

1. Where is the French paper? Ah, there it is. Give (fam.) it to me, will you, Paul?
2. Here is the ad. I'll read it to you (fam.).
3. Large double room with French family. Let's get over there!
4. You have a large room, madame? Could we see it?
5. I have two, gentlemen. I'll show them to you immediately.
6. It is very quiet. Would it be possible to put a desk and a lamp there?
7. Certainly, I have only to ask my husband for them.
8. Does he have those pieces of furniture? Yes, he has them in the attic.
9. Don't ask him for them today, madame.
10. We have two other tenants and he is with them now.
11. *I* like the room in the rear, but *they* prefer a room next to the bathroom.
12. Do you have many rooms? We have six.

CHAPTER FIVE

The Adjective: *Formation of the Feminine; Agreement of Adjectives; Position of the Adjective; Summary of the Position of Adjectives*
The Adverb: *Formation of the Adverb; Position of the Adverb*
Comparison of the Adjective and Adverb: *Comparing the Adjective; Comparing the Adverb*

AU LABORATOIRE DE LANGUES	IN THE LANGUAGE LABORATORY
HÉLÈNE – Je me sauve . . . Il faut que J'AILLE MAINTENANT au laboratoire. J'ai encore QUATRE LONGS EXERCICES à enregistrer avant jeudi et ce sont LES PLUS DIFFICILES jusqu'ici.	HELEN – I'll be running along . . . I have to go to the laboratory now. I still have four long exercises to record before Thursday and they are the most difficult up to now.
JEANNINE – Ça exige pas mal de temps, n'est-ce pas? Mais, ça vaut la peine!	JEANNINE – That takes quite a lot of time, doesn't it? But it's worth the trouble!
HÉLÈNE – C'est UN TRAVAIL BEAUCOUP PLUS EXIGEANT qu'on ne le croirait. Par exemple, hier je ne sais combien de fois j'ai dû effacer MON DISQUE MAGNÉTIQUE. C'était CHAQUE FOIS UNE PRONONCIATION PLUS HONTEUSE QUE LA DERNIÈRE.	HELEN – It's much more demanding work than you'd think. For example, yesterday I don't know how many times I had to erase my magnetic disc. Each time, it was a more disgraceful pronunciation than the last.
JEANNINE – Tu travailles toujours aux voyelles?	JEANNINE – Are you still working on the vowels?
HÉLÈNE – C'est CETTE MISÉRABLE U qui prend TOUT MON TEMPS!	HELEN – It's that awful "u" that takes all my time!
JEANNINE – Tu y parviendras car tu la PRONONCES PARFAITEMENT presque toujours. C'est en forgeant qu'on devient forgeron.	JEANNINE – You'll get there because you nearly always pronounce it perfectly. Practice makes perfect.

HÉLÈNE – C'est juste! -u, -u, *ju*ste. Voilà! Ça y est! Je crois que cette après-midi j'y réussirai complètement. Mais dans CETTE PETITE CABINE . . .

HELEN – That's right! -u, -u, That's right. There! There we are! I think I'll make a complete success of it this afternoon. But in that little booth . . .

JEANNINE – Et après, pourquoi n'empruntes-tu pas à la bibliothèque QUELQUES BANDES des GRANDS CLASSIQUES?

JEANNINE – And afterward, why don't you borrow a few tapes of the great classics from the library?

HÉLÈNE – BONNE IDÉE! Il y en a plusieurs de la COMÉDIE FRANÇAISE. C'est beaucoup MOINS COÛTEUX QUE D'ALLER au théâtre.

HELEN – A good idea! There are several by the Comédie Française. It's a lot less expensive than going to the theater.

I. THE ADJECTIVE

A. Formation of the Feminine

The feminine is regularly formed by adding *-e* to the masculine:

petit, petite
français, française

SPECIAL FEMININE FORMS

-X, -SE
honteux (ashamed), honteuse

-F, -VE
vif (lively), vive

-ER, -ÈRE
dernier (last), dernière

-EUR, -EUSE
rêveur (dreamy), rêveuse

BUT: meilleur, meilleure
supérieur, supérieure

-ATEUR, -ATRICE
consolateur (consoling), consolatrice

DOUBLING FINAL CONSONANT

-EL, -ELLE
solennel (solemn), solennelle

-EIL, -EILLE
pareil (similar), pareille

-IEN, -IENNE
italien (Italian), italienne

-ON, -ONNE
mignon (cute), mignonne

-S, -SSE
gros (big, bulky), grosse

MUTE E – same in feminine
magnétique, magnétique
fidèle (faithful), fidèle

NO RULE GOVERNING THE FEMININE

franc (candid, frank), franche
faux (false), fausse
doux (gentle, sweet) douce
frais (fresh), fraîche
favori (favorite), favorite
sec (dry), sèche
public, publique
beau (beautiful, fine), belle
mou (soft), molle

fou (foolish), folle
nouveau (new), nouvelle
vieux (old), vieille

NOTE: The last five adjectives have an alternate masculine form to be used before a masc. sing. noun beginning with a vowel or *h* mute: *bel, mol, fol, nouvel, vieil.*

EXAMPLE:
un vieil exercice

NOTE: Adjectives are pluralized according to the same rules that hold for nouns.

Exercise 1

Give the feminine of the following adjectives:

1. excellent, ______
2. cher (dear), ______
3. difficile, ______
4. frais (fresh), ______
5. coûteux, ______
6. révélateur (revealing), ______
7. ancien (ancient, former), ______
8. heureux (happy), ______
9. faux, ______
10. bon, ______
11. premier, ______
12. nouveau, ______
13. doux, ______
14. flatteur (flattering), ______
15. exceptionnel, ______
16. beau, ______
17. vieux, ______
18. candide, ______

B. Agreement of Adjectives

An adjective must agree in number and gender with the noun it modifies. If an adjective modifies more than one noun, it is masculine plural if all are masculine or if the nouns are of mixed gender; it is feminine plural if all the nouns are feminine.

EXAMPLES:

des laboratoires et des bibliothèques exceptionnels
des salles de classe et des bibliothèques pleines (full) d'étudiants

Exercise 2

Translate the following (the adjectives "expensive" and "excellent" will follow nouns):

1. a large booth
2. some old tapes
3. some expensive records and tapes
4. a good pronunciation
5. some excellent libraries and classrooms (salles de classe)

C. Position of the Adjective

Generally the following rules explain the position of the adjective:

1. *After the noun* is found an adjective that adds something *essential* by serving to distinguish the noun it modifies from other nouns of the same category.

EXAMPLES:

mon disque magnétique
un exercice difficile
un professeur exigeant

2. *Before the noun* are found adjectives of weaker force (a) that express a quality usually associated with the noun, or (b) that are subjectively used, or (c) the following adjectives of common occurrence, which fall into the classifications of *beauty, age, goodness,* and *size*:

   beauty: beau (beautiful), vilain (ugly), laid (ugly)
   age: jeune (young), vieux (old)
   goodness: bon (good), mauvais (bad), méchant (naughty)
   size: petit (small), grand (large), gros (big in bulk), court (short), long (long)

EXAMPLES:

les fameux classiques
ma misérable prononciation
quatre longs exercices; cette petite cabine

Also, if an adjective is used merely as an ornament, without full descriptive force, it precedes.

EXAMPLE:

un magnifique laboratoire

3. *Of varying position.* Other considerations enter into the position that an adjective may occupy. An adjective used figuratively precedes; the same adjective used literally follows. Thus, the following adjectives vary in meaning according to position:

BEFORE	AFTER
	nouveau
new (different)	new (newly acquired)
une nouvelle robe	une robe nouvelle
(a new dress)	(a new dress)
	pauvre
poor (to be pitied)	poor (without money)
le pauvre étudiant	l'étudiant pauvre
(the poor student)	(the poor student)
	dernier
last (of a series)	last (final) (most recent)
la dernière classe	l'année dernière
(the last class)	(last year)
	prochain
next (of a series)	next (to come, in time expressions)
la prochaine fois	la semaine prochaine
(the next time)	(next week)
	ancien
former	ancient
un ancien élève	une ville ancienne
(a former student, an alumnus)	(an ancient city)

Exercise 3

Translate:

1. a large laboratory
2. a new exercise
3. a demanding professor
4. an excellent pronunciation
5. a long assignment (devoir)
6. a fine recording (enregistrement)
7. French theaters
8. a disgraceful diction

9. an easy exercise
10. a magnificent library
11. the poor student works hard (travaille dur)
12. the difficult vowel *u*
13. an intelligent young man
14. each miserable time
15. the long and short vowels

Summary of the Position of Adjectives:

BEFORE NOUN (weak position; adjective not stressed)	AFTER NOUN (strong position; adjective emphatically used)
1. To express a quality already associated with the noun: le fameux Arc de Triomphe	**1.** To add a distinguishing quality: un travail exigeant
2. Figurative meaning: le pauvre étudiant	**2.** Literal meaning: l'étudiant pauvre
3. Subjectively used: la misérable voyelle *u*	**3.** Objectively used: un disque magnétique
4. List of common adjectives of beauty, age, goodness, size: quatre longs exercices	
5. Indefinite adjectives: chaque fois	

NOTE: If two adjectives are used with the same noun, they occupy the position that they would occupy if they were used singly:

un long exercice difficile (a long, difficult exercise)

If both follow, they are joined by *et*:

une diction claire et soignée (a clear and careful pronunciation)

II. THE ADVERB

A. Formation of the Adverb

Most adverbs can be formed from the corresponding adjective by adding *-ment* to the feminine form of the adjective:

complète, complètement
parfaite, parfaitement

NOTE: 1. *-ment* is added to the masculine of the adjective if the adjective ends in a vowel:

absolu, absolument; infini, infiniment

2. Adjectives ending in a nasal, such as *-ant*, or *-ent* change these syllables to *-am* and *-em* respectively before adding *-ment*:

courant, couramment (fluently)
évident, évidemment

B. Position of the Adverb

Adverbs are generally placed after the verbs they modify:

Tu la prononces parfaitement. (You pronounce it perfectly.)

NOTE: The adverb *tout*, meaning "quite," "entirely," is invariable before the adjective it modifies, except when it is used before a feminine adjective beginning with a consonant or aspirate *h*:

Ces disques sont *tout neufs*. (These records are quite new.)
Cette bande est *toute neuve*. (This tape is quite new.)

EXERCISE 4

Give the adverb formed from the following adjectives:

1. complet _______
2. sec _______
3. infini _______
4. franc _______
5. galant _______
6. résolu (resolute) _______
7. différent _______
8. cruel _______
9. vif _______
10. facile _______

III. COMPARISON OF THE ADJECTIVE AND ADVERB

A. Comparing the Adjective

POSITIVE	COMPARATIVE	SUPERLATIVE
expensive (coûteux)	more expensive than (plus coûteux que)	the most expensive (le plus coûteux)
	as expensive as (aussi coûteux que)	
	less expensive than (moins coûteux que)	

1. Naturally, the adjective and the article become feminine or plural as the noun demands:

   des bandes plus coûteuses que les nôtres (tapes more expensive than ours)

2. Where the adjective follows the noun, there will be two articles necessary in the construction of the superlative:

   les étudiants les plus intelligents (the most intelligent students)

3. Where the adjective precedes the noun, the comparative and the superlative are identical:
   le plus beau laboratoire (the finer laboratory)
   le plus beau laboratoire (the finest laboratory)
4. As in English, the adjectives "good" (bon) and "bad" (mauvais) have irregular comparative and superlative forms:
   bon, meilleur, le meilleur (good, better, best)
   mauvais, pire, le pire (bad, worse, worst)

B. Comparing the Adverb

POSITIVE	COMPARATIVE	SUPERLATIVE
easily (facilement)	more easily than (plus facilement que)	the most easily (le plus facilement)
	as easily as (aussi facilement que)	
	less easily than (moins facilement que)	

1. In the superlative of the adverb the *le* is always invariable.
2. The comparative and superlative of *mauvais* are *pis* and *le pis*; the comparative and superlative of *bien* are *mieux* and *le mieux*.

Exercise 5

Complete in French:

1. Les cabines sont *quite large.* Elles sont *larger than* les autres.
2. Les Français parlent *more rapidly than* les Américains.
3. Le laboratoire est *much more useful* (utile) *than you think.*
4. Est-ce que les disques magnétique sont *as faithful as* les bandes?
5. Ces exercices sont *less difficult than* les derniers.

Review Exercise

Translate:

1. We have a fine new laboratory.
2. I go there every afternoon to correct (corriger) my miserable pronunciation.
3. I record two short exercises on the magnetic disc and, if (si) I make any bad mistakes (fautes), I erase the recording.
4. I pronounce as carefully (soigneusement) as possible because I want to have as perfect a pronunciation as possible.
5. François has an excellent pronunciation, but Henry's pronunciation is worse than mine (la mienne).

6. It's harder work than you think, but it's worth the trouble.
7. When my precious (précieux) recordings have been made (ont été faits), I borrow some interesting (intéressant) tapes of the great French classics.
8. I listen to (écouter) the beautiful voices of famous actors of the Comédie Française.
9. The time goes by (passe) so (si) pleasantly (agréablement).
10. Someday (Un jour) I too shall have (j'aurai) a clear, perfect diction too.

CHAPTER SIX

The Imperfect Indicative: *Formation of the Imperfect Indicative; Translation and Use of the Imperfect Indicative*

UN COUP DE TÉLÉPHONE

MARIANNE – Mais comment ça se fait? Tu ne m'as pas appelée. J'ATTENDAIS ton coup de téléphone depuis deux heures AVANT DE SORTIR.

JEANNINE – Tout d'abord, c'est que *j'avais* l'après-midi complètement bloquée – une classe après l'autre, à partir de deux heures jusqu'à six heures.

MARIANNE – Mais *tu avais* les dix minutes entre les classes. . . .

JEANNINE – Ne me les rappelle pas, je t'en prie. La première fois que j'ai essayé, *les cabines téléphoniques étaient toutes occupées.*

MARIANNE – Et ensuite?

JEANNINE – La deuxième fois JE COMPOSAIS précisément le numéro quand le timbre a sonné qui *annonçait* la prochaine classe et j'ai dû raccrocher! J'ENRAGEAIS.

MARIANNE – *Tu n'avais pas de chance!* Voilà tout!

JEANNINE – Entre la troisième et la quatrième classe j'ai essayé de nouveau. J'Y COURAIS, paraît-il, à tout moment.

MARIANNE – Je comprends. Je comprends. Tu es pardonnée.

JEANNINE–Non, tu écouteras! La troisième fois, quand j'ai finalement réussi à composer ton numéro, voilà que *ta ligne était occupée!* Ah! *Si tu n'étais ma meilleure amie,* je ne t'appellerais plus jamais.

A TELEPHONE CALL

MARIANNE – But how is that? You didn't call me. I had been waiting for your call for two hours before going out.

JEANNINE – First of all, it's because I had a completely filled afternoon – one class after the other, from two to six o'clock.

MARIANNE – But you had the ten minutes between classes. . . .

JEANNINE – Please don't remind me of them. The first time I tried, the phone booths were all taken.

MARIANNE – And then?

JEANNINE – The second time, I was just dialing the number when the bell rang (announcing the) for the next class and I had to hang up! I was furious.

MARIANNE – You just weren't in luck! That's all!

JEANNINE – Between the third and fourth classes, I tried again. It seems I was running there every minute.

MARIANNE – I understand. I understand. You're forgiven.

JEANNINE – No, you'll hear me out! The third time, when I finally succeeded in dialing your number, your line was busy! Oh! If you weren't my best friend, I'd never call you again.

I. THE IMPERFECT INDICATIVE

A. Formation of the Imperfect Indicative

The imperfect indicative is formed in all three regular conjugations by removing the *-ons* of the first-person plural of the present indicative, and then by adding the personal endings given below:

Imperfect Indicative of the Three Conjugations: -ER, -IR, -RE

	NOUS COMPOS(ONS)	NOUS FINISS(ONS)	NOUS RÉPOND(ONS)
je	composAIS	finissAIS	répondAIS
tu	composAIS	finissAIS	répondAIS
il	composAIT	finissAIT	répondAIT
nous	composIONS	finissIONS	répondIONS
vous	composIEZ	finissIEZ	répondIEZ
ils	composAIENT	finissAIENT	répondAIENT

The above endings are the same for *all* verbs, even irregular verbs. The stem always has the same source: j'AVais, je VENais, je COURais. (The only exception, as to the stem, is in the verb *être,* where *j'étais* does not resemble *nous sommes.*)

The orthographic-changing verbs of the first conjugation in *-cer*, *-ger*, *-yer* also follow the pattern described above: je commençais, j'enrageais, j'essayais. Remember that in *-cer* verbs, *ç* must be used before *a* (je commençais, etc.); in *-ger* verbs, *ge* is used before *a* (j'enrageais). Where *i* follows the *c* or *g,* no cedilla or *e* is needed (nous commencions, nous enragions, vous commenciez, vous enragiez).

Exercise 1

Give the imperfect forms of the following:

1.	je (raccrocher)	je (choisir)	j' (attendre)
2.	elle (écouter)	elle (remplir)	elle (perdre)
3.	vous (essayer)	vous (finir)	vous (entendre)
4.	ils (commencer)	ils (réussir)	ils (répondre)
5.	tu (appeler)	tu (rougir)	tu (vendre)
6.	nous (enrager)	nous (finir)	nous (perdre)
7.	le timbre (sonner)	la classe (réussir)	la classe (attendre)
8.	les timbres (sonner)	les étudiants (réussir)	les classes (attendre)
9.	elle (manger)	nous (manger)	vous (manger)
10.	je (placer)	nous (placer)	ils (placer)

Exercise 2

Give the following forms of the imperfect (forms marked with the asterisk have a special stem):

aller (present tense: nous allons)	il ______
avoir (nous avons)	nous ______
connaître (nous connaissons)	elles ______
courir (nous courons)	vous ______
croire (nous croyons)	je ______
devoir (nous devons)	elle ______
dire (nous disons)	ils ______
dormir (nous dormons)	vous ______
écrire (nous écrivons)	nous ______
envoyer (nous envoyons)	j' ______
être*	il ______
faire (nous faisons)	tu ______
falloir*	il ______
lire (nous lisons)	vous ______
mettre (nous mettons)	je ______
pouvoir (nous pouvons)	nous ______
prendre (nous prenons)	je ______
recevoir (nous recevons)	tu ______
savoir (nous savons)	ils ______
venir (nous venons)	elles ______
voir (nous voyons)	vous ______
vouloir (nous voulons)	je ______

B. Translation and Use of the Imperfect Indicative

1. I was ____ing:

   Je commençais à composer le numéro . . . (I was beginning to dial the number . . .)

2. I used to ____:

   J'y courais à tout moment . . . (I used to run there every minute . . .)

3. I ____ed (during all that time):

   J'avais l'après-midi complètement bloquée. (I had the afternoon completely filled.)

4. I had been ____ing (for a certain length of time):

   J'attendais ton coup de téléphone depuis deux heures. (I had been waiting for your call for two hours.)

5. I was (in past description):
   J'étais furieuse. (I was furious.)
6. If you were ____, I would:
   Si tu n'étais ma meilleure amie, je ne t'appellerais plus jamais. (If you weren't my best friend, I'd never call you again.)

The imperfect indicative is used for:

1. Past action in progress
2. Repeated past action
3. More vivid narration in the past
4. "Had been ____ing" with expressions of time
5. Descriptions in the past
6. "IF" clause when conditional is used in the result

Exercise 3

Translate:

1. I was dialing.
2. She used to finish.
3. We heard (for a long time).
4. They had been waiting for ten minutes.
5. The telephone was ringing.
6. Were you answering?
7. He didn't listen.
8. I wasn't free.
9. Were you choosing?
10. They were furious.
11. We used to begin.
12. She had been calling for fifteen minutes.
13. If you heard the question you would answer it (vous y répondriez).
14. You used to succeed.
15. He was hanging up.

Review Exercise

Translate the English into French:

We had been waiting depuis trois heures le coup de téléphone de François, mais *if you knew* ce qui lui est arrivé, vous admireriez sa ténacité. *He had* l'après-midi complètement bloquée. C'est-à-dire (That is) qu' *he was free* pendant les dix minutes entre les classes. *He would go to the telephone booth* chaque fois mais *he never had* assez de temps pour nous appeler. La première fois, *he was just dialing the number* quand le timbre a sonné qui annonçait la prochaine classe. La deuxième fois *he wanted to call us* mais les cabines téléphoniques *were all taken*. La troisième fois, *he saw* (vivid narration) qu'une cabine *was free. He believed* (croire) *that he was in luck*. Mais *the line was busy! He was going* y renoncer (to give up) mais il a finalement réussi à avoir une réponse. Le pauvre François!

CHAPTER SEVEN

The Future Tense: *Formation of the Future Tense; Translation and use of the Future Tense*
The Conditional Tense: *Formation of the Conditional Tense; Translation and use of the Conditional Tense*
Verbs Irregular in the Future and Conditional Tenses

LA PARTIE DE FOOTBALL	THE FOOTBALL GAME
MARIANNE – Paul, mon cher frère, VOUDRAIS-TU faire quelque chose pour moi? Henri m'a invitée à l'accompagner samedi prochain à la partie de football contre Stansbury et je ne comprends rien au jeu. Si TU M'EXPLIQUAIS un peu ce qui SE PASSERA, JE ME DIVERTIRAIS. . . .	MARIANNE – Paul, dear brother, would you do something for me? Henry has asked me to accompany him next Saturday to the football game against Stansbury and I don't understand a thing about the game. If you explained to me a little what will go on, I would enjoy myself. . . .
PAUL – Qu'est-ce TU FERAIS, Marianne, si tu n'avais pas ton frère? Bon, je te l'explique – mais après, TU ME PRÉPARERAS une belle tarte aux pommes. Entendu?	PAUL – What would you do, Marianne, if you didn't have your brother? All right, I'll explain it to you – but afterward you'll prepare me a fine apple pie. Understood?
MARIANNE – Bon, j'y conviens.	MARIANNE – All right, I agree.
PAUL – Si tu m'apportes du papier, je T'EN FERAI un petit dessin. Voici ce que TU VERRAS. . . . IL Y AURA naturellement deux équipes. ON LANCERA LE BALLON . . .	PAUL – If you bring me some paper, I'll make you a little sketch of it! Here's what you'll see. . . . There will naturally be two teams. They'll kick the ball . . .
MARIANNE – Pourquoi lance-t-on le ballon?	MARIANNE – Why do they kick the ball?
PAUL – Pas de questions! TU ÉCOUTERAS d'abord . . . ON LANCERA le ballon et celui qui l'ATTRAPERA SE METTRA à courir.	PAUL – No questions! Listen first . . . They'll kick the ball, and the one who'll catch it will begin to run.
MARIANNE – De quel côté?	MARIANNE – In what direction?
PAUL – Du côté des adversaires, naturellement . . .	PAUL – In the direction of the opponents, naturally . . .

MARIANNE – Pourquoi?

PAUL – Pour arriver au but . . .

MARIANNE – Est-ce qu'IL PORTERA le ballon pendant qu'il court?

PAUL – Mais naturellement! S'il n'avait pas le ballon, IL SERAIT inutile de courir. . . .

MARIANNE – Et que FERONT les adversaires pendant tout ce temps-là?

PAUL – ILS TÂCHERONT de l'empêcher de faire un touchdown. LORSQUE TU VERRAS le jeu, TU COMPRENDRAS tout cela! Et maintenant . . . où est ma tarte aux pommes?

MARIANNE – Why?

PAUL – To reach the goal . . .

MARIANNE – Will he carry the ball while he runs?

PAUL – Well, naturally! If he didn't have the ball, it would be useless to run. . . .

MARIANNE – And what will the opponents do all that time?

PAUL – They'll try to prevent him from making a touchdown. When you see the play, you'll understand all that! And now . . . where's my apple pie?

I. THE FUTURE TENSE

A. Formation of the Future Tense

To the whole infinitive, which serves as stem (in verbs of the third conjugation, the final *-e* is dropped), the following endings are added: -AI, -AS, -A, -ONS, -EZ, -ONT.

Future Tense in the Three Conjugations

	PRÉPARER	FINIR	RÉPONDRE
je	préparerAI	finirAI	répondrAI
tu	préparerAS	finirAS	répondrAS
il	préparerA	finirA	répondrA
nous	préparerONS	finirONS	répdonrONS
vous	préparerEZ	finirEZ	répondrEZ
ils	préparerONT	finirONT	répondrONT

1. The endings are identical in *all* – even irregular – verbs. These endings will remind you of the forms of the verb AVOIR:
   j'*ai*, tu *as*, il *a*, nous (av)*ons*, vous (av)*ez*, ils *ont*.
2. Orthographic-changing verbs, like *préférer*, do not change the acute accent in the future tense:
   je préférerai, tu préféreras, il préférera, etc.

Exercise 1

Give the future of the following verbs:

1. j' (accompagner)	je (finir)	je (vendre)
2. vous (inviter)	vous (remplir)	vous (attendre)
3. ils (passer)	ils (punir)	ils (répondre)
4. nous (préparer)	nous nous (divertir)	nous (entendre)
5. elle (écouter)	elle (rougir)	elle (rendre)
6. tu (porter)	tu (bâtir)	tu (perdre)
7. elles (tâcher)	elles (vieillir)	elles (répondre)
8. il (lancer)	il se (divertir)	il (attendre)
9. le joueur (attraper)	le jouer (finir)	le joueur (attendre)
10. les joueurs (attraper)	les joueurs (finir)	les joueurs (attendre)

B. Translation and Use of the Future Tense:

Translation:

The future tense is translated as "shall," "will."

Uses:

1. A future action:

   . . . celui qui l'attrapera se mettra à courir.

2. Result clause when present is in *si* clause:

   Si tu m'apportes du papier, je ferai un petit dessin.

3. Hidden future: after words like *lorsque* (when), *dès que* and *aussitôt que* (as soon as) if the future is meant (and expressed in the main clause).

   Lorsque tu verras le jeu, tu comprendras tout cela.

   BUT: If "when" means "whenever" the present is used:

   Lorsqu'on attrape le ballon, on se met à courir. (When they catch the ball, they start running.)

   If the future is an immediate future ("right now"), the present is used:

   Bon, je te l'explique. (Good, I will explain it to you.)

Exercise 2

Translate the English into French:

1. *He will throw* le ballon.
2. *I shall invite* nos amis.
3. *When you go with Henry,* il vous expliquera le jeu.
4. *They will finish* la partie avant quatre heures.
5. Dès que son frère lui *explains* le jeu, elle lui fera une tarte aux pommes.
6. *When the player catches the ball,* ses adversaires tâchent de l'empêcher d'arriver au but.

7. *We shall carry* le ballon.
8. *Will you throw the ball?*
9. Si vous m'expliquez le football, *I'll prepare an apple pie.*
10. Donne-moi le papier et *I'll explain it to you* tout de suite.

II. THE CONDITIONAL TENSE

A. Formation of the Conditional Tense

To the stem of the future (which is the whole infinitive in regular verbs with final *-e* dropped in the third conjugation), the endings -AIS, -AIS, -AIT, -IONS, -IEZ, -AIENT are added as follows:

je	porterAIS	remplirAIS	perdrAIS
tu	porterAIS	remplirAIS	perdrAIS
il	porterAIT	remplirAIT	perdrAIT
nous	porterIONS	remplirIONS	perdrIONS
vous	porterIEZ	remplirIEZ	perdrIEZ
ils	porterAIENT	remplirAIENT	perdrAIENT

The endings of the conditional are identical in *all* verbs — even in the irregular ones. Note that these endings are the same as the endings of the imperfect tense.

B. Translation and Use of the Conditional Tense

The conditional tense is translated as "should" and "would," which have several interpretations.

should {
- would (conditional tense in a result clause):
  - Je me divertirais. (I would amuse myself.)
- ought to (*devoir* in the conditional tense):
  - Je devrais comprendre le football, mais je n'y comprends rien. (I should [ought to] understand football, but I don't understand a thing about it.)

would {
- Result of an action:
  - Si tu m'expliquais un peu ce qui se passera, je me divertirais.
- Willingness:
  - Voudrais-tu faire quelque chose pour moi? (Would you be willing?)
- "used to" (imperfect):
  - Il attrapait le ballon chaque fois qu'on le lui lançait. (He would catch the ball each time they threw it to him.)

Exercise 3

Translate the English into French:

1. *He would invite*
2. *They would accompany*
3. *I would have a good time*
4. *You would finish*
5. *You should (ought to) finish*
6. *Would you wait* si j'arrivais en retard?
7. *Would you explain the game to me?*
8. Si Marianne ne lui préparait pas la tarte aux pommes, *Paul wouldn't explain football to her.*
9. *Would it be useless to run,* s'il n'avait pas le ballon?
10. Si le joueur n'attrapait pas le ballon, qu'est-ce qui *would happen* (arriver: to happen)?

III. VERBS IRREGULAR IN THE FUTURE AND CONDITIONAL TENSES

The future stem is all that has to be learned; the endings are the same as for the future and conditional of regular verbs.

Exercise 4

From the listed future stems of irregular verbs, give the following forms:

VERB	STEM		FUTURE	CONDITIONAL
1. acquérir: (to acquire)	ACQUERR-	(vous)	______	______
2. aller: (to go)	IR-	(j')	______	______
3. avoir: (to have)	AUR-	(elle)	______	______
4. courir: (to run)	COURR-	(vous)	______	______
5. cueillir: (to gather)	CUEILLE-	(elles)	______	______
6. devoir: (to have to)	DEVR-	(je)	______	______
7. envoyer: (to send)	ENVERR-	(nous)	______	______
8. être: (to be)	SER-	(ils)	______	______

9. faire: (to do, to make)	FER-	(tu)	______	______
10. falloir: (to be necessary)	FAUD-	(il)	______	______
11. mourir: (to die)	MOURR-	(il)	______	______
12. pleuvoir: (to rain)	PLEUVR-	(il)	______	______
13. pouvoir: (to be able)	POURR-	(je)	______	______
14. recevoir: (to receive)	RECEVR-	(vous)	______	______
15. savoir: (to know, to know how)	SAUR-	(elles)	______	______
16. valoir: (to be worth)	VAUD-	(ils)	______	______
17. venir: (to come)	VIENDR-	(nous)	______	______
18. voir: (to see)	VERR-	(je)	______	______
19. vouloir: (to wish, to want)	VOUDR-	(vous)	______	______

Review Exercise

Translate the English into French:

Samedi prochain, *Marianne will accompany Henry to the football game.* Si Paul ne lui explique pas le jeu, *she won't understand a thing about it* (about it: y). *But he will explain it to her. Would he explain it to his sister* si elle ne lui préparait pas la tarte aux pommes? *Yes, he would do it* quand même (anyway). Si elle lui apporte du papier, *he'll make a little sketch for her* (to her). "*When you* (fam.) *go to the game, here's what you'll see!*" lui dit-il. "*There will naturally be two teams! They will kick the ball* et celui *who catches it will run* du côté du but. *As soon as he starts running,* les adversaires *will try to prevent him* de faire un touchdown. Peut-être qu'il (maybe he) *will be able* arriver au but, *maybe it will be necessary* lancer le ballon à un autre joueur de son équipe." "*Will he run* s'il ne porte pas le ballon?" "Non, *it would be useless! You* (fam.) *will learn* (apprendre) le reste *when you see* le jeu. *You will have a good time,* j'en suis sûr. *You shouldn't have* beaucoup de questions.

CHAPTER EIGHT

The Past Indefinite: *Formation of the Past Indefinite; Translation of the Past Indefinite; Intransitive Verbs of Motion That Use* Être *as Auxiliary*

How the Past Participle Agrees: *If the Auxiliary Is* Avoir; *If the Verb Belongs to the List of Intransitive Verbs of Motion Taking* Être *as an Auxiliary; If the Verb Is Reflexive*

Distinction Between Past Indefinite and Imperfect Tenses

Past Participles of Some Irregular Verbs

LA GRIPPE	THE FLU
JEANNINE – Où est ta sœur, Paul? JE L'AI ATTENDUE avant la classe d'anglais, mais ELLE N'EST PAS VENUE et JE SUIS ENTRÉE un peu en retard.	JEANNINE – Where is your sister, Paul? I waited for her before English class, but she didn't come and I entered a little late.
PAUL – ELLE EST RESTÉE à la maison aujourd'hui, Jeannine. ELLE A PERDU la voix. Je crois qu'ELLE A PRIS froid samedi à la partie de football. Hier, elle se plaignait d'avoir des frissons et de la fièvre et ON A FAIT VENIR le médecin.	PAUL – She stayed home today, Jeannine. She lost her voice. I think she caught cold at the football game Saturday. Yesterday she was complaining of having chills and fever and we sent for the doctor.
JEANNINE – C'est la grippe! Moi aussi J'AI ATTRAPÉ une laryngite la semaine passée. Heureusement JE ME SUIS REPOSÉ LA VOIX et JE ME SUIS COMPLÈTEMENT REMISE en un jour.	JEANNINE – It's the flu. I caught laryngitis last week, too. Fortunately, I rested my voice and I recovered completely in one day.
PAUL – C'est ce qu'il faut faire. Le médecin LUI A FAIT une injection, je crois, et ELLE S'EST GARGARISÉE avec quelque solution QU'IL A RECOMMANDÉE. Ce matin, elle parlait. . . .	PAUL – That's what you have to do. The doctor gave her an injection, I believe, and she gargled with some solution that he recommended. This morning, she was talking. . . .
JEANNINE – La pauvre! Alors, je ne vais pas l'appeler. Je ne veux pas la faire parler.	JEANNINE – The poor thing! Then I'm not going to call her. I don't want to make her talk.

PAUL – Oh, la paix QUI EST DESCENDUE sur notre maison! Chaque fois qu'elle essayait de parler, c'est ce que nous lui disions.	PAUL – Oh, the peace that descended on our house! Each time she tried to talk, that's what we said to her.
JEANNINE – Tu es méchant, Paul!	JEANNINE – You're mean, Paul!
PAUL – C'était pour la taquiner.	PAUL – That was to tease her.

I. THE PAST INDEFINITE

A. Formation of the Past Indefinite

The past indefinite (*le passé indéfini* or *le passé composé*) is made up of the present of the auxiliary verb and a past participle: -er-verb past participles end in -é (recommander, recommandé); -ir-verb past participles end in -i (finir, fini); -re-verb past participles end in -u (attendre, attendu). The auxiliary is usually *avoir*. The auxiliary is *être* with reflexive verbs and with a special group of intransitive verbs which will be listed below.

The Past Indefinite of Verbs of the Three Conjugations and of One Verb Conjugated with Être

	FIRST CONJUGATION	SECOND CONJUGATION	THIRD CONJUGATION
j'	ai recommandé	ai fini	ai attendu
tu	as recommandé	as fini	as attendu
il / elle	a recommandé	a fini	a attendu
nous	avons recommandé	avons fini	avons attendu
vous	avez recommandé	avez fini	avez attendu
ils / elles	ont recommandé	ont fini	ont attendu

EXAMPLE OF A VERB CONJUGATED WITH ETRE

je suis venu(e)
tu es venu(e)
il (elle) est venu(e)
nous sommes venu(e)s
vous êtes venu(e) (s)
ils (elles) sont venu(e)s

The past participle stands outside the negation or interrogation:

Elle n'est pas venue. (She didn't come.)

Le médecin ne m'a pas fait d'injection. (The doctor didn't give me any injection.)

Marianne a-t-elle pris froid? (Did Marianne catch cold?)

S'est-elle reposé la voix? (Did she rest her voice?)

B. Translation of the Past Indefinite

The past indefinite is translated as: "______ed," "has ______," "have ______," "did ______."

C. Intransitive Verbs of Motion That Use Être as Auxiliary

The past participles are formed as would be expected, except for the three that are given:

aller (to go)
arriver (to arrive)
venir (to come, past participle *venu*; compounds: *revenir*, to come back; *devenir*, to become)
entrer (to enter, to go in; compound: *rentrer*, to return)
tomber (to fall)
rester (to remain, to stay)
naître (to be born, past participle *né*)
mourir (to die, past participle *mort*)
partir (to leave, to go away, to depart)
sortir (to leave, to go out)
monter (to go up)
descendre (to go or come down)
retourner (to return, to go back)

NOTE: If *monter, descendre, sortir,* and *rentrer* are used transitively, with the meanings, respectively, of "to bring up," "to bring down," "to take out," "to bring back in," they are conjugated with *avoir*.

EXERCISE 1

Translate:

1. I caught
2. You finished
3. She waited
4. They have recommended
5. We didn't select
6. You (fam.) didn't lose
7. I haven't called
8. You did tease
9. Have we tried?
10. Did he speak?
11. Haven't you left?
12. Didn't she come?

13. He stayed
14. You went
15. He didn't fall
16. Did you arrive?
17. I entered
18. You (fam.) went down
19. He rested
20. I gargled
21. You recovered
22. Did they rest their voices?
23. He didn't recover
24. You complained (to complain: *se plaindre;* past participle, *plaint*)

II. HOW THE PAST PARTICIPLE AGREES

Note that the agreement is always determined *by going back.* Also remember that a direct object is the word that answers "whom" or "what." There are three sorts of agreement:

A. *If the auxiliary is avoir,* agreement is with the *direct object if it precedes:*

Je l'ai attendue. (I waited for her.)

BUT: There is no agreement if the direct object follows:

Elle a perdu la voix. (She lost her voice.)

or if the preceding object is indirect:

Il lui a fait une injection. (He gave her an injection.)

No agreement is necessary in the past participle *fait* + an infinitive; *vu* and *entendu* agree when the direct preceding object performs the action indicated in the infinitive:

Nous les avons *fait* venir. (We sent for them.)
Je l'ai *entendue* tousser. (I heard her coughing.)
Il nous a *vus* attendre. (He saw us waiting.)

EXERCISE 2

Translate the English into French:

Où est Marianne? Elle est absente aujourd'hui à cause d'une laryngite *that she caught* à la partie de football. *She lost her voice completely.* On a fait venir le médecin. Quelle solution *did he recommend? He gave her an injection,* je crois.

B. *If the verb belongs to the list of intransitive verbs of motion taking* être *as an auxiliary,* agreement is with the subject:

Elle n'est pas venu*e*. (She didn't come.)
Je suis entré*e*. (I went in.)
Elle est resté*e*. (She stayed.)

Exercise 3

Translate the English into French:

1. Jeannine *arrived* de bonne heure mais *she didn't enter* immédiatement dans la classe d'anglais.
2. Ensuite, *she went* demander à Paul: "*Did your sister stay home today*?"
3. Paul explained: "Marianne *didn't come* aujourd'hui. *She didn't go out*."
4. Jeannine et Paul *went down* à la classe de français.

C. *If the verb is reflexive*, agreement is with the preceding direct object:

Elle *s'*est complètement remis*e*. (She completely recovered.)

Elle s'est reposé la voix. (No agreement) (She rested her voice.)

Quelles *questions* s'est-elle fait*es*? (What questions did she ask herself?)

Note that since the preceding direct object is usually the reflexive pronoun, it is well always to look first at the *me, te, se,* etc. To determine whether or not these are the direct object, it is often helpful to translate the expression literally:

Elle s'est assise. (She seated herself.)

Also, when the expression contains a preposition, the *me, te, se* are usually the direct object of the verb because any noun that might follow is usually object of the preposition:

Elle s'est servie de cette solution. (She used that solution.)

Here, *solution* is object of the preposition *de*, leaving *se* as direct object of the verb.

Exercise 4

Translate the English into French:

Lorsqu'on a demandé à Marianne ce qu'elle avait (what was the matter with her), *she complained* d'avoir des frissons et de la fièvre. Jeannine a dit *that she rested her voice and completely recovered* en un jour. Jeannine et Paul *spoke to each other* (se parler) avant la classe d'anglais et lorsque Paul *told her* que sa sœur avait une laryngite, Jeannine *said to herself:* Je ne vais pas l'appeler; je ne veux pas la faire parler.

Exercise 5

Translate the English into French:

We waited for Marianne mais *she didn't come* ce jour-là. À cause d'une laryngite *that she caught* samedi passé, *she stayed home. The doctor gave her* une solution avec laquelle (with which) *she gargled. The injection that he gave her* lui a fait du bien (did her good). *She has almost* (presque) *completely recovered* en un jour. *I called her and I heard her speak.* Elle m'a dit *that she rested her voice toute* la journée. *Did her brother tease her?* Naturellement, il lui a dit: *Oh, the peace that has descended on our house! Jeannine didn't go* la voir parce qu'elle a pris froid, elle aussi (too).

Summary of the Agreement of Past Participles	
KIND OF VERB	AGREEMENT
Auxiliary *avoir*	Direct preceding object
With *être*	Subject
Reflexive	*Se,* etc., if this pronoun is direct object (or with any other preceding direct object)

III. DISTINCTION BETWEEN PAST INDEFINITE AND IMPERFECT TENSES

PAST INDEFINITE

1. has ______, have ______
2. did ______
3. ______ed

Simple past in English is to be interpreted as the French *passé composé* if the implication is "on that occasion" or "as I look back":

Moi aussi j'ai attrapé une laryngite. (I caught laryngitis too.)

Je me suis complètement remise en un jour. (I completely recovered in one day.)

IMPERFECT

1. used to (would)
2. was ______ing, were ______ing
3. ______ed

Simple past in English is to be interpreted as the French imperfect if the implication is "during that time" or if the meaning of "used to" or "was or were ______ing" suits the sense.

Hier elle se plaignait. (Yesterday she was complaining.)

Chaque fois qu'elle essayait de parler, nous lui disions . . . (Each time she tried to speak we told her . . .)

The one essential difference between these two tenses is that the past indefinite indicates a completed action, the end of which is either expressed or in view:

j'ai attrapé (I caught)

je me suis reposé la voix (I rested my voice)

whereas the imperfect indicates an action in progress or in some way suspended with no reference to its having been completed:

elle se plaignait (she was complaining)

chaque fois qu'elle essayait de parler... (each time she tried to speak...)

IV. PAST PARTICIPLES OF SOME IRREGULAR VERBS

Give the following forms of the past indefinite:

eu (from avoir: to have)	je ______
connu (connaître: to know)	vous ______
couru (courir: to run)	ils ______
cru (croire: to believe)	nous ______
dû (due) (devoir: to have to)	elle ______
dit (dire: to say, to tell)	elles ______
écrit (écrire: to write)	vous ______
été (être: to be)	il ______
fait (faire: to do, to make)	je ______
fallu (falloir: to be necessary)	il ______
lu (lire: to read)	nous ______
mis (mettre: to put)	ils ______
ouvert (ouvrir: to open)	vous ______
pris (prendre: to take)	je ______
reçu (recevoir: to receive)	il ______
su (savoir: to know, to know how)	elles ______
venu (venir: to come)	nous ______
vécu (vivre: to live)	vous ______
vu (voir: to see)	je ______
voulu (vouloir: to wish, to want)	elles ______

CHAPTER NINE

The Compound Tenses: *The Past Indefinite, the Future Perfect, the Pluperfect, the Conditional Perfect, the Preterit Perfect*

À LA BIBLIOTHÈQUE	AT THE LIBRARY
MARIANNE – Je croyais que c'était toi, Jeannine, derrière ce tas de livres.	MARIANNE – I thought that it was you, Jeannine, behind that stack of books.
JEANNINE – Ah, Marianne! Oui, c'est moi. Et je ne sais vraiment pas ce que J'AURAI DÉCOUVERT QUAND JE LES AURAI TOUS CONSULTÉS.	JEANNINE – Ah, Marianne! Yes, it's me. And I really don't know what I'll have found out when I have consulted them all.
MARIANNE – Mais ils portent tous sur ton sujet. Du moins tu auras une belle bibliographie.	MARIANNE – But they all have to do with your subject. At least you'll have a fine bibliography.
JEANNINE – SI SEULEMENT J'AVAIS GARDÉ le premier titre QUE J'AVAIS CHOISI, JE N'AURAIS PAS RENCONTRÉ tant d'obstacles. Mais ça ira. Et ton travail, Marianne, ça marche?	JEANNINE – If I had only kept the first title that I had chosen, I wouldn't have met so many obstacles. But it will be all right. And how about your paper, Marianne, is it coming along?
MARIANNE – Assez bien, Jeannine. Mais il le faut, car j'en ai deux à remettre avant Noël. Pour le premier, il a fallu préparer un plan. SI JE M'ÉTAIS SERVIE d'un plan pour l'autre aussi, JE LES AURAIS DÉJÀ TERMINÉS, les deux.	MARIANNE – Pretty well, Jeannine. But it has to because I have two of them to hand in before Christmas. For the first one, I had to prepare an outline. If I had used an outline for the other too, I would have the two of them finished by now!
JEANNINE – Alors tu as pas mal de recherches à faire encore.	JEANNINE – Then you have quite a lot of research still to do.
MARIANNE – Il n'y a qu'une référence de plus à vérifier et J'AURAIS PU SORTIR ce livre aujourd'hui SI JE N'AVAIS LAISSÉ ma carte à la maison. C'est si embêtant!	MARIANNE – There's only one more reference to check, and I could have taken out that book today if I hadn't left my card at home. It's so annoying!
JEANNINE – Mais voici ma carte, Marianne. Sors le livre à mon nom! Où est la bibliothécaire?	JEANNINE – Why here's my card, Marianne. Take the book out in my name! Where's the librarian?
MARIANNE – Jeannine! Tu es un ange! Comme ça je pourrai tout taper à la machine ce soir.	MARIANNE – Jeannine! You're an angel! That way, I can type everything up this evening.

THE COMPOUND TENSES

TENSE	FORMATION	TRANSLATION	EXAMPLE
Past Indefinite	For full treatment, consult preceding chapter.		
Future Perfect	Future auxiliary + past particple j'aurai consulté tu auras consulté il aura consulté nous aurons consulté vous aurez consulté ils auront consulté	"shall have ____ed" or "will have ____ed" Often after "when" (lorsque, quand) and "as soon as" (dès que, aussitôt que), the English appears as "when you have ____ed" instead of "when you will have ____ed".	J'aurai découvert quand je les aurai tous consultés.
Pluperfect	Imperfect auxiliary + past particple j'avais choisi tu avais choisi il avait choisi nous avions choisi vous aviez choisi ils avaient choisi	"had ____ed" Besides being used independently, this tense is also found in the if-clause when the conditional perfect is in the result clause.	Si seulement j'avais gardé le premier titre que j'avais choisi, je n'aurais pas rencontré tant d'obstacles.
Conditional Perfect	Conditional auxiliary + past participle j'aurais pu tu aurais pu il aurait pu nous aurions pu vous auriez pu ils auraient pu	"would have ____ed" "should have ____ed" This tense is used in the result clause when the pluperfect is in the if-clause. When "should have ____" means "ought to have ____" the conditional perfect of the verb *devoir* is needed. Ex.: J'aurais dû consulter ce livre. (I should have consulted that book.)	Si seulement j'avais gardé le premier titre que j'avais choisi, je n'aurais pas rencontré tant d'obstacles. J'aurais pu sortir ce livre aujourd'hui si je n'avais pas laissé ma carte à la maison.
Preterit Perfect	Consult the chapter on the past definite (le passé défini or le passé simple), of which this tense is a companion tense.		

Exercise 1

Translate:

A. The Future Perfect

1. I shall have kept
2. You will have chosen
3. He will have heard
4. She will have prepared
5. We shall have arrived
6. They shall have gone out

B. The Pluperfect

1. I had kept
2. You had chosen
3. He had heard
4. She had prepared
5. We had arrived
6. They had gone out

C. The Conditional Perfect

1. I would have kept
2. You would have chosen
3. He would have heard
4. She would have prepared
5. We would have arrived
6. They would have gone out

Exercise 2

Translate the English into French:

Marianne ne savait pas ce qu'elle *would have discovered* lorsqu' *she'd have consulted* tous ces livres. *If she had only kept* son premier titre, *she wouldn't have met* tant d'obstacles. Pourquoi *had she chosen* l'autre sujet et pourquoi *had she decided* à le changer? *Would her work have gone along better if she had kept* le premier titre? *If only she had used* un plan, le travail *would have been* beaucoup moins difficile. *If Marianne hadn't left* sa carte à la maison, *she could have take out* le livre dont elle avait besoin. *When she has checked* une référence de plus, elle commencera à taper à la machine son travail. *As soon as the work has been typed,* elle le remettra à son professeur. Et votre travail, comment marche-t-il? *When you have finished* toutes les lectures requises, vous faudra-t-il (will it take you) longtemps pour l'écrire? *If I hadn't spent* tant de temps à faire mes recherches, *I'd have completed my paper already.*

CHAPTER TEN

The Sequence of Tenses in If-Clause Sentences

LE JOUR D'ACTIONS DE GRÂCES	THANKSGIVING DAY
MME DESJARDINS – Encore de la dinde, Laurent? Des patates, du chou-fleur, des . . . ?	MRS. DESJARDINS – Some more turkey, Laurence? Some sweet potatoes, cauliflower, some . . . ?
LAURENT – Non, merci, madame. Le dîner a été tout à fait délicieux, surtout la dinde avec la gelée d'airelles!	LAURENCE – No, thank you, madame. The dinner was just delicious, especially the turkey with cranberry jelly.
MME DESJARDINS – Bon, alors, SI VOUS NOUS EXCUSEZ, MARIANNE ET MOI NOUS IRONS CHERCHER le dessert.	MRS. DESJARDINS – All right, then, if you'll excuse us, Marianne and I will go and get the dessert.
MARIANNE – C'est la spécialité de Maman pour le Jour d'Actions de grâces! Moi je l'attends toute l'année. . . . Tu éteins les lumières, Paul, n'est-ce pas?	MARIANNE – It's Mother's specialty for Thanksgiving Day! I wait all year for it. . . . You'll put out the lights, won't you, Paul?
PAUL – Bien sûr, Marianne!	PAUL – Of course, Marianne!
M. DESJARDINS – C'est une petite cérémonie que nous observons chaque année, Laurent . . . Ah, voilà Maman qui apporte le pouding aux fruits!	MR. DESJARDINS – It's a little ceremony we observe each year, Laurence . . . Ah, there's Mother bringing the fruit pudding.
MME DESJARDINS – Nous y versons du cognac. Ensuite nous l'allumons. Marianne, tu as les assiettes? Voilà. Tout le monde est servi?	MRS. DESJARDINS – We pour brandy over it. Then we light it. Do you have the plates, Marianne? There you are. Is everyone served?
LAURENT – C'est le couronnement du banquet, madame! SI CE N'ETAIT UNE INDISCRÉTION, EST-CE QUE JE POURRAIS vous prier de me révéler le secret de votre recette, madame? C'est pour ma mère en France. Je voudrais la lui envoyer pour la Noël.	LAURENCE – It's the crowning of the banquet, madame! If it weren't indiscreet, could I (would I be able to) ask you to reveal the secret of your recipe to me, madame? It's for my mother in France. I would like to send it to her for Christmas.
MME DESJARDINS – Mais certainement, Laurent! Et SI JE VOUS DISAIS d'où je tiens cette recette, VOUS	MRS. DESJARDINS – Why, certainly, Laurence! And if I told you where I got this recipe, you would prize

L'ESTIMERIEZ encore davantage. Je la tiens d'une vieille famille française de Québec où nous avons passé bien des années lorsque Marianne et Paul étaient enfants.

it even more. I have it from an old French family of Québec, where we spent many years when Marianne and Paul were children.

LAURENT – Vous êtes si aimable, madame. Sans parler du plaisir de la compagnie de ta chère famille, Paul, figure-toi que SI TU N'AVAIS PAS EU la bonté de m'inviter chez toi, J'AURAIS PASSÉ une journée bien nostalgique au dortoir.

LAURENCE – You are so kind, madame. Not to mention the pleasure of your dear family's company, Paul, just imagine that, if you hadn't been good enough to invite me to your home, I would have spent a very lonely day in the dormitory.

PAUL – Et figure-toi que SI TU N'ÉTAIS PAS VENU aux États-Unis comme étudiant d'échange, NOUS N'AURIONS JAMAIS FAIT LA CONNAISSANCE de notre cher ami Laurent!

PAUL – And just imagine that if you hadn't come to the United States as an exchange student, we would never have met our dear friend Laurence!

THE SEQUENCE OF TENSES IN IF-CLAUSE SENTENCES

IF CLAUSE	RESULT CLAUSE
1. Present	Future (also possible: present or imperative)
Si vous nous excusez . . . (If you will excuse us . . .)	Marianne et moi nous irons chercher le dessert. (Marianne and I will go and get the dessert.)
2. Imperfect	Conditional
Si je vous disais d'où je tiens cette recette . . . (If I told you where I got this recipe . . .)	vous l'estimeriez encore davantage. (you would prize it even more.)
3. Pluperfect	Conditional perfect
Si tu n'avais pas eu la bonté de m'inviter . . . (If you hadn't been good enough to invite me . . .)	j'aurais passé une journée nostalgique. (I would have spent a lonely day.)

EXERCISE 1

Translate the English into French:

1. *If you like* la dinde, *you'll find it* encore plus délicieuse avec de la gelée d'airelles.
2. *If we don't have* de cognac, *we shall not light* le pouding aux fruits.

3. *If Mrs. Desjardins gives* la recette à Laurent, *he will be able to send it* à sa mère pour la Noël.

Exercise 2

Translate the English into French:

1. *Laurence would prize* encore davantage le pouding aux fruits *if he knew* que c'est une vieille recette québecoise.
2. Si Marianne *had* le pouding aux fruits tous les dimanches, *would it be* un régal (a treat)?
3. *Would the turkey be* si délicieuse *if we didn't have* la gelée d'airelles?

Exercise 3

Translate the English into French:

1. *If Mrs. Desjardins had not invited* Laurent à passer chez eux le Jour d'Actions de grâces, *he would have spent* une journée bien nostalgique au dortoir.
2. Si la famille Desjardins *had not gone* au Canada, Mme Desjardins *couldn't have* (wouldn't have been able) faire ce délicieux pouding.
3. *If Laurence hadn't come* en Amérique, Marianne et Paul *would not have made* sa connaissance.

Exercise 4

Match the following:

1. Si nous y réfléchissions,	elle n'aurait pas pu l'allumer.
2. Si Paul n'éteint pas les lumières,	Mme Desjardins n'aurait jamais trouvé cette belle recette.
3. Si Mme Desjardins n'avait pas versé de cognac sur le pouding,	nous ne pourrons pas voir la belle flamme bleue.
4. Si on avait la dinde tous les jours,	nous trouverions que nous avons bien des bénédictions.
5. Si la famille Desjardins n'était pas allée au Canada,	ce ne serait plus un régal.

Review Exercise

Translate the English into French:

If Laurence had not met Marianne and Paul à l'université, son séjour (his stay) en Amérique *would have been* moins agréable car il parlait très peu l'anglais. *How would he have spent Thanksgiving Day* si les Desjardins *had not invited him to have dinner* chez eux? *Where would he have gone? How would he have enjoyed himself* (se divertir)? *If he didn't have these good friends, he certainly would be* très malheureux (unhappy). *If Marianne and Paul and their parents* go un jour en France, *Laurence and his mother will receive them* avec le plus grand plaisir.

CHAPTER ELEVEN

The Demonstrative Adjective and Pronoun: *The Demonstrative Adjective; The Demonstrative Pronoun; Neuter Demonstrative Pronouns*
Some Indefinite Adjectives and Pronouns
The Verb "Devoir"

À L'AÉRODROME	AT THE AIRFIELD
PAUL – Tu es certain, Laurent, que Georges DEVAIT prendre l'avion de six heures?	PAUL – Are you sure, Laurence, that George was to take the six-o'clock plane?
LAURENT – C'est ce qu'il m'a dit, Paul. Je ne sais vraiment pas ce qui a bien pu lui arriver.	LAURENCE – That's what he told me, Paul. I really don't know what could have happened to him.
MARIANNE – C'est sans doute que Georges a pris tant de plaisir à revoir sa famille qu'IL A DÛ remettre son retour au dernier moment.	MARIANNE – It's just that George took such pleasure in seeing his family again that he must have put off his return till the last minute.
LAURENT – C'est probablement CELA, Marianne. Est-ce que NOUS DEVRIONS consulter l'horaire pour savoir à quelle heure atterrira le prochain avion de Boston?	LAURENCE – That's probably it, Marianne. Should we consult the schedule to find out when the next plane from Boston lands?
PAUL – Si vous m'excusez, j'irai chercher CETTE INFORMATION. Un instant.	PAUL – If you'll excuse me, I'll go and get that information. Just a minute!
LAURENT – CES QUATRE JOURS de vacances que vous avez pour le Jour d'Actions de grâces sont épatants, Marianne!	LAURENCE – These four days of vacation that you have for Thanksgiving are wonderful, Marianne!
PAUL – Il y a le vol de sept heures qui DOIT arriver ici à huit heures dix.	PAUL – There's the seven-o'clock flight that is to arrive here at eight ten.
MARIANNE – Nous avons donc une heure d'attente. . . . Allons voir les décollages, voulez-vous, et après nous prendrons une tasse de café.	MARIANNE – Then we have one hour to wait. . . . Let's go see the take-offs, shall we, and afterward we'll have a cup of coffee.
PAUL ET LAURENT – Bonne idée!	PAUL AND LAURENCE – Good idea!

LAURENT – Mais regardez tous CES VOYAGEURS!	LAURENCE – But look at all those passengers!
PAUL – CHAQUE FOIS qu'il y a une fête, c'est comme ÇA. Il y en a QUELQUES-UNS qui rentrent le samedi mais la plupart des voyageurs attendent le dimanche soir pour rentrer.	PAUL – Every time there is a holiday, it's like that. There are some who come home on Saturday, but the majority of the travelers wait for Sunday night to come home.
MARIANNE – Vous voyez CET AVION-LÀ? Non, non, pas CELUI-CI – CELUI-LÀ, à gauche. C'est un jet, non?	MARIANNE – Do you see that plane? No, no, not *this* one – *that* one, on the left. It's a jet, isn't it?
PAUL – Non, Marianne. Ce sont CEUX QUI n'ont pas d'hélices.	PAUL – No, Marianne. They are the ones that don't have any propellers.
MARIANNE – Ah, je vois! Et il y a une différence aussi pour les ailes, n'est-ce pas?	MARIANNE – Oh, I see! And there's a difference in the wings too, isn't there?
PAUL – C'est ÇA. Tu vois CELLES DE CELUI QUI est sur la piste de décollage et puis CELLES de CE JET qui est sur le point de décoller?	PAUL – That's right. Do you see those of the one that's on the runway and then those of that jet that is just about to take off?
MARIANNE – Ah, oui, Paul! Un jour je vais voler, moi aussi!	MARIANNE – Oh, yes, Paul! Someday I'm going to fly, too!

I. THE DEMONSTRATIVE ADJECTIVE AND PRONOUN

A. The Demonstrative Adjective

The adjective that translates "this," "that," "these," or "those" agrees in gender and number with the noun it modifies. The forms of the demonstrative adjective are:

MASCULINE SINGULAR	FEMININE SINGULAR	ALL PLURALS
CE (ce jet)	CETTE (cette information)	CES (ces quatre jours, ces familles)

1. CET (instead of CE) is used before a masculine singular noun beginning with a vowel or nonaspirate "h":

   cet avion (this plane)
   cet homme (this man)

2. If "this" is emphasized in English, such emphasis is expressed in French by adding -CI after the noun; if "that" is stressed, -LÀ is added. Such stress is found especially in contrasts:

   Vous voyez cet avion-là? (Do you see *that* plane?)

Exercise 1

Place the correct form: CE, CET, CETTE, CES before the following nouns:

1. _____ jet
2. _____ jets
3. _____ piste de décollage
4. _____ avion
5. _____ décollage
6. _____ café
7. _____ atterrissage
8. _____ jour
9. _____ vacances
10. _____ tasse
11. _____ famille
12. _____ heure
13. _____ voyageur
14. _____ hélices
15. _____ différence
16. *this* vol et *that* vol
17. *these* avions, pas *those* avions
18. *this* décollage et *those* décollages
19. *these* hélices et *those* hélices
20. *this* atterrissage et *that* atterrissage

B. The Demonstrative Pronoun

Meaning "this (one)," "that (one)," "these (ones)," "those (ones)," "the one(s)," "he who," "she who," "they who," "those who," the demonstrative pronoun, just as any other pronoun, stands in the place of a noun. It must, therefore, be masculine or feminine, singular or plural, like the noun it replaces. The forms of the demonstrative pronoun are:

	MASCULINE	FEMININE
Singular	CELUI	CELLE
Plural	CEUX	CELLES

1. Just as in the case of the demonstrative adjective, *-ci* and *-là* are added when the English stresses "this" and "that," respectively, if it is necessary to distinguish. If a *de* phrase or a *qui*, or *que* clause follows, *-ci* and *-là* are never added:

   Pas celui-ci, celui-là, à gauche... (not this one, that one, on the left...)

   Tu vois celles de celui qui est sur la piste de décollage? (Do you see those of the one that's on the runway?)

2. Another meaning of *celui-ci* and *celui-là* is "the latter" and "the former," respectively. Note that, no matter how the English reads, the French always places *celui-ci* first:

   Le pilote et le co-pilote sont des aviateurs très expérimentés; celui-ci a plus de dix mille heures d'expérience et celui-là est spécialiste en jets. (The pilot and co-pilot are very experienced aviators; the former is a specialist in jets, and the latter has more than ten thousand hours of experience.)

3. Often a possessive expression such as "Peter's," "Mary's" occurs. Here we must change the expression to "that (those) of Peter," etc.: *celui (ceux) de Pierre; celui (ceux) de Marie.*

C. Neuter Demonstrative Pronouns

These are *ceci* (this) and *cela* (that), familiar form *ça* (that). These pronouns stand for ideas or abstractions and thus can have no gender or number. Generally *ceci* (this) refers to an idea that is about to be expressed; *cela* (that) refers back to an idea that has been expressed:

Ceci va vous plaire: nous allons prendre un jet et nous serons à Washington dans une heure. (This is going to please you: we're going to take a jet and we'll be in Washington in an hour.)

C'est sans doute que Georges a pris tant de plaisir à revoir sa famille qu'il a dû remettre son retour au dernier moment. C'est probablement *cela*, Marianne. (It's just that George had such a good time seeing his family again that he must have put off his return till the last minute. That's probably it, Marianne.)

Exercise 2

Translate the italicized words:

1. ce jet et *the one* que vous voyez là-bas
2. ces avions-ci et *those* de l'autre hangar
3. cette piste de décollage-ci et *that one*
4. ces atterrissages-ci et *those*
5. Quel pilote? *The one* qui vient d'atterrir.
6. Quels voyageurs? *The ones* qui descendent.
7. (les vols) *this one* et *that one*
8. (les tasses) *these,* pas *those*
9. (les hélices) *this one* et *that*
10. (les avions) *this* et *those*
11. *This* est très agréable: nous allons survoler (fly over) la ville de New-York.
12. Est-ce que *that* vous plaît?

II. SOME INDEFINITE ADJECTIVES AND PRONOUNS

The following list of indefinite adjectives and pronouns can be learned simply as vocabulary. Note that with the pronouns, *en* has to be used to complete the thought.

INDEFINITE ADJECTIVES	INDEFINITE PRONOUNS	
quelque[s] (some) Quelques voyageurs sont descendus. (Some passengers got off.)	**quelqu'un[e] (someone)**	**quelques-un[e]s (some [ones])** Il y en a quelques-uns qui rentrent le samedi. (There are some who come home on Saturday.)
chaque (each) Chaque fois (Each time)	**chacun[e] (each [one])** Chacune des fois (Each of the times)	
quelconque (some or other C'est une fête quelconque. (It's some holiday or other.)	**quiconque (whoever)** Quiconque vole . . . (Whoever flies . . .)	

1. *Quelques* and *des* both translate as "some"; *quelques* is "some" in the sense of "a few"; *des* is more vague.
2. The word *plusieurs* (several) never takes *de* but is followed by the noun immediately:

   Il y a plusieurs jets qui décollent. (There are several jets taking off.)
3. Note the meaning of the following composite words:

   n'importe qui, anyone
   n'importe quand, anytime
   n'importe comment, anyhow
   n'importe où, anywhere

Exercise 3

Match the French with the English:

1. chaque avion	whoever takes a jet
2. quelques-uns des pilotes	some plane or other
3. vous pouvez demander à n'importe qui	each plane
4. chacun des décollages	I would fly anwhere
5. n'importe qui vous le dira	each of the take-offs
6. quiconque prend un jet	some of the pilots
7. un avion quelconque	you can ask anyone
8. quelques pistes de décollage	several hours
9. je volerais n'importe où	anyone will tell you
10. plusieurs heures	some runways

III. THE VERB "devoir"

It is extremely important to note the meanings of the verb *devoir* in the following tenses:

TENSE	MEANING	EXAMPLE
Present	must	Je dois me dépêcher. (I must hurry.)
	is (supposed) to	Il y a un vol qui doit arriver... (There is a flight that is to arrive...)
Imperfect	had to (for some time)	Je devais me dépêcher. (I had to hurry.)
	was (supposed) to	Georges devait prendre l'avion de six heures. (George was to take the six-o'clock plane.)
Past Indefinite	had to (on an occasion)	J'ai dû me dépêcher ce matin. (I had to hurry this morning.)
	must have	Il a dû remettre son retour. (He must have put off his return.)
Conditional	should, ought to	Est-ce que nous devrions consulter...? (Should we consult...?)
Conditional Perfect	should have, ought to have	Nous aurions dû arriver à huit heures. (We should have [ought to have] arrived at eight o'clock.)

Exercise 4

Translate:

1. *I am to* décoller.
2. *They were to* atterrir.
3. *You must have waited.*
4. *You should have arrived.*
5. *He should (ought to) fly.*
6. *Must I put off?*
7. *Was she to land?*
8. *Did you have to fly?*
9. *I shall not have to wait.*
10. *The plane shouldn't have taken off.*
11. *Shouldn't the jet arrive?*
12. *We shouldn't have waited.*

Review Exercise

Translate the English into French:

Georges *was to* prendre l'avion de sept heures, mais quand l'avion a atterri, il n'était pas là. *He must have* remettre son retour mais *he should have* nous le dire. Il y a un deuxième vol qui *is to* décoller de Boston à huit heures. *He should* arriver donc à neuf heures parce que c'est un jet. Ah, voilà un avion qui arrive! Non, il y en a deux! Ce *must be George's*. Lequel? (Which one?) *This one or that one*? *That one, the one* qui n'a pas d'hélices. Ah, vous savez que les jets n'ont pas d'hélices? Mais naturellement, je sais *that*. J'en ai vu *some* sur la piste de décollage et Paul m'a fait remarquer (showed me) *several differences* entre les deux types. Je me connais en avions (I'm an authority on planes). *Those that have* les ailes horizontales sont des avions traditionnels; *those that have the ones* en forme de la lettre V, ce sont des jets. *That jet is landing*. Allons voir si Georges est là! Ah oui, le voilà! Où ça? (Where?) *That* garçon qui descend. *Each time* que je crois le voir il y a *some passengers* qui passent devant lui. Allons à sa rencontre! (Let's go and meet him!)

CHAPTER TWELVE

The Possessive Adjective

The Possessive Pronoun

The Cardinal and Ordinal Numbers: *The Cardinal Numbers; The Ordinal Numbers; Fractions; Special Uses of the Numbers*

AU GRAND MAGASIN	IN THE DEPARTMENT STORE
MARIANNE – Il n'est que deux heures et demie . . . non, deux heures et quart. Nous avons largement le temps d'admirer le décor jusqu'à trois heures.	MARIANNE – It's only half-past two . . . no, a quarter after two. We have plenty of time to admire the decorations until three o'clock.
HÉLÈNE – C'est bien! . . . Voilà le Père Noël, Marianne. Tu le vois avec SES RENNES, SES NAINS, et SON GRAND SAC rouge? Non, non! Là-bas, au fond.	HELEN – That's right! . . . There's Santa Claus, Marianne. Do you see him with his reindeer, his elves, and his big red bag? No, no! Over there, at the back.
MARIANNE – C'est bien lui! Mais c'est tout un pays féerique autour de lui. Ah, comme c'est mignon! Tu vois? Le Père Noël a SA PIPE et voilà que le petit nain a LA SIENNE À LUI.	MARIANNE – Indeed that's him! Why, it's a whole fairyland around him. Oh, how cute! You see? Santa Claus has his pipe and there the little dwarf has his.
HÉLÈNE – Regarde comme ils travaillent à LEURS JOUETS!	HELEN – Look how they're working on their toys!
MARIANNE – Voilà le carillon qui commence à jouer les noëls. D'où est-ce que ça vient?	MARIANNE – There are the chimes beginning to play the carols. Where are they coming from?
HÉLÈNE – De la crèche, Marianne. La voilà à gauche . . . Tu la vois?	HELEN – From the manger, Marianne. There it is on the left . . . Do you see it?
MARIANNE – Comme c'est beau! Le décor est magnifique! Il y a tant de belles choses à voir que nous allons oublier de faire NOS ACHATS.	MARIANNE – How beautiful it is! The decorations are splendid! There are so many beautiful things to see that we're going to forget to do our shopping.

HÉLÈNE – Attends que je trouve MA LISTE, Marianne . . . Tu as LA TIENNE?	HELEN – Wait till I find my list, Marianne . . . Do you have yours?
MARIANNE – Un instant. Ah, oui. Voici LA MIENNE. Nous voilà munies de NOS LISTES . . . Par où est-ce que nous commençons? Voyons. Un sac à main pour MA MÈRE, un tricot pour MON PÈRE.	MARIANNE – Just a second. Ah, yes. Here's mine. Now we're fortified with our lists . . . Where do we begin? Let's see. A handbag for my mother, a sweater for my father.
HÉLÈNE – Moi, j'achète un porte-monnaie pour MON FRÈRE. Commençons par le rayon de la maroquinerie pour TON SAC À MAIN et MON PORTE-MONNAIE. En avant! Courage!	HELEN – I'm buying a wallet for my brother. Let's start with the leather goods department for your bag and my wallet. Forward! Courage!
MARIANNE – Très bien! Ensuite nous irons au rayon de la bijouterie pour le collier de perles, au rayon de la parfumerie pour le petit vaporisateur, et au rayon de la mercerie pour les cravates et les gants.	MARIANNE – Fine! Then we'll go to the jewelry department for the pearl necklace, to the perfume department for the little atomizer, and to the haberdashery department for the ties and gloves.
HÉLÈNE – Avec cela, nous aurons fait presque tous NOS ACHATS et ce n'est aujourd'hui que le dix-neuf décembre. Voilà des progrès!	HELEN – At that point, we shall have made almost all our purchases and today is only December nineteenth. That's progress!

I. THE POSSESSIVE ADJECTIVE

	WITH MASCULINE SINGULAR NOUN	WITH FEMININE SINGULAR NOUN	WITH ALL PLURAL NOUNS
MY:	MON	MA	MES
YOUR:	TON	TA	TES
HIS or HER:	SON	SA	SES
OUR:	NOTRE	NOTRE	NOS
YOUR:	VOTRE	VOTRE	VOS
THEIR:	LEUR	LEUR	LEURS

1. Agreement is with the thing possessed, not with the possessor:
   Le Père Noël a *sa pipe*. (Santa Claus has his pipe.)
2. The possessive is expressed before each noun:
   Voici les étrennes pour *mon père* et *ma mère*. (Here are the gifts for my father and mother.)

3. *Mon, ton,* and *son* (instead of *ma, ta,* and *sa*) are used before a feminine noun beginning with a vowel or h mute:

   Voilà mon idée. (That is my idea.)

4. To distinguish between "her father" (son père) and "his father" (son père), add son père *à elle* and son père *à lui*:

   Marianne a un tricot pour son père à elle tandis que Laurent a des gants pour son père à lui. (Marianne has a sweater for *her* father, while Laurence has gloves for *his* father.)

Exercise 1

Translate:

(her) sac à main	(their) liste	(my) collier
(his) pipe	(your) tricots	(her) perles
(our) pays	(her) porte-monnaie	(your) vaporisateur
(his) nains	(your) idée (corresponding to *tu*)	(his) cravates
		(their) gants

Exercise 2

Go through the above list of nouns, expressing before each (1) my, (2) his, (3) your (corresponding to *vous*), (4) her, (5) our, (6) their.

II. THE POSSESSIVE PRONOUN

	STANDING FOR A MASCULINE SINGULAR WORD	STANDING FOR A FEMININE SINGULAR WORD	STANDING FOR MASCULINE PLURAL WORDS	STANDING FOR FEMININE PLURAL WORDS
MINE:	LE MIEN	LA MIENNE	LES MIENS	LES MIENNES
YOURS: (corresponding to *tu*)	LE TIEN	LA TIENNE	LES TIENS	LES TIENNES
HIS or HERS:	LE SIEN	LA SIENNE	LES SIENS	LES SIENNES
YOURS: (correspond-to *vous*)	LE VÔTRE	LA VÔTRE	LES VÔTRES	LES VÔTRES
OURS:	LE NÔTRE	LA NÔTRE	LES NÔTRES	LES NÔTRES
THEIRS:	LE LEUR	LA LEUR	LES LEURS	LES LEURS

1. By thinking first of the noun that is meant and of the article that you would use with it, you will automatically select the correct pronoun:

   sa pipe et la mienne (his pipe and mine)

2. If it is necessary to emphasize *his*, as for example, to distinguish it from *hers*, *à lui* is added for "his" and *à elle* for "hers."

   Le Père Noël a sa pipe et ce petit nain a la sienne à lui. (Santa Claus has his pipe and this little dwarf has *his*.)

Exercise 3

Translate the italicized words:

1. mon sac à main et *hers*
2. leur pays et *ours*
3. sa pipe et *mine*
4. nos tricots et *yours* (pl.)
5. ma liste et *his*
6. son porte-monnaie et *mine*
7. mon idée et *yours*
8. nos perles et *theirs*
9. notre pays et *theirs*
10. ses cravates et *mine*

Exercise 4

Give the possessive pronoun that would replace the noun at the head of each column:

	le porte-monnaie	*la liste*	*les gants*	*les cravates*
MINE	______	______	______	______
HIS	______	______	______	______
OURS	______	______	______	______
HERS	______	______	______	______
THEIRS	______	______	______	______
YOURS (corresponding to *vous*)	______	______	______	______

Exercise 5

Translate the English into French:

J'ai *my list* et je vais avec *my friend* Jeannine au grand magasin. Jeannine aussi a *her list*. Elle va acheter *her Christmas presents* pendant que moi j'achète *mine*. Avez-vous déjà achète *yours*? *My brother* n'achète jamais *his* avant la veille de Noël (Christmas Eve). Mais mes deux sœurs achètent *theirs* au mois d'octobre. Voyons la liste. Pour *my father*, une pipe parce que *his* est très vieille (old); pour *my mother*, un sac à main bleu parce que *hers* est noir et *her* robe nouvelle est bleue. Pour *my* petite sœur, une poupée (doll) et pour *my* petit frère, une locomotive come *yours*, pour *his* train électrique. Est-ce que nous avons tous *our* paquets? Nous avons *ours*. Est-ce que *your friends* ont *theirs*? Très bien alors! Nous sommes très contents de *our* achats.

III. THE CARDINAL AND ORDINAL NUMBERS

A. The Cardinal Numbers

1	un	6	six	11	onze	16	seize
2	deux	7	sept	12	douze	17	dix-sept
3	trois	8	huit	13	treize	18	dix-huit
4	quatre	9	neuf	14	quatorze	19	dix-neuf
5	cinq	10	dix	15	quinze	20	vingt

From 20 to 100, it is necessary to learn only 30, 40, 50, etc., and to combine these with the above, using hyphens in all cases (except the "ones" where *et* replaces the hyphen in 21, 31, 41, 51, 61, 71):

21	vingt et un	34	trente-quatre	56	cinquante-six
22	vingt-deux	41	quarante et un	57	cinquante-sept
23	vingt-trois	45	quarante-cinq	61	soixante et un
31	trente et un	51	cinquante et un	67	soixante-sept

There are no single words for 70, 80, or 90. On arriving at 70, one continues on through the teens:

70	soixante-dix	75	soixante-quinze
71	soixante et onze	76	soixante-seize
72	soixante-douze	77	soixante-dix-sept
73	soixante-treize	78	soixante-dix-huit
74	soixante-quatorze	79	soixante-dix-neuf

The words for 80 are *quatre-vingts*. Note that from here on, the *s* of *vingts* drops and the *et* is not used with the "one"; 90 continues right on from *quatre-vingt-dix*:

81	quatre-vingt-un	94	quatre-vingt-quatorze
82	quatre-vingt-deux	95	quatre-vingt-quinze
83	quatre-vingt-trois	96	quatre-vingt-seize

The following are the basic forms after 100 (*cent*):

200	deux cents
250	deux cent cinquante (note the dropping of the *s* of *cent* when a number follows immediately)
1,000	mille (*mil* in dates; otherwise *mille* is invariable)
2,000	deux mille
1,000,000	un million (de) + noun
1,000,000,000	un milliard (de) + noun

B. The Ordinal Numbers

The English -th, in sixth, seventh, eighth, etc., is equal to the French *-ième* in *sixième, septième, huitième.* Note the special forms:

1st premier
4th quatrième (the *e* of *quatre* drops before *-ième* and in all forms where the cardinal ends in *-e*: *onzième, douzième, treizième, quatorzième, quinzième*)
5th cinquième (*u* is inserted)
9th neuvième (*f* changes to *v*)

C. Fractions

Just as in English, fractions use the cardinal for the numerator and the ordinal for the denominator. The definite article is used if the numerator is plural:

un cinquième (one fifth)
un huitième (one eighth)
les trois septièmes (three sevenths)

Un demi (one half), *un tiers* (one third), and *un quart* (one quarter) are special forms.

D. Special Uses of the Numbers:

1. *In telling time.* The nearest hour is always told first. "After" is expressed by *et* with *quart* (quarter) and *demie* (half); otherwise it is unexpressed. "To" is expressed by *moins.*

Quelle heure est-il? (What time [hour] is it?)
Il est trois heures. (It is three o'clock.)
Il est trois heures dix (3:10).
Il est trois heures et quart (3:15).
Il est trois heures et demie (3:30).
Il est quatre heures moins vingt (less twenty) (3:40).
Il est quatre heures moins un (or *le*) quart (3:45).
Il est quatre heures précises (4:00 exactly).
Il est midi (12:00 noon).
Il est minuit (12:00 midnight).
Il est une heure du matin (1:00 A.M.).
Il est huit heures du soir (8:00 P.M.).

2. *Expressing the date.* The article, the cardinal number (except for "first," *premier*), and the month are used:

Quel jour du mois est-ce (*or* sommes-nous) aujourd'hui? (What day of the month is today?)

C'est (Nous sommes) aujourd'hui le onze février dix-neuf (mil neuf) cent soixante-cinq. (Today is the eleventh of February, 1965.)

3. *Measuring surfaces.* The wording here is to be noted:

Ce comptoir est long de dix pieds et large de trois pieds *or* Ce comptoir a dix pieds de long (de longueur) sur trois pieds de large (de largeur). (This counter is ten feet long by three feet wide.)

4. *Telling or comparing ages.* The use of the verb *avoir* is to be noted:

Quel âge ce nain a-t-il? (How old is that dwarf?)

Il a vingt ans. (He is twenty years old.)

Combien d'années le Père Noël a-t-il de plus que le nain? *or* De combien d'ans le Père Noël est-il plus âgé que le nain? (How much older is Santa Claus than the dwarf?)

Le Père Noël est de quarante ans plus âgé que le nain *or* Le Père Noël a quarante ans de plus que le nain. (Santa Claus is forty years older than the dwarf.)

5. *Expressing titles of rulers.* The cardinal number is used (except *premier*):

Louis quatorze (XIV), Henri quatre (IV), François premier (I).

6. *Expressing the idea of "about."* The suffix *-aine* can be added to a cardinal number:

une dizaine (about ten)

une vingtaine (about twenty)

Exercise 6

Translate the following:

four	sixty-five	third
fifteen	seventy-two	fifth
twenty	eighty-seven	twenty-ninth
twenty-six	ninety-three	thirty-seventh
forty-nine	one hundred thirty-six	fifty-second
fifty-eight	one million three thousand	ninety-third

Translate the English into French:

1. Quelle heure est-il? *It's eleven o'clock. It's five minutes after eleven. It's a quarter after eleven. It's half-past eleven. It's a quarter to twelve* (noon). *It's noon.*
2. Quel jour du mois est-ce aujourd'hui? *Today is the fourteenth of December, nineteen hundred sixty-five.*

3. Regardez combien de personnes écoutent le carillon! Il y en a *about fifty.*
4. Cette boîte *is two feet long by one foot wide.*
5. Quel âge cet enfant a-t-il? *He's five years old.*
6. Est-il plus âgé que sa petite sœur? *Yes, he's one year older.*
7. Combien de rois de France pouvez-vous nommer? *Louis IX, Henry IV, Louis XIV, Francis I.*
8. A quelle heure êtes-vous arrivé à l'université ce matin? Je suis arrivé *at ten o'clock.*
9. Combien font trente et cinquante? Trente et cinquante font *eighty.* Combien font quatre-vingt-dix moins quarante? Quatre-vingt-dix moins quarante font *fifty.* Combien font deux fois trente? Deux fois trente font *sixty.*

CHAPTER THIRTEEN

The Relative Pronoun: *The Simple Relative Pronouns; The Double or Compound Relative Pronouns*

DANS LE TRAIN	ON THE TRAIN
PAUL – Il faut faire la queue devant le guichet!	PAUL – We have to stand in line before the ticket window.
LAURENT – Écoutez! Si vous prenez mes skis, moi je prendrai les billets. Ensuite je vous retrouverai à la salle d'attente.	LAURENCE – Listen! If you take my skis, I'll get the tickets. Then I'll meet you in the waiting room.
HENRI – C'est une très bonne idée! Mais c'est MOI qui IRAI chercher les billets.	HENRY – That's a very good idea! But I'm the one who will go and get the tickets.
....	....
HENRI – Encore deux heures et nous voilà. Ensuite, trois belles journées de patinage et de ski!	HENRY – Two hours more and there we are. Then, three fine days of skating and skiing!
LAURENT – Les montagnes couronnées de neige. C'est CE QUE nous avons dans mon pays.	LAURENCE – Mountains crowned with snow. That's what we have in my country.
PAUL – Ce sont des scènes QUI font penser à la Savoie, n'est-ce pas, Laurent?	PAUL – They're scenes that remind you of Savoie, aren't they, Laurence?
LAURENT – Oui, en effet. C'est un paradis à cette époque de l'année.	LAURENCE – Yes, indeed. It's a paradise at this time of the year.
PAUL – Henri, comment est cette auberge QUE tu nous as recommandée?	PAUL – Henry, how is that inn that you recommended to us?
HENRI – Tout à fait magnifique! C'est un endroit DONT la réputation devient de plus en plus répandue. Il y a là TOUT CE QU'ON pourrait souhaiter, des repas épatants, l'atmosphère alpestre . . .	HENRY – Just great! It's a spot whose reputation is becoming more and more widespread. There's all you could wish for there, wonderful meals, an Alpine setting . . .
PAUL – Et des propriétaires QUI ne parlent que le français, n'est-ce pas, Henri?	PAUL – And owners who speak only French, right, Henry?
HENRI – C'est juste!	HENRY – Just so!

LAURENT – Magnifique! Et le billet d'aller et retour ne coûte pas cher.

LAURENCE – Great! And the round-trip ticket isn't expensive.

HENRI – J'ai oublié de vous dire qu'il y a un beau lac SUR LEQUEL on peut patiner à cœur joie.

HENRY – I forgot to tell you that there's a fine lake where you can skate to your heart's content.

PAUL – Quelle chance! Si nous allions prendre le déjeuner . . . Mais le wagon-restaurant est probablement pas mal bondé à cette heure-ci.

PAUL – What luck! Suppose we go have lunch . . . But the dining car is probably quite crowded at this hour.

HENRI – Ça ne fait rien. Il faut se fortifier – SANS QUOI il sera impossible de grimper les collines.

HENRY – That's nothing. We have to fortify ourselves – without which it'll be impossible to climb the hills.

I. THE RELATIVE PRONOUN

The relative pronouns have the following forms and are used as follows:

A. The Simple Relative Pronouns

SUBJECT	OBJECT
QUI, who, which, that: des propriétaires qui ne parlent que le français (proprietors who speak only French.) une idée qui est très bonne (an idea that is very good)	QUE, whom, which, that: le skieur que nous avons salué (the skier whom we greeted) cette auberge que tu nous as recommandée (that inn that you recommended to us)

OBJECT OF PREPOSITION

QUI, whom:
le patineur à qui (the skater to whom)

LEQUEL, which (things):
un beau lac sur lequel (a beautiful lake on which)

QUOI, which (referring back to an idea; also for things):
Il faut se fortifier – sans quoi il sera impossible. (We have to fortify ourselves – without which it'll be impossible.)

DONT, word containing the preposition *de* and meaning "whose," "of whom," "of which":

un endroit dont la réputation devient de plus en plus répandue (a spot whose reputation is becoming more and more widespread)

1. When *qui* is used preceded by a pronoun (*moi, toi, lui, elle,* etc.), the verb following *qui* takes the form that matches the pronoun. Note the translation:

   C'est moi qui irai chercher les billets. (I am the one who will go and get the tickets.)

2. *Lequel* (*laquelle, lesquels, lesquelles*) contracts into *auquel, à laquelle, auxquels, auxquelles* when used with the preposition *à*; into *duquel, de laquelle, desquels, desquelles* when used with *de*. *Lequel* and its various forms may also be used for persons or things to refer back to an antecedent in a more specific way:

   les collines et le lac, lequel je puis voir de ma fenêtre (the hills and the lake, which I can see from my window)

3. *Dont*, "whose," "of whom," "of which," must be followed by this order: subject, verb, object (if there is one):

   C'est un endroit dont la réputation devient de plus en plus répandue. (It's a spot whose reputation is becoming more and more widespread.)

   Dont may not be used if any other preposition is involved in the expression. In such a case, *qui* is used for persons (also *lequel*), and *lequel* is used for things:

   Marianne avec le frère de qui . . . (Marianne with whose brother . . .)

   La Savoie, parmi les montagnes de laquelle il y a tant de villages pittoresques, est une des plus belles régions du monde. (Savoie, in the mountains of which there are so many picturesque villages, is one of the most beautiful regions in the world.)

4. *Où* (where) can replace expressions of place involving a preposition, such as *dans lequel, sur lequel,* and is used to translate "on which" referring to time:

   l'auberge *dans laquelle* or *où* (the inn in which *or* where)
   le jour *où* (the day on which)

Exercise 1

Insert the pronoun *qui* or *que* to complete the following sentences:

1. I'll give you these valises that I am carrying: Je vous donne ces valises _____ je porte.
2. That is a round-trip ticket that is expensive: C'est un billet d'aller et retour _____ coûte cher.
3. It's an inn that everyone knows: C'est une auberge _____ tout le monde connaît.
4. It is a scene that reminds me of my country: C'est une scène _____ me fait penser à mon pays.
5. This is a waiting room that I always find crowded: Voici une salle d'attente _____ je trouve toujours bondée.

B. The Double or Compound Relative Pronouns

CE QUI, what (that which) as subject:

Je sais *ce qui* vous fait penser à votre pays. (I know what makes you think of your country.)

CE QUE, what (that which) as object:

C'est ce que nous avons dans mon pays. (That's what we have in my country.)

CE DONT, what (that of which):

Ce dont vous avez besoin ce sont des patins affilés. (What [that of which] you [have] need is sharpened skates.)

If you have trouble recognizing "which" as a subject or as an object, just remember that it is a subject (*qui*) when it is followed by a verb in English; if it is followed by any other part of speech in English, it is an object (*que*):

Mountains *that are* crowned with snow always remind me of Savoie. (The verb follows "that." Therefore it is the subject and *qui* is used.) Les montagnes *qui* sont couronnées de neige me font penser toujours à la Savoie.

Marianne is wearing the skates *that I* had sharpened. (The pronoun follows "that." Therefore it is object and *que* is used.) Marianne porte les patins *que* j'ai fait affiler.

Exercise 2

Match the following:

1. L'auberge _______ nous avons passé les trois journées est magnifique.	dans laquelle or où
2. Voilà le guichet _______ il faudra faire la queue.	dont

3. ________ enchante Laurent, ________ les montagnes couronnées de neige.
4. Allons déjeuner au wagon-restaurant, après ________ nous serons bien fortifiés.
5. Il y a ici ________ on pourrait souhaiter.
6. Cette colline ________ la pente (slope) est très raide (steep) est la favorite des skieurs.
7. Laurent est un skieur ________ nous avons énormément d'admiration.
8. ________ j'ai envie ________ de voir les Alpes.
9. La salle d'attente ________ est là à gauche est toute petite.
10. Cette colline ________ vous voyez là-bas est la plus haute (highest) de toutes.
11. Ce sont les mêmes patineurs ________ nous avons parlé hier.
12. ________ nous avons besoin ce sont des patins affilés.

qui
à la porte de laquelle
ce qui . . . ce sont
quoi
à qui
devant lequel
ce dont . . . c'est
pour l'agilité de qui
tout ce qu'
ce dont
que

Review Exercise

Translate the English into French:

La Savoie est une région *whose natural beauty* est d'une renommée toute particulière. Dans la blancheur de ses vallées alpestres, entourées de montagnes *among whose snowy peaks* (pics) flottent des nuages, on se sent protégé, transporté dans un monde d'une beauté presque irréelle *in which* règnent la solitude et la paix. Mon père, *who* est né dans le beau village de Saint-Jean-de-Maurienne, nous a raconté les plaisirs de son enfance, *which* il n'oubliera jamais – les joies de grimper les montagnes, l'alpenstock à la main, l'édelweiss au chapeau. "Vous rappelez-vous les magnifiques passages *in which* Jean-Jacques Rousseau fait la description des paysages savoyards?" "Eh bien! *All that he wrote* est vrai, je vous assure," nous a dit Laurent enthousiasmé. C'est surtout Chamonix, la belle station d'hiver, *which* fait la joie des touristes et des amateurs de sports. *What attracts* (to attract, *attirer*) les skieurs ce sont ces pentes raides *on which* on glisse à toute vitesse ou bien ces pics *which*, s'élançant vers les cieux, jettent le défi aux alpinistes.

CHAPTER FOURTEEN

The Interrogative Adjective and the Interrogative Pronoun: *"What?" Which Forms to Use; "Who?" and "Whom?"; "Which?"*

AU BUREAU DE POSTE

HÉLÈNE – QU'EST-CE QUE TU FAIS maintenant, Jeannine?

JEANNINE – Il faut que j'aille au bureau de poste, Hélène, pour envoyer en France la lettre du Cercle Français.

HÉLÈNE – QUELLE LETTRE, Jeannine?

JEANNINE – Celle qu'on envoie aux Éditions Lorimard pour les dix livres.

HÉLÈNE – À QUOI est-ce que je pensais? J'oubliais la lettre et le fait que tu es secrétaire du cercle.

JEANNINE – Paul m'a dit qu'il faudra avoir un mandat-poste.

HÉLÈNE – Pourquoi ça, Jeannine? QU'EST-CE QUI T'EMPÊCHE d'envoyer les deux billets de dix dollars?

JEANNINE – Ce n'est pas permis, dit-il. Alors, je m'en vais.

....

JEANNINE – Pardon, monsieur. QUELLE SERAIT LA MEILLEURE FAÇON d'envoyer en France une lettre urgente contenant vingt dollars?

L'EMPLOYÉ – Il faudra un mandat-poste pour l'argent et vous pourriez recommander la lettre et l'envoyer par avion.

AT THE POST OFFICE

HELEN – What are you doing now, Jeannine?

JEANNINE – I have to go to the post office, Helen, to send the French Club's letter to France.

HELEN – What letter, Jeannine?

JEANNINE –The one that they're sending to Lorimard Publishing Company for the ten books.

HELEN – What was I thinking of? I was forgetting the letter and the fact that you are secretary of the club.

JEANNINE – Paul told me that I'll have to have a money order.

HELEN – Why so, Jeannine? What stops you from sending the two ten-dollar bills?

JEANNINE – It isn't allowed, he says. So, I'm off.

....

JEANNINE – Excuse me, sir. What would be the best way to send an urgent letter containing twenty dollars to France?

THE CLERK – You'll need a postal money order for the money and you could register the letter and send it by air mail.

JEANNINE – Ah, merci. Et où puis-je avoir le mandat-poste?	JEANNINE – Oh, thank you. And where can I get the money order?
L'EMPLOYÉ – Au guichet d'en face, mademoiselle.	CLERK – At the opposite window, miss.
JEANNINE – LEQUEL? Oh, oui, celui-là. Merci bien.	JEANNINE – Which one? Oh, yes, that one. Thank you very much.
....	....
L'EMPLOYÉ – Un mandat-poste pour la somme de vingt dollars? Bon. QUI L'ENVOIE et À QUI l'envoyez-vous, mademoiselle?	CLERK – A money order for the sum of twenty dollars? Very well. Who is sending it and to whom are you sending it, miss?
JEANNINE – Voici l'enveloppe, monsieur. Vous avez ici le nom du destinataire et celui de l'expéditeur.	JEANNINE – Here is the envelope, sir. Here you have the name of the addressee and that of the sender.
L'EMPLOYÉ – Et voici votre mandat-poste, mademoiselle.	CLERK – And here is your money order, miss.
JEANNINE – Merci, monsieur. Je voudrais recommander la lettre et l'envoyer par avion.	JEANNINE – Thank you, sir. I'd like to register the letter and send it by air mail.
L'EMPLOYÉ – Ce monsieur-là, au guichet No. 3, vous indiquera les timbres nécessaires.	CLERK – That gentleman, at Window No. 3, will indicate to you the necessary stamps.

I. THE INTERROGATIVE ADJECTIVE AND THE INTERROGATIVE PRONOUN

A. "What?"

1. QUEL (QUELLE, QUELS, QUELLES)	+ noun, or + *être* and a noun: Quelle lettre? (What letter?) Quelle serait la meilleure façon? (What would be the best way?)
2. QU'EST-CE QUI	As subject: Qu'est-ce qui t'empêche . . .? (What prevents you . . .?)
3. QU'EST-CE QUE (with uninverted verb)	As object: Qu'est-ce que tu fais maintenant? (What are you doing now)
QUE (with inverted verb)	Que fais-tu maintenant? (What are you doing now?)

4. QU'EST-CE QUE C'EST QUE (or the shortened form QU'EST-CE QUE)

   To ask a definition:

   Qu'est-ce que c'est qu'un mandat-poste? (What is a postal money order?)

5. QUOI

   After a preposition or standing alone:

   À quoi est-ce que je pensais? (What was I thinking of?)

   Quoi? Vous ne savez pas ce que c'est qu'un mandat-poste? (What? You don't know what a postal money order is?)

Remember that an interrogative pronoun asks a question and never can have an antecedent. When "what" means "that which," it is the compound relative pronoun discussed in Chapter XIII.

B. "Who?" and "Whom?"

1. QUI (or long form QUI EST-CE QUI)

   WHO:

   Qui l'envoie? (Who is sending it?)

   Qui est-ce qui l'envoie? (Who is sending it?)

2. QUI (with inverted verb) QUI EST-CE QUE (without inversion)

   WHOM:

   Qui voyez-vous? (Whom do you see?)

   Qui est-ce que vous voyez? (Whom do you see?)

3. QUI

   WHOM, after preposition:

   À qui l'envoyez-vous? (To whom are you sending it?)

As will be noted from the above, *qui* can be used at all times for persons, whether as subject, as object, or after a preposition.

C. "Which (one[s])?"

LEQUEL (LAQUELLE, LESQUELS, LESQUELLES)

Whenever "which" means "which one" or "which ones":

Au guichet d'en face, mademoiselle. Lequel? (At the opposite window, miss. Which one?)

Exercise 1

From the following list, select the forms that correctly complete the sentences below:

quels	quoi
qu'est-ce qui	qui
qu'est-ce que	qui est-ce qui
que (qu')	qui est-ce que
qu'est-ce que c'est qu'	laquelle

1. ________ un philatéliste?
2. ________ faut-il avoir pour envoyer de l'argent en France?
3. ________ timbres désirez-vous?
4. ________ t'a dit qu'il faut un mandat-poste?
5. Voici les deux lettres. ________ voulez-vous recommander?
6. Qui avez-vous consulté? ________ vous avez consulté?
7. Dans ________ avez-vous mis l'argent?
8. ________ vous avez dit au facteur quand il a apporté votre courrier (mail)?
9. ________arrive (happens) si la lettre s'égare (goes astray)?
10. ________ avez-vous dit au facteur quand il a apporté le colis (package)?

Review Exercise

Translate the English into French:

Pourquoi ne jetez-vous pas la lettre dans la boîte aux lettres (to mail: *jeter dans la boîte aux lettres*)? *What* lettre? Celle que vous envoyez en France. Non, il faut que j'aille au bureau de poste. Pourquoi? *What* voulez-vous faire au bureau de poste? Il y a deux raisons pour lesquelles je vais au bureau de poste. Tout d'abord, il faut que j'aie un mandat-poste. *What?* Un mandat-poste. Mais *what is* un mandat-poste? Je crois (I believe) que c'est une espèce (kind) de chèque postal. Et *what is* l'autre raison? Ensuite, il me faut (I need) un timbre spécial parce que j'envoie la lettre par avion. Savez-vous ce qu'on appelle (calls) la personne *to whom* on envoie une lettre? Non, *what* on l'appelle? On l'appelle le destinataire. Et savez-vous ce qu'on appelle la personne qui envoie la lettre? Non. *What* l'appelle-t-on? On l'appelle l'expéditeur. *Who* (in two ways) vous a dit tout cela? C'est mon frère qui me l'a dit. *What* est dans cette enveloppe? Deux billets de dix dollars et ma lettre. *Which* (one)? Celle du Cercle Français. *Of what* est-il question (is it a question)? Il est question de dix livres français que nous voulons commander chez Lorimard.

CHAPTER FIFTEEN

The Use of Ce or Il (Elle, Ils, Elles) with Être
The Causative Use of Faire

CHEZ LE DENTISTE	AT THE DENTIST'S
HENRI – Cette misérable dent m'a tellement fait souffrir que je ne puis laisser passer un jour de plus sans VOUS LA FAIRE EXAMINER, docteur.	HENRY–This miserable tooth has been so painful that I can't let one day more go by without having you look at it, Doctor.
LE DENTISTE – Toujours le même Henri! Vous vous brossez les dents tous les jours et puis, c'est fini! VOUS NE LES FAITES EXAMINER PAR VOTRE DENTISTE que lorsqu'ELLES VOUS FONT SOUFFRIR.	THE DENTIST – Always the same Henry! You brush your teeth every day and then, that's the end! You have your dentist examine them only when they make you suffer.
HENRI – C'est ma faute, docteur, je l'avoue. Mais CE DOIT ÊTRE UNE CAVITÉ ÉNORME. IL ME SEMBLE que le nerf est complètement exposé.	HENRY – It's my fault, Doctor, I admit. But it must be an enormous cavity. It seems to me that the nerve is completely exposed.
LE DENTISTE – Bien, FAITES-MOI VOIR la dent dont IL S'AGIT. C'EST CETTE MOLAIRE à droite? En effet, ELLE EST CARIÉE.	THE DENTIST – All right, let me see the tooth in question. Is it this molar on the right? It really is decayed.
HENRI – Est-ce qu'IL FAUDRA l'arracher, docteur?	HENRY – Will you have to extract it, Doctor?
LE DENTISTE – Je crois que nous pourrons la sauver, mais tout ce que nous pourrons faire aujourd'hui C'EST radiographer la dent. Si ELLE EST SAINE, nous la plomberons la prochaine fois.	THE DENTIST – I think we'll be able to save it, but all we can do today is X-ray the tooth. If it's sound, we'll fill it the next time.
HENRI – C'EST LE GUIGNON LE PLUS CRUEL que d'avoir mal aux dents et deux examens le lendemain!	HENRY – It's the cruelest bad luck having a toothache and two exams the next day!
LE DENTISTE – C'EST EMBÊTANT mais IL VOUS FAUDRA de la patience, Henri. Et des aspirines!	THE DENTIST – It's annoying but you'll need patience, Henry. And some aspirin!

I. THE USE OF *CE* OR *IL* (*ELLE, ILS, ELLES*) WITH *ÊTRE*

CE

1. Before a noun:
   C'est cette molaire. (It's this molar.)
2. Before a pronoun:
   C'est moi. (It's I.)
3. Before a superlative:
   C'est le guignon le plus cruel. (It's the cruelest bad luck.)
4. Referring back to an idea:
   C'est embêtant! (It's annoying!)

IL (ELLE, ILS, ELLES)

1. Before an adjective:
   Elle est cariée. (It is decayed.)
2. Before a noun when referring back to a specific antecedent:
   Connaissez-vous le docteur Dulac? Il est le frère de notre professeur. (Do you know Dr. Dulac? He is our professor's brother.)
3. In impersonal expressions:
   Il me semble que ... (It seems to me that . . .)

If *devoir* or *pouvoir* is used with *être*, the main verb is still *être* and the above rules apply:

Ce doit être la molaire à droite. (It must be the molar on the right.)

Before any verb other than *être*, *il* (*elle, ils, elles*) must be used:

Il a mal aux dents. (He has a toothache.)

Exercise 1

Translate the English into French:

1. *It is* cette dent à gauche qui me fait tellement souffrir.
2. *It is* cariée.
3. Je vais donc voir le docteur Dulac. *He has been* (present tense) mon dentiste depuis dix ans.
4. *He is* un très bon dentiste.
5. *It was he* qui a arraché mes deux dents de sagesse (wisdom teeth) l'année passée.
6. J'avais cru (I had thought) *that they were sound* mais *it wasn't true* (vrai).
7. Les dents de sagesse sont quelquefois curieuses. On dit (It is said) *that they are* les dernières (last) dents à arriver et les premières à partir.
8. Est-ce qu'il faudra arracher la dent ou bien *will it be possible* de la sauver?
9. Je ne sais pas encore (yet). *It will be* la radiographie qui décidera la question.
10. Tout ce que je sais *is* que *it must be* une cavité énorme.

II. THE CAUSATIVE USE OF FAIRE

Whenever one person has something done by another, the verb *faire* must be used:

> Henri fait examiner la dent par le dentiste. (Henry has the dentist examine the tooth.)

Note the following about this construction:

1. The English translation is usually "has," "gets," but we must always transpose the English into terms of *to make* before translating into French.

   > The dentist has (gets) the tooth X-rayed (The dentist makes to X-ray the tooth). (Le dentiste fait radiographier la dent.)

2. *Faire* is nearly always directly followed by the infinitive:

   > The dentist has the gentleman wait until next week (The dentist makes to wait the gentleman until next week). (Le dentiste fait attendre le monsieur jusqu'à la semaine prochaine.)

3. If pronouns are involved, they go before *faire*:

   > . . . sans vous la faire examiner, docteur. (. . . without having you examine it, Doctor.)

   Unless in an affirmative imperative:

   > Faites-moi voir. (Let me see.)

4. If *faire* has an object and if the infinitive has an object, the object of *faire* becomes indirect:

   > We had him examine the tooth. (Nous lui avons fait examiner la dent.)

   Here " him" being the object of *faire*, and "the tooth" the object of *examiner*, "him" becomes indirect.

   If this indirect object is a noun, *par* or *à* can be used:

   > Vous ne les faites examiner par votre dentiste que losqu'elles vous font souffrir. (You have your dentist examine them only when they make you suffer.)

5. The past participle of *faire* + an infinitive is invariable:

   > Le dentiste nous a fait attendre. (The dentist had us wait.)

Exercise 2

Translate:

1. The dentist has the tooth X-rayed.
   The dentist has it X-rayed.
   The dentist has it X-rayed by the nurse (l'infirmière).
   The dentist has her X-ray it.

Have the dentist X-ray the tooth.
Have him X-ray the tooth.
Have him X-ray it.

2. The dentist had the tooth X-rayed.
The dentist had it X-rayed.
The dentist had it X-rayed by the nurse.
The dentist had her X-ray it.

3. The dentist will have the tooth X-rayed.
The dentist will have it X-rayed.
The dentist will have it X-rayed by the nurse.
The dentist will have her X-ray it.

Exercise 3

Translate the English into French:

1. J'ai mal aux dents. *Have the dentist examine them.*
2. De quelles dents s'agit-il? De ces deux molaires *that I had filled* l'année passée.
3. Est-ce que le dentiste peut nous recevoir immédiatement? Non, *he'll have us wait* jusqu'à trois heures.
4. *Get him to examine* ce bridge aussi.
5. *I got him to examine it* la dernière fois.
6. *He'll have you come in* dans un moment.
7. Regardez ces deux dames qui sortent (are coming out). Il leur donne rendez-vous pour la prochaine fois. Regardez! *He is making them write it* dans leur carnet (little book).
8. Voilà l'infirmière. *He always makes her write it* aussi.
9. Demain lorsque je reviendrai, il aura ma radiographie (X-ray) et *he'll show it to me* (to show: *faire voir*).
10. J'aime mieux *to have the tooth extracted* que de *have it drilled.*

Review Exercise

Translate the English into French:

Qu'est-ce que tu as, Henri? J'ai mal aux dents, Paul. *It's a molar* qu'il faut *to get extracted. Have you had it X-rayed*, Henri? Oui, mais *it is* cariée et je crois *that it is impossible* de la sauver. Moi je préfère *to have a tooth extracted* que de *to have it drilled.* Est-ce que tu connais le docteur Dulac? *He is my dentist* aussi. Lui et son frère sont dentistes. *They are* très capables, tous les deux. J'ai mal aux dents et deux examens demain. *It's bad luck* qui me poursuit (pursues). *It's annoying* mais ce qu'il vous faut *is patience.*

CHAPTER SIXTEEN

The Past Definite: ***Formation of the Past Definite; Translation and Use of the Past Definite; Verbs Irregular in the Past Definite Tense***

The Past Anterior: ***Formation of the Past Anterior; Translation and Use of the Past Anterior***

Distinction Between the Past Definite, Past Indefinite, and Imperfect

UN CONFÉRENCIER AU CERCLE FRANÇAIS

MARIANNE – Je propose que le procès-verbal soit adopté à l'unanimité.

HENRI – J'appuie la proposition de Marianne.

JACQUES – Très bien. Le procès-verbal est adopté à l'unanimité. Et maintenant, j'ai l'honneur de vous présenter notre illustre conférencier, M. Charles Leduc, professeur de littérature française, qui nous parlera sur la "Vie et les œuvres de Molière" . . . M. Leduc.

M. LEDUC – M. le Directeur, M. le Président, chers amis: Jean-Baptiste Poquelin, mieux connu sous le nom de Molière, NAQUIT à Paris, en 1622. À l'âge de vingt ans, Molière OBTINT sa licence en droit mais cette carrière FUT vite abandonnée dès qu'il EUT FAIT la connaissance d'une famille d'acteurs, les Béjart. Avec eux, il FONDA l'Illustre Théâtre. Ne trouvant pas de succès à Paris, ils FIRENT des tournées des provinces, ce qui SERVIT à établir une réputation solide. Ce FUT pendant ces pérégrinations que Molière ENRICHIT

A LECTURER AT THE FRENCH CLUB

MARIANNE – I move that the minutes be adopted unanimously.

HENRY – I second Marianne's motion.

JAMES – All right. The minutes are adopted unanimously. And now, I have the honor to present to you our distinguished lecturer Mr. Charles Leduc, professor of French literature, who will speak to us on the "Life and Works of Molière" . . . Mr. Leduc.

MR. LEDUC – Mr. Director, Mr. President, friends: Jean-Baptiste Poquelin, better known by the name of Molière, was born in Paris, in 1622. At the age of twenty, Molière obtained his law degree, but this career was quickly abandoned as soon as he had made the acquaintance of a family of actors, the Béjarts. With them he founded the Illustrious Theater. Not finding success in Paris, they toured the provinces, which served to establish a solid reputation. It was during these travels that Molière enriched his knowledge of human nature and

sa connaissance de la nature humaine et TROUVA l'inspiration. À PEINE FUT-IL RENTRÉ à Paris en 1658, que Molière et ses acteurs ATTIRÈRENT l'attention du Roi Louis XIV. Celui-ci lui ACCORDA une pension. En 1665, sa troupe DEVINT la Troupe du Roi. Mais Molière se surmenait car il était à la fois auteur, directeur de la troupe, et acteur dans ses propres comédies. Ce FUT précisément en jouant le rôle principal dans sa comédie *Le Malade Imaginaire* qu'il SUCCOMBA à la phtisie dont il souffrait depuis des années.

found inspiration. Scarcely had he returned to Paris in 1658 when Molière and his actors attracted the attention of King Louis XIV. The latter granted him a pension. In 1665, his troupe became the King's Troupe. But Molière was overworking for he was at the same time author, director of the troupe, and actor in his own comedies. It was just while playing the principal role in his comedy *Le Malade Imaginaire* that he succumbed to tuberculosis, from which he had been suffering for years.

Pour Molière, comme pour Boileau, "rien n'est beau que le vrai." Tout ce qui est faux, tout ce qui est artificiel, il le déteste. C'est pour cela qu'il s'attaque aux mœurs et au langage affectés des "Précieuses ridicules" et aux momeries du "Bourgeois gentilhomme" qui veut être ce qu'il n'est pas. L'œuvre de Molière est caractérisée par une vérité et une profondeur psychologiques, égalées seulement par son talent pour le comique. Son œuvre comporte des farces, des comédies-ballets, des comédies de mœurs et surtout des comédies de caractère. C'est dans cette dernière catégorie qu'on trouve ses chefs-d'œuvre: *le Tartuffe* (l'hypocrite), *l'Avare*, et *le Misanthrope*.

For Molière, as for Boileau, "nothing but the true is beautiful." Everything that is false, everything that is artificial, he detests. That is why he attacks the affected manners and language of the ridiculous "*précieuses*" and the mummery of the "Would-be Gentleman," who wants to be what he is not. Molière's work is characterized by a psychological truth and depth equaled only by his comic talent. His work includes farces, comedy-ballets, comedies of manners, and especially comedies of character. It's in this latter category that his masterpieces *Tartuffe* (The Hypocrite), *The Miser*, and *The Misanthrope* are found.

I. THE PAST DEFINITE

A. Formation of the Past Definite

The past definite (*le passé défini* or *le passé simple*) is formed in all three regular conjugations by removing the *-er*, *-ir*, *-re* of the infinitive and by adding the personal endings given below:

PAST DEFINITE OF THE THREE CONJUGATIONS

	fonder	*finir*	*répondre*
je	fondAI	finIS	répondIS
tu	fondAS	finIS	répondIS
il	fondA	finIT	répondIT
nous	fondÂMES	finÎMES	répondÎMES
vous	fondÂTES	finÎTES	répondÎTES
ils	fondÈRENT	finIRENT	répondIRENT

Since in most irregular verbs the endings are the same as for *-ir* and *-re* verbs, it is necessary to learn only the stem of the *je* form in order to master the verb in all forms of the past definite.

The same form will serve later as stem for the imperfect subjunctive (see Chapter XVIII).

Exercise 1

Give the following forms:

1. Je (trouver) ______, (finir) ______, (rendre) ______
2. Vous (attirer) ______, (enrichir) ______, (attendre) ______
3. Il (observer) ______, (réussir) ______, (vendre) ______
4. Nous (étudier) ______, (punir) ______, (entendre) ______
5. Elles (fonder) ______, (réunir: to bring together) ______, (perdre) ______
6. Tu (succomber) ______, (accueillir: to welcome) ______, (répandre: to spread) ______
7. Ils (se surmener) ______, (se réunir: to get together) ______, (s'attendre) ______
8. Elle (prier) ______, (finir) ______, (rendre) ______

B. Translation and Use of the Past Definite

This tense translates the English "____ed" and "did ____." In translation it resembles the past indefinite, but it is used only in an intended narrative, where we deliberately set out to relate, such as in an anecdote, historical passage, or biography. It is a tense usually found in written, rather than conversational or spoken, French. It can, however, be found in the spoken relation of any series of events.

Exercise 2

Translate the English into French:

1. Molière *founded,* avec les Béjart, l'Illustre Théâtre.
2. Mais cette troupe *did not succeed* dans la capitale.

3. Alors Molière et ses acteurs *took refuge* (se réfugier: to take refuge) dans les provinces.
4. Ces pérégrinations *enriched* l'expérience de Molière.
5. *He found there* énormément (a tremendous amount) de matière pour ses caractères.
6. *The actors established* leur réputation dans les provinces.
7. Quand Molière et sa troupe *came back* à Paris, le roi les *welcomed.*
8. *He granted* à Molière une pension.
9. *He gave* à la troupe le nom de Troupe du Roi.
10. La gloire de Molière *spread* (se répandre: to spread) partout.

C. Verbs Irregular in the Past Definite Tense

The stem is all that has to be learned; the endings carry through whatever vowel appears in the *je* form, to which are added the usual *-s, -s, -t, ^mes, ^tes, -rent*:

je *craign*is: tu craignis, il craignit, nous craignîmes, vous craignîtes, ils craignirent

je *cour*us: tu courus, il courut, nous courûmes, vous courûtes, ils coururent

If the *je* form of the irreglar verb ends in *-ai*, the verb is treated as if it were a regular first-conjugation verb.

j'*envoy*ai: tu envoyas, il envoya, nous envoyâmes, vous envoyâtes, ils envoyèrent

It will be useful also to note that the final vowel that appears in the past participle of an irregular verb is often the same as that appearing in the ending of the past-definite forms:

cour*u*, je cour*us*; voul*u*, je voul*us*; cueill*i*, je cuell*is*

Exercise 3

Give the following forms of the past definite:

		LE PASSÉ DÉFINI
1. acquérir (to acquire)	J'ACQUIS	vous ______
2. aller (to go)	J'ALLAI	elle ______
3. avoir (to have)	J'EUS	nous ______
4. courir (to run)	JE COURUS	ils ______
5. cueillir (to gather)	JE CUEILLIS	tu ______

6. devoir (to have to, to owe)	JE DUS	il ______
7. envoyer (to send)	J'ENVOYAI	elles ______
8. être (to be)	JE FUS	nous ______
9. faire (to do, to make)	JE FIS	il ______
10. falloir (to be necessary)	IL FALLUT	
11. mourir (to die)	JE MOURUS	elles ______
12. pleuvoir (to rain)	IL PLUT	
13. pouvoir (to be able)	JE PUS	vous ______
14. recevoir (to receive)	JE REÇUS	elle ______
15. savoir (to know, to know how)	JE SUS	ils ______
16. valoir (to be worth)	JE VALUS	tu ______
17. venir (to come)	JE VINS*	elles ______
18. voir (to see)	JE VIS	nous ______
19. vouloir (to wish, to want)	JE VOULUS	il ______

* Note the irregularities of the verb *venir* in the past definite: je vins, tu vins, il vint, nous vînmes, vous vîntes, ils vinrent.

II. THE PAST ANTERIOR

A. Formation of the Past Anterior

The past anterior is a compound tense, of limited use, which is made up of the past definite of the auxiliary *avoir* or *être* and the past participle:

j'eus fondé (I had founded)	je fus venu(e) (I had come)
tu eus fondé	tu fus venu(e)
il eut fondé	il fut venu
nous eûmes fondé	nous fûmes venu(e)s
vous eûtes fondé	vous fûtes venu(e)(s)
ils eurent fondé	ils furent venus

Exercise 4

Give the following forms:

The auxiliary is *avoir:*		The auxiliary is *être:*	
je (j')	(inspirer) ______	je (j')	(aller) ______
vous	(enrichir) ______	vous	(venir) ______
elle	(répondre) ______	elle	(arriver) ______
nous	(protéger) ______	nous	(rentrer) ______
tu	(établir) ______	tu	(rester) ______
ils	(perdre) ______	ils	(partir) ______

B. Translation and Use of the Past Anterior

The past anterior is a companion tense to the past definite and translates "had" + a past participle. It is used only:

1. In a subordinate clause introduced by a time expression such as *dès que, aussitôt que* (as soon as); *quand, lorsque* (when); *après que* (after); *à peine* (scarcely) + an inverted verb and *que.*
2. When the main verb is in the past definite:

   Dès qu'il eut fait la connaissance des Béjart, le droit fut vite abandonné. (As soon as he had made the acquaintance of the Béjarts, law was quickly abandoned.)

   À peine fut-il rentré à Paris en 1658 que Molière et ses acteurs attirèrent l'attention du Roi Louis XIV. (Scarcely had he come back to Paris in 1658 when Molière and his actors attracted the attention of King Louis XIV.)

Exercise 5

Translate the English into French:

1. *Scarcely had Molière obtained* sa licence en droit *when he abandoned* cette carrière.
2. *After Molière and his troupe had gone* aux provinces, *he found* l'inspiration de ses comédies.
3. *As soon as the Illustre Théâtre had attracted* l'attention du roi, *a pension was granted* à Molière.
4. *When the troupe had established* une réputation solide, *Molière and the actors went back* à Paris.
5. *After he had arrived* au succès, *Molière succumbed* à la phtisie.

III. DISTINCTION BETWEEN THE PAST DEFINITE, PAST INDEFINITE, AND IMPERFECT

PAST DEFINITE	PAST INDEFINITE	IMPERFECT
1. Intended narration as in an anecdote, biography, etc.	1. Narration within conversation	1. Vivid narration in the past
		2. Repeated, habitual events
2. Series of events	2. Independent events	
3. Remote distant past, entirely unrelated to present	3. Recent past or past with repercussion in present	3. Action in progress in the past

Exercise 6

Translate the English into French:

Has our lecturer arrived, Jacques? *Yes, Marguerite, he and another professor came half an hour ago* (il y a une demi-heure). *They were chatting* (to chat: *bavardar*) *with our director in his office* (dans son bureau). *He used to give courses* (to give a course: *faire un cours*) à l'Université de M. Leduc. Ah, voici notre conférencier qui entre. Notre président le présente aux membres du Cercle. Il commence à parler: Jean-Baptiste Poquelin *was born* à Paris en 1622. *He undertook* (to undertake: *entreprendre*) la carrière de droit mais *he abandoned it* et *established* l'Illustre Théâtre avec une famille d'acteurs, les Béjart. *Molière and his actors didn't find* de succès à Paris. Alors *they decided* de faire une tournée en province. Là, *he observed* la vie. *He used to spend* des heures entières (hours on end) à étudier les gens. *It was* pendant ces pérégrinations que sa troupe *established its reputation* et que Molière *found* son art.

CHAPTER SEVENTEEN

Formation of the Present Subjunctive
Formation of the Past Subjunctive
Uses of the Subjunctive: ***After Verbs of Wishing, Forbidding, Preventing, Preferring; After an Expression of Doubt; After an Expression of Emotion; After an Impersonal Expression; After*** **Croire** ***or*** **Penser** ***Used Negatively or Interrogatively; After Certain Indefinite Words***

LA TÉLÉVISION	TELEVISION
MME DESJARDINS – CROYEZ-VOUS QUE CE SOIT possible de faire les réparations avant ce soir?	MRS. DESJARDINS – Do you think it will be possible to make the repairs before this evening?
LE DÉPANNEUR – Oui, madame, je crois que ça peut bien s'arranger.	REPAIRMAN – Yes, madam, I think that can be arranged.
MME DESJARDINS – JE NE VEUX PAS QUE VOUS VOUS DÉPÊCHIEZ. C'est seulement qu'il y aura ce soir un programme que NOUS NE VOUDRIONS PAS MANQUER.	MRS. DESJARDINS – I don't want you to hurry. It's just that there is a program this evening that we wouldn't like to miss.
LE DÉPANNEUR – Je ferai tout mon possible, madame.	REPAIRMAN – I'll do my best, madam.
MME DESJARDINS – Vous voyez? QUOI QU'ON FASSE, il y a toujours ces rayures et l'image est tout de travers.	MRS. DESJARDINS – You see? Whatever you do, there are always those lines and the picture is all crooked.
LE DÉPANNEUR – Où avez-vous l'antenne? IL EST POSSIBLE QUE LA TEMPÊTE DE LA SEMAINE PASSÉE L'AIT DESSERRÉE quelque peu.	REPAIRMAN – Where do you have the antenna? It's possible that last week's storm loosened it somewhat.
MME DESJARDINS – Ah oui. C'est vrai. Pour cela, IL FAUDRA MONTER sur le toit. C'est par ici.	MRS. DESJARDINS – Ah yes. That's true. You'll have to go up on the roof for that. It's this way.

LE DÉPANNEUR – J'ai ajusté l'antenne. Je crois que cela fera l'affaire.

MME DESJARDINS – Bon! Essayons les différents canaux! IL ME SEMBLE QUE C'EST TRÈS BIEN!

LE DÉPANNEUR – En effet. JE DOUTE QU'ON PUISSE avoir une image plus nette.

MME DESJARDINS – C'est juste. JE SUIS BIEN CONTENTE QUE CE NE SOIT PAS le tube cathodique. Ça coûte si cher!

LE DÉPANNEUR – Non, madame, heureusement. JE SUIS CERTAIN QUE VOUS N'AUREZ PLUS de difficultés.

REPAIRMAN – I adjusted the antenna. I think that will do the trick.

MRS. DESJARDINS – Fine! Let's try the different channels. It seems to me that it's all right.

REPAIRMAN – Indeed. I doubt that you can have a clearer picture.

MRS. DESJARDINS – That's right. I'm very glad that it isn't the picture tube. That is so expensive!

REPAIRMAN – No, madam, fortunately. I am sure that you won't have any more difficulties.

I. FORMATION OF THE PRESENT SUBJUNCTIVE

The present subjunctive (*le présent du subjonctif*) is formed by adding to the stem of the third-person plural (ils) of the present indicative the following endings: *-e, -es, -e, -ions, -iez, -ent.* These endings are the same for all verbs except *avoir* and *être.*

je	doutE	finissE	répondE
tu	doutES	finissES	répondES
il	doutE	finissE	répondE
nous	doutIONS	finissIONS	répondIONS
vous	doutIEZ	finissIEZ	répondIEZ
ils	doutENT	finissENT	répondENT

1. In irregular verbs, where the present-indicative *nous* stem differs from the *ils* stem, the stem of the *nous* form of the present indicative serves as stem for the *nous* and *vous* forms of the present subjunctive.

ILS PRENNENT	NOUS PRENONS
je *prenne*	nous *prenions*
tu *prennes*	vous *preniez*
il *prenne*	
ils *prennent*	

2. Three common verbs have special stems:
faire – FASS: je fasse, tu fasses, il fasse, nous fassions, vous fassiez, ils fassent
pouvoir – PUISS: je puisse, tu puisses, il puisse, nous puissions, vous puissiez, ils puissent
savoir – SACH: je sache, tu saches, il sache, nous sachions, vous sachiez, ils sachent

3. *Avoir* and *être* have each a special stem and special endings:
avoir: j'aie, tu aies, il ait, nous ayons, vous ayez, ils aient
être: je sois, tu sois, il soit, nous soyons, vous soyez, ils soient

Exercise 1

Give the following present subjunctive forms:

1.	je (réparer) _____	je (remplir) _____	je (perdre) _____
2.	elle (monter) _____	elle (choisir) _____	elle (entendre) _____
3.	vous (manquer) _____	vous (punir) _____	vous (vendre) _____
4.	ils (douter) _____	ils (se divertir) _____	ils (attendre) _____
5.	tu (fermer) _____	tu (finir) _____	tu (vendre) _____
6.	nous (regarder) _____	nous (se réunir) _____	nous (rendre) _____
7.	le dépanneur (desserrer) _____	. . . (réussir) _____	. . . (descendre) _____
8.	les tubes cathodiques (coûter) _____	. . . (éclaircir) _____	. . . (rendre) _____

Exercise 2

Give the following present subjunctive forms:

1. je (prendre) _____, nous _____
2. elle (venir) _____, vous _____
3. vous (boire) _____, il _____
4. ils (faire) _____, je _____
5. tu (voir) _____, nous _____
6. nous (dire) _____, elle _____
7. je (savoir) _____, vous _____
8. elles (aller) _____, nous _____
9. elle (devoir) _____, vous _____
10. le téléspectateur (viewer) (ouvrir: to turn on) _____
11. les réclames (commercials) (pouvoir) _____
12. le dépanneur (craindre) _____

II. FORMATION OF THE PAST SUBJUNCTIVE

The **past subjunctive** is made up of the present subjunctive of the auxiliary *avoir* or *être* and the past participle. (It is similar to the *passé composé* of the indicative except that the auxiliary is in the subjunctive.)

J'AIE réparé	JE SOIS venu(e)
TU AIES réparé	TU SOIS venu(e)
IL AIT réparé	IL SOIT venu
NOUS AYONS réparé	NOUS SOYONS venu(e)s
VOUS AYEZ réparé	VOUS SOYEZ venu(e) (s)
ILS AIENT réparé	ILS SOIENT venus

Exercise 3

Give the following forms of the past subjunctive (the verbs marked with an asterisk are conjugated with *être*):

1. je (manquer) _____	je (choisir) _____	je (répondre) _____
2. elle (arriver*) _____	elle (se divertir*) _____	elle (descendre*) _____
3. vous (fermer) _____	vous (finir) _____	vous (perdre) _____
4. ils (monter*) _____	ils (se réunir*) _____	ils (attendre) _____
5. tu (écouter) _____	tu (réussir) _____	tu (entendre) _____
6. nous (regarder) _____	nous (partir*) _____	nous (vendre) _____
7. le dépanneur (desserrer) _____	. . . (sortir*) _____	. . . (rendre) _____
8. les tubes cathodiques (coûter) _____	. . . (éclaircir) _____	. . . (répandre) _____

III. USES OF THE SUBJUNCTIVE

Basically, the indicative is the mood used to express facts objectively:

Ce n'est pas le tube cathodique. (It is not the picture tube.)

The subjunctive is usually used to show a person's attitude about the fact or to express it subjectively:

Je suis bien contente que ce ne SOIT pas le tube cathodique. (I'm very glad that is isn't the picture tube.)

Thus, we can see that *the subjunctive does not occur in a main clause.* The subjunctive is to be used in the dependent clause because of some element in the main clause that requires it. *It is therefore the content of the main clause that must be watched*, especially, too, because the French subjunctive cannot be recognized from the English wording. What elements, therefore, in the main clause cause a subjunctive in the dependent clause? We may visualize them as follows:

The subjunctive is used in the subordinate clause when in the main clause there is:

- **A.** verb of wishing, forbidding, etc.
- **B.** expression of doubt
- **C.** expression of emotion
- **D.** impersonal expression
- **E.** *croire* or *penser* interrogatively or negatively
- **F.** one of certain indefinite words (*qui que* [whoever], *quoi que* [whatever], etc.)

A. After Verbs of Wishing, Forbidding, Preventing, Preferring in the main clause a subjunctive is used in the dependent clause when the second verb has a subject of its own.

We would like the repairman to come immediately.

In such cases, note that the sentence must be expanded, first in English, so as to read:

We would like *that* the repairman come immediately.

Thus:

Nous voudrions que le dépanneur vienne immédiatement.

If the second verb has the same subject as the first, the second verb is an infinitive and not a subjunctive. Note the difference:

Je ne veux pas que vous vous dépêchiez. (I do not want you to hurry.)

Nous ne voudrions pas manquer . . . (We wouldn't want to miss . . .)

Exercise 4

Translate the English into French:

1. *I wish that you could see* ce programme ce soir.
2. *Paul wants to examine* les tubes mais Maman défend (forbids) *him to lay a hand on* (mettre la main sur) *the set* (l'appareil).
3. Préféreriez-vous que *we change programs* (changer de: to change) ou bien *do you want to wait for* la fin de celui-ci?
4. L'image est un petit peu déformée (out of shape) mais *that will not prevent my father from seeing* la lutte (wrestling) ce soir.
5. Les téléspectateurs préfèrent-ils *that programs be interrupted* par les réclames ou bien que l'on soit obligé de payer les programmes que l'on *wishes to see*?

B. After an Expression of Doubt in the main clause, the subjunctive is used in the dependent clause (this will also be seen under the study of Impersonal Expressions, below):

Je doute qu'on puisse avoir une image plus nette. (I doubt that one [you] can have a clearer picture.)

Exercise 5

Translate the English into French:

1. Je doute *that there is* une émission en français à la télévision.
2. Paul doute *that the repairman will come before five o'clock.*
3. Nous doutons *that last week's storm has loosened the aerial.*

C. After an Expression of Emotion in the main clause, the subjunctive is used if the second verb has a subject of its own. Otherwise, the second verb is in the infinitive:

Je suis bien contente que ce ne soit pas le tube cathodique. (I'm very glad that it isn't the picture tube.)

Je suis bien content de savoir cela. (I'm very glad to know that.)

Exercise 6

From the list of expressions of emotion given below, select one that will serve as main clause for the dependent clauses:

avoir peur, craindre (to fear, to be afraid)
être content, être heureux (to be glad)
regretter (to be sorry)
c'est dommage (it's a pity, it's too bad)
s'étonner (to be surprised)

1. ______ que mon récepteur de télévision soit détraqué (out of order).
2. ______ que le dépanneur puisse le réparer avant ce soir.
3. ______ que vous ne sachiez quand ce programme se présentera.
4. ______ que vous n'ayez pas consulté le journal.
5. Les téléspectateurs ______ que ce programme ait été interrompu par tant de réclames.

D. An Impersonal Expression in the main clause usually calls for the subjunctive in the dependent clause if the statement made refers to some specific person or thing.

Il est possible que la tempête de la semaine passée l'ait desserrée quelque peu. (It is possible that last week's storm loosened it somewhat.)

Some of the more common impersonal expressions requiring the subjunctive are the following:

il faut que il est nécessaire que	it is necessary that
il est bon que	it is good that
il est convenable que il convient que	it is proper (suitable, fitting) that
il est essentiel que	it is essential that
il est faux que	it is false that
il est juste que	it is fair (right) that
il est important que il importe que	it is important that
il est naturel que	it is natural that
il est possible que	it is possible that
il est temps que	it is time that
il semble que	it seems that
il se peut que	it may be that
il vaut mieux que	it is better that

1. The infinitive, instead of the subjunctive, can be used after the expressions above, with the exception of *il se peut que*:

(a) When the impersonal expression applies generally, and not to any specific person or thing:

Il est important de ne pas manquer ce programme. (It is important not to miss that programme.)

BUT: Il est important que nous ne manquions pas ... (It is important for us not to miss . . .)

(b) In some cases even though a special person is involved:

Il me faut renoncer à mon programme favori ce soir. (I must [It is necessary for me to] give up my favorite program this evening.)

All expressions above, except *il faut, il semble, il vaut mieux*, require *de* before the infinitive.

Il est nécessaire de faire venir le dépanneur. (It is necessary to send for the repairman.)

2. The indicative is used after the following: *il paraît que, il* (*me te, nous, vous, leur*) *semble que, il est probable que, il est sûr que, il est certain que*:

Il est certain que la télévision a le moyen d'instruire le grand public. (It is certain that television has the means of educating the masses.)

Exercise 7

Match each of the following main clauses with a suitable dependent clause:

1. Notre récepteur de télévision est détraqué. Il faudra . . .	que nous ne soyons pas obligés de le remplacer nous-mêmes.
2. Est-il vrai . . .	que le dépanneur examine immédiatement l'antenne.
3. Oui, c'est vrai! Il est bon . . .	que nous fassions venir le dépanneur.
4. Il vaut toujours mieux . . .	que nous puissions avoir notre programme après tout.
5. Il se peut . . .	que le tube cathodique soit garanti?

E. After *Croire* or *Penser* Used Negatively or Interrogatively:

Croyez-vous qu'il soit possible de faire les réparations avant ce soir? (Do you think it will be possible to make the repairs before this evening?)

Je ne crois pas que toutes ces réclames soient nécessaires. (I don't believe that all those commercials are necessary.)

BUT: With the affirmative or negative-interrogative use, *croire* and *penser* take the indicative:

Oui, madame, je crois que ça peut bien s'arranger. (Yes, madam, I think that that can be arranged.)

Ne croyez-vous pas que le dépanneur peut le réparer immédiatement? (Don't you think that the repairman can repair it immediately?)

Exercise 8

Translate the English into French:

1. Croyez-vous que les téléspectateurs *enjoy* (prendre plaisir à) ces programmes de crime et de violence?
2. Je ne crois pas *that it is* un divertissement (entertainment) convenable.
3. Je ne crois pas *that one can* se reposer pendant la nuit après avoir regardé ces horreurs.
4. Ne croyez-vous pas que les programmes *should be more varied*?
5. Bien sûr! A vrai dire (to tell the truth), je suis las (weary) de voir toujours la même histoire. Je crois que ceux qui préparent les programmes *haven't* beaucoup d'imagination.

F. After Certain Indefinite Words, as *qui que* (whoever); *quoi que* (whatever); *quel(le) (s) que* (whichever or whatever, used as an adjective); *quelque* (or *si*) + adjective or adverb + *que* (however, no matter how):

Quoi qu'on fasse, il y a toujours ces rayures... (Whatever you do, there still are those lines...)

Si coûteuse que soit l'émission, elle n'est pas du tout intéressante. (However costly the broadcast may be, it isn't at all interesting.)

Exercise 9

Translate the English into French:

1. *However interesting the broadcast may be*, le téléspectateur y prend toujours un plus grand plaisir si c'est une émission en direct (live).
2. C'est parce que, *no matter how good the acting* (le jeu) *may be*, ce sont les actions et les réactions spontanées qui sont les plus naturelles.
3. *Whoever we may be*, nous avons tous la passion de la vérité (love for truth).
4. *However long the commercials may have been*, je ne les ai pas trouvées ennuyeuses (boring) parce que celui qui les présentait avait le don (gift) de la pantomime.
5. *Whatever that actor* (cet acteur) *said and whatever he did*, c'était si bien exécuté (performed) qu'on se croyait toujours en présence de la réalité.

Review Exercise

Words needed in this translation are given in the vocabulary below.

to guess: *deviner*
to let know: *faire savoir*
to imagine: *se faire une idée*
simple: *simple*
scene: *la scène*
to use: *se servir de*
to need: *avoir besoin de*
to wave: *faire signe de la main*
to applaud: *applaudir*
obey: *obéir à*
to respond to: *répondre à*
guests: *les invités*
to get (tickets): *prendre, se procurer (les billets)*
late: *tard*
to realize: *se rendre compte de*
most of us: *la plupart d'entre nous*

Translate the English into French:

I doubt that you can guess où j'ai été hier soir. Eh bien, mon frère et moi nous avons assisté à l'émission de mon programme favori. *It's too bad you were not with us, but it was impossible to let you know* à temps. *I think it's impossible for viewers* to imagine tous les préparatifs nécessaires même à une émission si peu prétentieuse (elaborate). *No matter how simple the scene may be, it seems they use* (one uses) une quantité d'appareils photographiques. *It is amazing that they need* tant de techniciens. *It may be that it's only a commercial* qu'on présente mais tout de même *you are* (one is) *astonished to see* toute une équipe (crew) de techniciens. *They forbid* (one forbids) *the guests to wave* devant les appareils et *it is important that they applaud* à des moments donnés et *that they respond* à certain signes. Naturellement *it is fitting that guests obey* ces règles. Comme cela, les programmes peuvent se dérouler (unfold) dans une atmosphère d'ordre et de décorum. *I am very glad that Paul was able to get* les billets mais *I'm sorry that we got them so late and that we went without you.* Le langage en pantomime dont on se sert pour avertir les acteurs de la fin du programme ou de *whatever interruption it may be,* est on ne peut plus amusant (most amusing). *But, I don't think that the viewer realizes* toutes les rigueurs de la vie devant les appareils photographiques. *I doubt that most of us would want to be* de tels esclaves de la précision.

CHAPTER EIGHTEEN

Other Uses of the Subjunctive: *After Certain Conjunctions; After a Denial or General Negation in the Main Clause; After an Indefinite Antecedent in the Main Clause; After a Superlative, as Antecedent of the Pronoun Introducing the Dependent Clause*

The Imperfect and Pluperfect Subjunctive: *Formation of the Imperfect Subjunctive; Formation of the Pluperfect Subjunctive.*

À LA RECHERCHE D'UNE SITUATION POUR L'ÉTÉ

PAUL – (Lisant à Marianne un article du journal) "... et AVANT QUE LE BANDIT EÛT GLISSÉ au caissier sa demande pour trois mille dollars, la police qui était depuis deux semaines sur sa piste le saisit SANS MÊME QUE LE BANDIT SÛT de quoi il s'agissait."

MARIANNE – Et pourtant on se moque de la police en disant qu'ils ne se tiennent pas en éveil. Mais ça c'est LE PLUS GROS MENSONGE QUE J'AIE JAMAIS ENTENDU.

PAUL – Tu lis trop de romans policiers Marianne. C'est pour faire ressortir l'habileté du détective.... Laurent! Tu as eu de la chance aujourd'hui?

LAURENT – Non, Paul. En tout cas, JE N'AI PAS DE PROMESSES QUI SOIENT vraiment définitives.

MARIANNE – Mais quelle sorte de poste cherches-tu pour l'été, Laurent?

LOOKING FOR A POSITION FOR THE SUMMER

PAUL – (Reading an article from the newspaper to Marianne) "... and before the bandit had slipped his demand for three thousand dollars to the teller, the police who had been on his trail for two weeks seized him without the bandit's even knowing what it was all about."

MARIANNE – And yet they make fun of the police, saying that they aren't on the alert. Why, that's the biggest lie I ever heard.

PAUL – You read too many detective stories, Marianne. That's to bring out the cleverness of the detective. ... Laurence! Did you have any luck today?

LAURENCE – No, Paul. Anyway, I don't have any promises that are really definite.

MARIANNE – But what kind of a job are you looking for for the summer, Laurence?

LAURENT – UN POSTE QUI ME PERMETTE d'utiliser ma connaissance du français et de la comptabilité.	LAURENCE – A job that would let me use my knowledge of French and bookkeeping.
PAUL – Et tu connais également la sténographie et la dactylographie, n'est-ce pas?	PAUL – And you also know stenography and typing, don't you?
LAURENT – C'est juste! Mais mon anglais n'est pas trop fort.	LAURENCE – That's right! But my English isn't too good.
MARIANNE – Ça ne fait rien. IL N'Y A PAS BEAUCOUP DE CANDIDATS QUI PUISSENT offrir le français, la comptabilité, la sténographie et la dactylographie.	MARIANNE – That doesn't matter. There aren't many applicants that can offer French, bookkeeping, stenography, and typing.
LAURENT – C'est très encourageant tout ce que vous dites.	LAURENCE – What you say is very encouraging.
MARIANNE – Fais voir le journal, Paul. Voyons les petites annonces . . . Tiens! En voici une précisément qui cherche UN SECRÉTAIRE BILINGUE QUI SACHE LE français et . . . Oh non! C'est pour le français et l'espagnol. Mais en voici une autre et c'est tout fait pour toi, Laurent. Écoute! "Maison française cherche comptable." Attends QUE JE DÉCOUPE l'annonce. Voilà, Laurent.	MARIANNE – Let's see the paper, Paul. Let's see the ads . . . Look! Here's one precisely that is looking for a bilingual secretary who knows French and . . . Oh no! It's for French and Spanish. But here's another and it's just made for you, Laurence. Listen! "French firm seeks bookkeeper." Wait till I cut out the ad. There you are, Laurence.
LAURENT – Merci mille fois, Marianne. J'irai demain matin.	LAURENCE – Thanks a thousand times, Marianne. I'll go tomorrow morning.
MARIANNE ET PAUL – Bonne chance, Laurent!	MARIANNE AND PAUL – Good luck, Laurence!

I. OTHER USES OF THE SUBJUNCTIVE

A. Certain Conjunctions, such as those listed below, are followed by the subjunctive.

afin que pour que	in order that
avant que	before

bien que } although
quoique }
à moins que unless
jusqu'à ce que until
(which shortens to *que* with the verb *attendre*)
de peur que } for fear that
de crainte que }
sans que without
de sorte que } so that
de façon que }
pourvu que provided that

1. If the second verb has a subject of its own, the subjunctive is to be used. If the one subject applies to both verbs, an infinitive is used with the prepositional form of the above expressions:

Avant que Marianne ait trouvé la petite annonce, Laurent n'avait rien de définitif. (Before Marianne found the ad, Laurence had nothing definite.)

BUT:

Avant de trouver la petite annonce, Laurent n'avait rien de définitif. (Before finding the ad, Laurence had nothing definite.)

2. When the infinitive is to be used rather than the subjunctive, some of the conjunctions change to prepositions as follows:

afin que	becomes	afin de
avant que	"	avant de
à moins que	"	à moins de
de peur que	"	de peur de
sans que	"	sans
pour que	"	pour
de façon que	"	de façon à

3. When *de sorte que* shows purpose, it takes the subjunctive; when it shows result, it takes the indicative.

Contrast:

Laurent cherche un poste de secrétaire bilingue de sorte qu'il puisse utiliser sa connaissance du français. (Laurence is looking for a position as bilingual secretary so that he may use his knowledge of French.)

BUT: Laurent a un poste de secrétaire bilingue de sorte qu'il peut utiliser sa connaissance du français. (Laurence has a position as bilingual secretary so that he is able to use his knowledge of French.)

Exercise 1

Translate the English into French:

1. Paul dit qu'on se moque de la police dans les romans policiers *so that the detective may be more admired.*
2. La police était sur la piste du bandit pendant deux semaines *without being ready to seize him until he entered the bank.*
3. *Provided that the applicant has a knowledge of typing,* je crois qu'on l'engagera.
4. Marianne sait le français, la sténographie et la dactylographie, *so that she too can be a bilingual secretary.*
5. *Unless the applicant can offer French and Spanish,* cette maison n'a pas de place pour lui.

B. A Denial or General Negation in the Main Clause causes the subjunctive to be used in the dependent clause.

Je n'ai pas de promesses qui soient vraiment définitives. (I have no promises that are really definite.)

Il n'y a pas beaucoup de candidats qui puissent offrir ... (There aren't many applicants who can offer ...)

Exercise 2

Translate the English into French:

1. Cette maison-là *doesn't want any applicants who can't offer* la sténographie et la dactylographie.
2. *There isn't any detective story where the police are more intelligent* que le détective.
3. *There is nobody who reads more detective stories* que Marianne.
4. *It isn't that Laurence hasn't been able to find a position,* c'est seulement qu'il veut utiliser sa connaissance de la comptabilité.
5. *We have never had any applicant who has come here* avec plus d'expérience.

C. An Indefinite Antecedent in the Main Clause is followed by the subjunctive in the dependent clause. When the pronoun introducing the subordinate clause refers back to an antecedent that is vague, the subjunctive is needed in the subordinate clause:

Un poste qui me permette d'utiliser ma connaissance du français . . . (A position [some position] that may let me use my knowledge of French . . .)

If, however, the antecendent is specific and definite, the indicative will follow it.

Laurent a un poste qui lui permet d'utiliser sa connaissance du français. (Laurence has a position [a definite one] which lets him use his knowledge of French.)

Exercise 3

Translate the English into French:

1. "As-tu *any promises that are* vraiment définitives?" demanda Paul.
2. "Pas jusqu'ici," répondit Laurent. "Ce que je cherche c'est *a French firm that needs a bookkeeper.*"
3. "Tu parles bien l'anglais, Laurent. Ne préférerais-tu pas travailler pour *an American firm that is well known and that can offer a good salary*?"
4. "Ce serait difficile pour moi, Paul, parce que mon fort c'est la comptabilité et je ne connais pas les termes en anglais. Pour commencer, il me faudra donc *a position that permits me to use* ma langue maternelle, quelque chose comme le travail mi-temps (part time) *that you found for me* le semestre passé.
5. A-t-on jamais vu *a girl who reads the classified ads more attentively* que Marianne?

D. A Superlative, as Antecedent of the Pronoun Introducing the Dependent Clause, necessitates the use of the subjunctive. The adjectives *seul, premier, unique* also convey superlative force:

C'est le plus gros mensonge que j'aie jamais entendu. (It's the biggest lie I've ever heard.)

Often the idea of "ever" will fit in, even though it is not expressed.

Exercise 4

Translate the English into French:

1. Laurent est *the most ambitious young man that one can find.*
2. Marianne *has the biggest collection of detective stories that I have ever seen.*
3. *The only detective story that Laurence ever read* c'est Sherlock Holmes.
4. Les petites annonces sont quelquefois *the most interesting reading* (lecture, f.) *that one can do.*
5. *The best thing that you can study,* si vous désirez devenir secrétaire bilingue, c'est la sténographie française.

II. THE IMPERFECT AND PLUPERFECT SUBJUNCTIVE

These forms are never found in conversational French, but are frequently used in literary French. Generally, when used, the imperfect subjunctive follows a main clause verb that is in the past. The pluperfect expresses "had" and a past participle in the dependent clause. In conversational French, the present subjunctive replaces the imperfect; the perfect replaces the pluperfect.

La police le saisit sans même que le bandit sût . . . (The police seized him without the bandit's even knowing . . .)

Avant que le bandit eût glissé . . . la police le saisit . . . (Before the bandit had slipped . . . the police seized him . . .)

A. Formation of the Imperfect Subjunctive

The final letter of the past definite (*passé simple*) *je* form is removed and to the remaining stem are added the endings: *-sse, -sses, -ˆt, -ssions, -ssiez, -ssent.* This rule holds for all verbs, regular and irregular.

Imperfect Subjunctive of the Three Conjugations

(*Past Definite*)	JE CHERCHAI	JE SAISIS	J'ENTENDIS
je	cherchaSSE	saisiSSE	entendiSSE
tu	cherchaSSES	saisiSSES	entendiSSES
il	cherchâT	saisîT	entendîT
nous	cherchaSSIONS	saisiSSIONS	entendiSSIONS
vous	cherchaSSIEZ	saisiSSIEZ	entendiSSIEZ
ils	cherchaSSENT	saisiSSENT	entendiSSENT

EXERCISE 5

Give the following forms of the imperfect subjunctive:

1. je (demander) _____	je (saisir) _____	je (perdre) _____
2. elle (glisser) _____	elle (finir) _____	elle (attendre) _____
3. vous (annoncer) _____	vous (remplir) _____	vous (entendre) _____
4. ils (encourager) _____	ils (salir) _____	ils (rendre) _____
5. tu (découper) _____	tu (embellir) _____	tu (répondre) _____
6. nous (se moquer) _____	nous (choisir) _____	nous (vendre) _____
7. la maison (désirer) _____	. . . (choisir) _____	. . . (attendre) _____
8. les candidats (utiliser) _____	. . . (finir) _____	. . . (répondre) _____

Going back to Chapter XVI, Exercise 3, change all these forms to the imperfect subjunctive.

B. Formation of the Pluperfect Subjunctive

This tense is made up of the imperfect subjunctive of the auxiliary verb *avoir* or *être* and a past participle. It is similar to the pluperfect of the indicative, except that the auxiliary here is in the subjunctive.

j'	EUSSE cherché	je	FUSSE venu(e)
tu	EUSSES cherché	tu	FUSSES venu(e)
il	EÛT cherché	il	FÛT venu
nous	EUSSIONS cherché	nous	FUSSIONS venu(e)s
vous	EUSSIEZ cherché	vous	FUSSIEZ venu(e) (s)
ils	EUSSENT cherché	ils	FUSSENT venus

Exercise 6

Change to the pluperfect subjunctive the verbs of the preceding exercise.

THE SUBJUNCTIVE IS USED AFTER

1. certain conjunctions
2. a denial
3. an indefinite antecedent
4. a superlative

Review Exercise

Where the imperfect or the pluperfect subjunctive is possible in the literary translation, use them, then show the substitution of the present or the perfect, as used in the conversational sequence. Translate:

1. Before Laurence came in, Marianne and Paul were reading.
2. Marianne had bought a new detective story that she hoped to finish that evening.
3. "It is the most thrilling plot [*intrigue*, f.] *I've ever read*," she told Paul, "and I was just looking for one that would have a different ending [*dénouement*, m.]."
4. I don't like a plot that is easy to guess (*facile à deviner*).
5. The best detective story that was ever written was one that I read a few years ago.
6. One cold winter (of winter: *d'hiver*) day in January, a woman was killed.
7. The only things that they found were a turned-over (*renversé*) glass that had contained water, a book, and a stain on the rug.

8. She had been stabbed (*poignarder:* to stab), but there was no weapon (*arme,* f.) that the police could see, so that it was really difficult to know where to begin.
9. They contacted all the relatives (*parent,* m.) and friends and even acquaintances (*connaissance,* f.) who could help them.
10. But there was no one who knew (*connaître*) any motive (*mobile,* m.) that would explain the murder (*meurtre,* m.).
11. They waited until the analysis (*analyse,* f.) came back from the laboratory.
12. Unless they found some indication in it that would give them an idea (*idée,* f.), the case (*cas,* m.) could not be solved (*résolu*).
13. But when they received the report (*rapport,* m.), they learned that the stain was – water!
14. Suddenly, one of the police detectives had an idea. Water! Winter!
15. The only answer that was possible was that the weapon was an icicle (*glaçon,* m.).
16. And in fact (*en effet*) that was the clue (*piste,* f.) that gave them the answer (*solution,* f.).
17. The woman had been stabbed by an icicle.
18. "I never would have guessed it!" exclaimed (*s'écrier:* to exclaim) Marianne. "That's the most original plot I ever heard!"

CHAPTER NINETEEN

The Passive: *Formation and Use*
Substitutes for the Passive: *On (one); Reflexive*

LE CARNAVAL	THE CARNIVAL
MARIANNE – Mais regardez tous les préparatifs QUI ONT ÉTÉ FAITS PAR LES GARÇONS!	MARIANNE – But look at all the preparations that have been made by the boys!
HÉLÈNE – C'est joli comme tout! Regardez les lanternes QUI ONT ÉTÉ SUSPENDUES à travers la promenade.	HELEN – It's as pretty as can be! Look at the lanterns that have been hung across the promenade.
JEANNINE – Et cette grosse tente à toit rayé . . . Oh, regardez les fontaines!	JEANNINE – And that big tent with the striped roof . . . Oh, look at the fountains!
MARGUERITE – Comme c'est beau cette eau couleur de vin QUI SE JETTE dans l'air.	MARGARET – How pretty that wine-colored water is that is sprayed up into the air.
MARIANNE – Voyez-vous les jolies petites tables QU'ON A MISES là-bas au coin? Ce n'est pas pour rien que PAUL S'INQUIÉTAIT ce matin lorsque le temps était à la pluie.	MARIANNE – Do you see the pretty little tables that were put over there in the corner? It's not for nothing that Paul was worried this morning when it looked like rain.
HÉLÈNE – Ç'aurait été une catastrophe s'il avait plu ce soir!	HELEN – It would have been a catastrophe if it had rained this evening!
MARGUERITE – Allons chercher les sandwiches et les petits fours. ON APPRÊTE LE BUFFET. Voilà QU'ON APPORTE les caisses de boissons non-alcooliques et les glaces.	MARGARET – Let's go get the sandwiches and the cakes. The buffet is being prepared. There are the cases of soft drinks and the ice cream being brought in.
MARIANNE – Et voilà les garçons qui viennent. LEUR TRAVAIL EST FAIT! Félicitations, Henri, Paul, Laurent. Les décors sont épatants!	MARIANNE – And there are the boys coming. Their work is done! Congratulations, Henry, Paul, Laurence. The decorations are wonderful!
JEANNINE – C'est un véritable mardi-gras que vous avez préparé.	JEANNINE – It's a real mardi-gras you've prepared.

LES GARÇONS – Merci, Marianne, merci, Jeannine! Mais regardez les rafraîchissements que vous avez préparés.

THE BOYS – Thanks, Marianne, thanks Jeannine! But look at the refreshments that you've prepared.

HÉLÈNE – Quel sera le programme?

HELEN – What will the program be?

HENRI – ON COMMENCERA LES FESTIVITÉS à neuf heures par les feux d'artifice. Ensuite, la sauterie . . .

HENRY – The festivities will be begun at nine o'clock with the fireworks. Then, the dance . . .

MARGUERITE – Ah, oui! L'orchestre est déjà là.

MARGARET – Ah, yes! The orchestra is there already.

PAUL – Et ce sera par la tombola qu'ON CLÔTURERA LA FÊTE.

PAUL – And it will be with the raffle that the celebration will be closed.

JEANNINE – Voilà ce que j'attends. Voilà ma petite Citroën rouge que je vais gagner. C'est tellement mignon!

JEANNINE – That's what I'm waiting for. There is my little red Citroën that I'm going to win. It's so cute!

MARIANNE – En attendant, allons nous attabler, voulez-vous? La musique commence.

MARIANNE – While we're waiting, let's go sit down at a table, shall we? The music is beginning.

I. THE PASSIVE

A. Formation and Use

The passive is made up of *être* and a past participle, which must agree with the subject. "By" with the agent is usually *par*, unless with a verb of emotion or in an expression of an habitual condition, when it is translated by *de*:

Mais regardez tous les préparatifs qui ont été faits par les garçons. (But look at all the preparations that have been made by the boys.)

Regardez les lanternes qui ont été suspendues. (Look at the lanterns that have been hung.)

Le carnaval est une fête qui est aimée de tous les étudiants. (The carnival is a celebration that is loved by all the students.)

In translating "was" or "were" observe the usual difference between the *passé indefini* and the imperfect:

Regardez toutes les lanternes qui ont été (were = have been) suspendues . . .

Chaque année les lanternes étaient suspendues (were = used to be) . . .

Exercise 1

Translate the English into French:

1. Tous les préparatifs *will be made by the boys.*
2. Les rafraîchissements *were prepared by the girls.*
3. Cent caisses de Coca-Cola *were ordered* (to order: commander).
4. Chaque année une belle voiture *was offered* comme prix par la même maison.
5. Le carnaval *is loved by students and professors.*

II. SUBSTITUTES FOR THE PASSIVE

Since the passive construction is much less used in French than it is in English, it is important to note the following:

A. On (one)

ON can translate any English passive where there is no agent mentioned:

On apprête le buffet. (The buffet is being prepared.)

Voilà qu'on apporte les caisses. (There are the cases being brought [in].)

On commencera les festivités à neuf heures. (The festivities will be begun at nine o'clock.)

Whenever the passive subject would become an indirect object in the active voice, *on* must be used.

The students were given cakes and soft drinks. (Cakes and soft drinks were given *to the students.*) (On a donné aux étudiants des petits fours et des boissons non-alcooliques.)

Exercise 2

Translate the English into French:

1. *Pretty little tables will be put* là-bas au coin.
2. *The prizes will be drawn* (to draw: tirer) à dix heures.
3. *A big tent has been constructed* (construire) au milieu du terrain universitaire.
4. Chaque année *a beautiful car is given* comme prix.
5. *Although the dancing* (la danse) *hasn't been begun yet,* voilà la musique qui commence.

B. Reflexive

The reflexive is often used where the English passive implies repetition or an action that is habitually or continually true.

Comme c'est beau cette eau couleur de vin qui se jette dans l'air. (How beautiful that wine-colored water is that is sprayed into the air.)

Exercise 3

Translate the English into French:

1. Chaque année le terrain universitaire *is lighted up* (illuminer) à l'époque du carnaval.
2. *The color of the water is changed to* (en) *red* et les fontaines sont magnifiques.
3. *A pretty Citroën is seen* sur la promenade.
4. Il y a quelques années *tickets used to be sold* partout pour la tombola.
5. L'année prochaine, je crois que plusieurs innovations *will be added* (to add: ajouter) au programme.

Review Exercise

Vary the translation by using as many constructions as possible for each passive.

Translate:

1. At that university, the carnival is an institution that is loved by all.
2. It is promoted (*promu*) by professors, students, friends, and even the merchants (*les marchands*) of the neighborhood (*le voisinage*).
3. Prizes are contributed (*contribuer*) by some of the big companies.
4. The decorations are furnished (to furnish: *fournir*) by the boys, and the refreshments are prepared by the girls.
5. The students are usually given cakes and soft drinks and ice cream for the occasion.
6. Last year, the fountains were lighted up and lanterns were hung across the promenade.
7. All the beautiful colors of the rainbow (*l'arc-en-ciel*) were reflected (to be reflected: *se refléter*) in the sky as the fireworks burst (to burst: *éclater*) into the darkness (*l'obscurité*, f.) of the night.
8. It was so beautiful!

CHAPTER TWENTY

The Infinitive: ***Uses; Prepositions Required by Certain Verbs Before an Infinitive***
The Present Participle

LE DÉPART	THE DEPARTURE
MARIANNE – Oh, maman! Quelle joie! Mon premier voyage en France! IL EST TELLEMENT ÉMOUVANT DE FRANCHIR LA PASSERELLE.	MARIANNE – Oh, Mamma! What a delight! My first trip to France. It's so thrilling to cross the gangplank.
MME DESJARDINS – Je comprends bien, Marianne. Pour moi c'est mon quatrième voyage, SANS COMPTER mon premier voyage en Amérique, et IL EST TOUJOURS MAGNIFIQUE À CONTEMPLER.	MRS. DESJARDINS – I fully understand, Marianne. For me, it's my fourth trip, without counting my first trip to America, and it's always wonderful to think about.
MARIANNE – Mais METTRE LE PIED sur le sol français, ME TROUVER finalement à Paris, APRÈS L'AVOIR TANT DE FOIS REVU dans mon imagination, PASSER DEUX MOIS à Saint-Jean-de-Maurienne dont Papa parle si souvent, ALLER VOIR Carcassonne, Lourdes, la Côte d'Azur, VISITER Brangues et FAIRE MES HOMMAGES au tombeau de Paul Claudel . . . c'est RÉALISER mon plus doux rêve! Maman, c'est trop. Je rêve. Voilà tout.	MARIANNE – But putting my feet on French soil, finally being in Paris, after having seen it so often in my dreams, spending two months in Saint-Jean-de-Maurienne, which Daddy talks so often about, going to see Carcassonne, Lourdes, the Riviera, visiting Brangues and paying my respects at the tomb of Paul Claudel . . . it's realizing my fondest dream! Mamma, it's too much. I'm dreaming. That's all.
MME DESJARDINS – Non, chérie, c'est vrai. Mais, TOUT EN PARLANT, nous oublions D'ALLER à notre cabine retrouver Papa et Paul. Ils vont nous manquer.	MRS. DESJARDINS – No, dear, it's true. But while we're talking, we're forgetting to go to our cabin and meet Daddy and Paul. We're going to miss them.
MARIANNE – Mais nous serons tous ensemble au mois d'août.	MARIANNE – But we'll all be together in the month of August.

MME DESJARDINS – Il est déjà deux heures moins le quart. Dépêchons-NOUS donc DE TROUVER la cabine!

MRS. DESJARDINS – It's already a quarter to two. Let's hurry and find the cabin.

MARIANNE – Par ici, Maman, c'est sur le pont B. Ah, voilà la piscine! Nous voici! La porte est ouverte.

MARIANNE – This way, Mamma, it's on B Deck. Ah, there's the swimming pool. Here we are. The door is open.

PAUL (qui chante) – Bon voyage, Maman! Bon voyage, Marianne! Bon . . . !

PAUL (singing) – Bon voyage, Mamma! Bon voyage, Marianne! Bon . . . !

M. DESJARDINS – Du champagne POUR FÊTER l'occasion!

MR. DESJARDINS – Some champagne to celebrate the occasion!

MME DESJARDINS – Ils ont tout préparé pour nous – le champagne, les hors-d'œuvre et les fleurs! Comme c'est joli!

MRS. DESJARDINS – They've got everything ready for us – the champagne, the hors-d'oeuvre, and the flowers. How pretty it is.

M. DESJARDINS – Dans deux mois Paul et moi nous vous rejoindrons en Savoie. Et Laurent a une surprise. IL M'A PRIÉ DE NE RIEN DIRE. IL TIENT À l'ANNONCER lui-même.

MR. DESJARDINS – In two months Paul and I shall rejoin you in Savoie. And Laurence has a surprise. He asked me not to say anything. He's anxious to announce it himself.

LAURENT – Je vais rentrer en France avec M. Desjardins et Paul, et MAMAN VOUS INVITE À FAIRE UN SÉJOUR en villégiature chez nous!

LAURENCE – I'm going to go back to France with Mr. Desjardins and Paul, and Mother invites you to stay in the country with us!

I. THE INFINITIVE

A. Uses

The infinitive is used in French as:

1. Subject:

Mettre le pied sur le sol français, *me trouver* finalement à Paris, *passer* deux mois à Saint-Jean-de-Maurienne . . . (Putting my feet on French soil, being finally in Paris, spending two months at Saint-Jean-de-Maurienne . . .)

2. Object, or as predicative complement:

Mme Desjardins n'aime pas *aller* en France sans Papa et Paul. (Mrs. Desjardin doesn't like going to France without Daddy and Paul.)

Mettre le pied sur le sol français, c'est *réaliser* mon plus doux rêve. (Putting my feet on French soil is realizing my fondest dream.)

3. After a preposition:

C'est la quatrième fois *sans compter*... (It's the fourth time without counting...)

NOTE:

a. Most of these verbs appear in English as present participles.

b. The preposition *après* is always followed by the past infinitive. Thus it will occur as *après avoir* ____ or *après être* ____:

Après l'avoir revu dans mon imagination... (After having seen it in my dreams...)

c. The preposition *en* is always followed by the present participle, as will be seen below.

d. The preposition *pour* must always be expressed before an infinitive when the meaning "in order to" is understood. It is always necessary also before an infinitive that follows *trop, assez.*

Il y a du champagne *pour fêter* l'occasion. (There is some champagne to celebrate the occasion.)

Avez-vous *assez d'argent pour faire* un voyage en France? (Do you have enough money to take a trip to France?)

Exercise 1

Translate the English into French:

1. *Going to France, after having dreamed so long of it,* c'est un plaisir des plus rares.
2. *Spending two months in Paris and seeing* tous les monuments, c'est une joie incomparable.
3. *Do you like visiting museums?* Moi *I like visiting museums and traveling* à loisir (leisurely).
4. *After staying in Saint-Jean-de-Maurienne* pendant une ou deux semaines, nous comptons prendre le train pour la Suisse car nous ne voudrions pas retourner en Amérique *without seeing our friends.*
5. Marianne se croit alpiniste. Ça il faut voir, n'est-ce pas? *Seeing is believing!*

B. Prepositions Required by Certain Verbs Before an Infinitive

Certain verbs require the preposition *à* before an infinitive that follows directly; others take the preposition *de*; still others require no preposition:

SOME COMMON VERBS REQUIRING *à*	SOME COMMON VERBS REQUIRING *de*
aider (to help)	*cesser* (to stop)
apprendre (to learn, to teach)	*conseiller* (to advise)
commencer (to begin)	*craindre* (to fear)
continuer (to continue)	*décider* (to decide)
se décider (to make up one's mind)	*défendre* (to forbid)
s'habituer (to get used to)	*demander* (to ask)
inviter (to invite)	*se dépêcher* (to hurry)
obliger (to force)	*dire* (to tell, to say)
passer (to spend [time])	*empêcher* (to prevent)
renoncer (to give up)	*éviter* (to avoid)
réussir (to succeed)	*oublier* (to forget)
	permettre (to allow)
	refuser (to refuse)
	regretter (to regret)
	tâcher (to try)
	venir (to have just)

The following verbs need no preposition:

aimer (to like)	*laisser* (to let)
aller (to go)	*oser* (to dare)
compter (to intend)	*pouvoir* (to be able)
croire (to believe)	*préférer* (to prefer)
désirer (to wish)	*savoir* (to know how to)
devoir (to have to)	*sembler* (to seem)
entendre (to hear)	*valoir mieux* (to be better)
envoyer (to send)	*venir* (to come)
espérer (to hope)	*voir* (to see)
faire (to get, to have, to make)	*vouloir* (to want)
falloir (to have to)	

Exercise 2

Translate the English into French:

1. *Marianne and her mother are trying to find* leur cabine.
2. *They forgot to take their bearings* (s'orienter) lorsqu'elles sont arrivées à bord.
3. *It is not easy to find* parce que le paquebot est grand et luxueux.
4. Ah! Voilà un mousse (cabin boy) *who can help them to reach* (arriver à) le pont où se trouve la cabine.

5. *If they ask him to show them the way, he will tell them to return* au pont A.
6. *It is interesting to see* tous les voyageurs et les visiteurs.
7. *And it is thrilling to be aboard* (à bord) un magnifique paquebot.
8. Un jour, *I hope to visit* la France.
9. En effet, *I intend to spend the whole summer visiting* les monuments.
10. *My friend's mother has invited me to spend the summer* chez eux.
11. Je me demande si *I'll succeed in saving* (économiser) assez d'argent *in order to be able to make the trip* l'été prochain.
12. *I would like to be able to go and see all the places* dont j'ai entendu parler dans ma classe de français.

II. THE PRESENT PARTICIPLE

The present participle, which never agrees (unless used as an adjective), serves mainly to express:

1. *Means* by which something may be accomplished:

C'est en économisant son argent qu'un étudiant réussira un jour à faire un voyage en France. (It is by saving his money that a student will one day succeed in making a trip to France.)

2. *Simultaneity* of two actions, both referring to the subject:

Tout en parlant, nous oublions d'aller à notre cabine. (While [the whole time that] we're talking, we're forgetting to go to our cabin.)

Exercise 3

Translate the English into French:

1. *It is by traveling* qu'on élargit (broadens) son horizon intellectuel.
2. *Having seen* d'autres pays, on comprend mieux les problèmes d'autrui (other people), *while appreciating* (apprécier) d'autant plus (all the more) son propre pays.
3. *By spending* autant de temps que possible dans un milieu français, *one ends up* (to end up: *finir par*) *speaking* la langue beaucoup plus couramment.
4. *And all the while you enjoy yourself* (se divertir), on apprend mille choses utiles.
5. *By saving your money*, vous pourrez voyager.

INFINITIVE IS USED	PARTICIPLE IS USED
1. subject	1. means
2. object	2. simultaneity
3. after preposition	

Review Exercise

Translate:

1. Crossing the gangplank, Marianne realized that her sweetest dream was going to be fulfilled.
2. With her mother, she hoped to spend the summer seeing Paris and traveling to all the places that her father had told them to see.
3. Going to visit his native village in Savoie would be one of the most thrilling moments of the trip.
4. But she and her mother were forgetting that they would have to hurry because they had invited friends to come and celebrate the occasion.
5. Having gone up to (jusqu'à) A Deck, they tried to find their cabin but could not succeed in reaching it.
6. It was better to ask the cabin boy to help them to find it.
7. They had just passed the swimming pool when they saw Paul and he began to shout: "Bon voyage, Maman! Bon voyage, Marianne!"

THE THREE REGULAR CONJUGATIONS

INDICATIVE

I	II	III

The Present (*Le présent*)

I	II	III
je chante	je finis	je vends
tu chantes	tu finis	tu vends
il chante	il finit	il vend
nous chantons	nous finissons	nous vendons
vous chantez	vous finissez	vous vendez
ils chantent	ils finissent	ils vendent

The Imperfect (*L'imparfait*)

I	II	III
je chantais	je finissais	je vendais
tu chantais	tu finissais	tu vendais
il chantait	il finissait	il vendait
nous chantions	nous finissions	nous vendions
vous chantiez	vous finissiez	vous vendiez
ils chantaient	ils finissaient	ils vendaient

The Future (*Le futur*)

I	II	III
je chanterai	je finirai	je vendrai
tu chanteras	tu finiras	tu vendras
il chantera	il finira	il vendra
nous chanterons	nous finirons	nous vendrons
vous chanterez	vous finirez	vous vendrez
ils chanteront	ils finiront	ils vendront

The Conditional (*Le conditionnel*)

I	II	III
je chanterais	je finirais	je vendrais
tu chanterais	tu finirais	tu vendrais
il chanterait	il finirait	il vendrait
nous chanterions	nous finirions	nous vendrions
vous chanteriez	vous finiriez	vous vendriez
ils chanteraient	ils finiraient	ils vendraient

The Past Definite (*Le passé défini* ou *le passé simple*)

je chantai	je finis	je vendis
tu chantas	tu finis	tu vendis
il chanta	il finit	il vendit
nous chantâmes	nous finîmes	nous vendîmes
vous chantâtes	vous finîtes	vous vendîtes
ils chantèrent	ils finirent	ils vendirent

The Present Perfect (*Le passé indéfini* ou *le passé composé*)

j'ai chanté	j'ai fini	j'ai vendu
tu as chanté	tu as fini	tu as vendu
il a chanté	il a fini	il a vendu
nous avons chanté	nous avons fini	nous avons vendu
vous avez chanté	vous avez fini	vous avez vendu
ils ont chanté	ils ont fini	ils ont vendu

The Pluperfect (*Le plus-que-parfait*)

j'avais chanté	j'avais fini	j'avais vendu
tu avais chanté	tu avais fini	tu avais vendu
il avait chanté	il avait fini	il avait vendu
nous avions chanté	nous avions fini	nous avions vendu
vous aviez chanté	nous aviez fini	vous aviez vendu
ils avaient chanté	ils avaient fini	ils avaient vendu

The Future Perfect (*Le futur antérieur*)

j'aurai chanté	j'aurai fini	j'aurai vendu
tu auras chanté	tu auras fini	tu auras vendu
il aura chanté	il aura fini	il aura vendu
nous aurons chanté	nous aurons fini	nous aurons vendu
vous aurez chanté	vous aurez fini	vous aurez vendu
ils auront chanté	ils auront fini	ils auront vendu

The Conditional Perfect (*Le conditionnel antérieur*)

j'aurais chanté	j'aurais fini	j'aurais vendu
tu aurais chanté	tu aurais fini	tu aurais vendu
il aurait chanté	il aurait fini	il aurait vendu
nous aurions chanté	nous aurions fini	nous aurions vendu
vous auriez chanté	vous auriez fini	vous auriez vendu
ils auraient chanté	ils auraient fini	ils auraient vendu

The Past Anterior (*Le passé antérieur*)

j'eus chanté	j'eus fini	j'eus vendu
tu eus chanté	tu eus fini	tu eus vendu
il eut chanté	il eut fini	il eut vendu
nous eûmes chanté	nous eûmes fini	nous eûmes vendu
vous eûtes chanté	vous eûtes fini	vous eûtes vendu
il eurent chanté	ils eurent fini	ils eurent vendu

SUBJUNCTIVE

The Present Subjunctive (*Le présent du subjonctif*)

je chante	je finisse	je vende
tu chantes	tu finisses	tu vendes
il chante	il finisse	il vende
nous chantions	nous finissions	nous vendions
vous chantiez	vous finissiez	vous vendiez
ils chantent	ils finissent	ils vendent

The Imperfect Subjunctive (*L'imparfait du subjonctif*)

je chantasse	je finisse	je vendisse
tu chantasses	tu finisses	tu vendisses
il chantât	il finît	il vendît
nous chantassions	nous finissions	nous vendissions
vous chantassiez	vous finissiez	vous vendissiez
ils chantassent	ils finissent	ils vendissent

The Perfect Subjunctive (*Le passé du subjonctif*)

j'aie chanté	j'aie fini	j'aie vendu
tu aies chanté	tu aies fini	tu aies vendu
il ait chanté	il ait fini	il ait vendu
nous ayons chanté	nous ayons fini	nous ayons vendu
vous ayez chanté	vous ayez fini	vous ayez vendu
ils aient chanté	ils aient fini	ils aient vendu

The Pluperfect Subjunctive (*Le plus-que-parfait du subjonctif*)

j'eusse chanté	j'eusse fini	j'eusse vendu
tu eusses chanté	tu eusses fini	tu eusses vendu
il eût chanté	il eût fini	il eût vendu
nous eussions chanté	nous eussions fini	nous eussions vendu
vous eussiez chanté	vous eussiez fini	vous eussiez vendu
ils eussent chanté	ils eussent fini	ils eussent vendu

OBSERVATIONS ON THE TENSES OF IRREGULAR VERBS

In considering the forms of irregular verbs, it will be observed that certain patterns often emerge. Since irregular verbs usually have regular endings, except in the present indicative (and even here, a frequent pattern is *-s, -s, -t, -ons, -ez, -ent*), we might say that mastery of the tenses can often be reduced to knowledge of the verb *stems*. Is it even necessary to learn the stem of each of the tenses? Actually not, because with *four* basic forms, in most cases the student can arrive at all forms of the verb. Thus, while the following hints are in no way intended as rules and have no reference to the historical derivation of the tenses, it is hoped that they will simplify the learning of the conjugation of irregular verbs by pointing up patterns that repeat themselves.

The four elements upon which we can often build the rest of the verb and which we have therefore called basic forms are as follows:

1. the stem of the first-person plural (*nous*) of the present indicative, and sometimes also the stem of the third-person plural (*ils*) of the same tense
2. the stem of the first-person singular (*je*) of the future
3. the stem of the first-person singular (*je*) of the past definite
4. the past participle

BASIC FORM 1

Since the present indicative itself is extremely unpredictable, all its forms should be carefully learned. Special attention should, however, be directed to the stem of the first-person plural (*nous*), which we call Basic Form 1. It is repeated in the imperfect indicative, in the present participle, and, in many cases, throughout the entire present subjunctive. Where the stem of the third-person plural of the present indicative (*ils*) differs from that of *nous*, we call the stem of *nous* Basic Form 1a and the stem of *ils* Basic Form 1b. In such a case the dual stem is found also in the present subjunctive, with the stem of *ils* serving as stem for *je, tu, il*, and *ils*, and the stem of *nous* serving as stem for *nous* and *vous*. Thus:

PRESENT INDICATIVE

je vois

tu vois

il voit

nous VOYons (1a) — Imperfect: VOYais, VOYais, VOYait, VOYions, VOYiez, VOYaient; Present Participle: VOYant; Present Subjunctive for nous: VOYions; Present Subjunctive for vous: VOYiez

vous voyez

ils VOIent (1b) — Present Subjunctive for all other persons: je VOIe, tu VOIes, il VOIe, ils VOIent

BASIC FORM 2

The stem of the future tense (obtained by removing the final *-ai* from the *je* form) serves all persons of the future, as well as all persons of the conditional:

FUTURE STEM

je VERRai — Future: VERRai, VERRas, VERRa, VERRons, VERRez, VERRont; Conditional: VERRais, VERRais, VERRait, VERRions, VERRiez, VERRaient

BASIC FORM 3

The stem of the past definite (obtained by removing final *-s*, or in a verb like *aller* by removing final *-i* from the *je* form) is repeated throughout the imperfect subjunctive:

PAST DEFINITE STEM

je VIs — Past Definite: VIs, VIs, VIt, VÎmes, VÎtes, VIrent; Imperfect Subjunctive: VIsse, VIsses, VÎt, VIssions, VIssiez, VIssent

BASIC FORM 4

The past participle is used to construct all compound tenses with the appropriate auxiliary:

PAST PARTICIPLE VU — j'ai VU, j'avais VU, j'aurai VU, j'aurais VU, j'eus VU, j'aie VU, j'eusse VU

Where the above patterns are not followed and when special stems or entire forms must be learned, we have tried to draw attention to the form that needs special study.

TABLE OF IRREGULAR VERBS

Acquérir (to acquire, to get)

INDICATIVE

PRESENT	IMPERFECT	FUTURE	CONDITIONAL	PAST DEFINITE
	From Basic Form 1 (or 1a)		From Basic Form 2	
acquiers	*acquérais*	*ACQUERRai* (2)	*acquerrais*	*ACQUIs* (3)
acquiers	*acquérais*	*acquerras*	*acquerrais*	*acquis*
acquiert	*acquérait*	*acquerra*	*acquerrait*	*acquit*
ACQUÉRons (1a)	*acquérions*	*acquerrons*	*acquerrions*	*acquîmes*
acquérez	*acquériez*	*acquerrez*	*acquerriez*	*acquîtes*
ACQUIÈRent (1b)	*acquéraient*	*acquerront*	*acquerraient*	*acquirent*

SUBJUNCTIVE

PARTICIPLES	IMPERATIVE	PRESENT	IMPERFECT
From Basic Form 1 (or 1a):		From Basic Form 1 (or 1b): all singular and 3rd plural	From Basic Form 3
acquérant	acquiers	From Basic Form 1 (or 1a): 1st and 2nd plural	*acquisse*
ACQUIS (4)	acquérons	*acquière*	*acquisses*
j'ai *acquis*	acquérez	*acquières*	*acquît*
j'avais *acquis*		*acquière*	*acquissions*
j'aurai *acquis*		*acquérions*	*acquissiez*
j'aurais *acquis*		*acquériez*	*acquissent*
j'eus *acquis*		*acquièrent*	
j'aie *acquis*			
j'eusse *acquis*			

Aller (to go), conjugated with *être*

INDICATIVE

PRESENT	IMPERFECT	FUTURE	CONDITIONAL	PAST DEFINITE
vais	*all*ais	*IR*ai (2)	*ir*ais	*ALLai* (3)
vas	*all*ais	*ir*as	*ir*ais	*alla*s
va	*all*ait	*ir*a	*ir*ait	*alla*
ALLons (1)	*all*ions	*ir*ons	*ir*ions	*allâ*mes
allez	*all*iez	*ir*ez	*ir*iez	*allâ*tes
vont	*all*aient	*ir*ont	*ir*aient	*allè*rent

SUBJUNCTIVE

PARTICIPLES	IMPERATIVE	PRESENT	IMPERFECT
*all*ant	va	N.B. Special stem for all singular and 3rd plural:	*alla*sse
ALLÉ (4)	allons		*alla*sses
je suis *allé*(e)	allez	AILL-	*allâ*t
j'étais *allé*(e)		AILLe	*alla*ssions
je serai *allé* (e)		AILLes	*alla*ssiez
je serais *allé*(e)		AILLe	*alla*ssent
je fus *allé* (e)		*all*ions	
je sois *allé*(e)		*all*iez	
je fusse *allé*(e)		AILLent	

Asseoir (to seat)

N.B.: Since this verb occurs most frequently in its reflexive form, with the meaning "to sit down," "to take a seat," it will be conjugated reflexively here.

INDICATIVE

PRESENT	IMPERFECT	FUTURE	CONDITIONAL	PAST DEFINITE
je m'*assieds*	je m'*assey*ais	je m'*ASSIÉR*ai (2)	je m'*assiér*ais	je m'*ASSI*s (3)
tu t'*assieds*	tu t'*assey*ais	tu t'*assiér*as	tu t'*assiér*ais	tu t'*assis*
il s'*assied*	il s'*assey*ait	il s'*assiér*a	il s'*assiér*ait	il s'*assit*
nous nous ASSEY*ons* (1)	nous nous *assey*ions	nous nous *assiér*ons	nous nous *assiér*ions	nous nous *ass*îmes
vous vous *asseyez*	vous vous *assey*iez	vous vous *assiér*ez	vous vous *assiér*iez	vous vous *ass*îtes
ils s'*asseyent*	ils s'*assey*aient	ils s'*assiér*ont	ils s'*assiér*aient	ils s'*assi*rent

SUBJUNCTIVE

PARTICIPLES	IMPERATIVE	PRESENT	IMPERFECT
s'*assey*ant	assieds-toi	je m'*asseye*	je m'*assi*sse
ASSIS (4)	asseyons-nous	tu t'*asseyes*	tu t'*assi*sses
je me suis *assis*(e)	asseyez-vous	il s'*asseye*	il s'*assît*
je m'étais *assis*(e)		nous nous *assey*ions	nous nous *assi*ssions
je me serai *assis*(e)		vous vous *assey*iez	vous vous *assi*ssiez
je me serais *assis*(e)		ils s'*assey*ent	ils s'*assi*ssent
je me fus *assis*(e)			
je me sois *assis*(e)			
je me fusse *assis*(e)			

Avoir (to have)

INDICATIVE

PRESENT	IMPERFECT	FUTURE	CONDITIONAL	PAST DEFINITE
ai	*av*ais	*AUR*ai (2)	*aur*ais	*EU*s (3)
as	*av*ais	*aur*as	*aur*ais	*eu*s
a	*av*ait	*aur*a	*aur*ait	*eu*t
*AV*ons (1)	*av*ions	*aur*ons	*aur*ions	*eû*mes
avez	*av*iez	*aur*ez	*aur*iez	*eû*tes
ont	*av*aient	*aur*ont	*aur*aient	*eu*rent

SUBJUNCTIVE

PARTICIPLES	IMPERATIVE	PRESENT	IMPERFECT
N.B. Special stem for Present Participle: AY-	N.B. Special forms:	N.B. Special stems:	From Basic Form 3
*AY*ant	AIE	AIE	*eu*sse
EU (4)	AYONS	AIES	*eu*sses
	AYEZ	AIT*	*eû*t
		AYONS	*eu*ssions
		AYEZ	*eu*ssiez
		AIENT	*eu*ssent

* Note the ending "-t."

Battre (to beat)

INDICATIVE

PRESENT	IMPERFECT	FUTURE	CONDITIONAL	PAST DEFINITE
bats	battais	BATTRai (2)	battrais	BATTIs (3)
bats	battais	battras	battrais	battis
bat	battait	battra	battrait	battit
BATTons (1)	battions	battrons	battrions	battîmes
battez	battiez	battrez	battriez	battîtes
battent	battaient	battront	battraient	battirent

SUBJUNCTIVE

PARTICIPLES	IMPERATIVE	PRESENT	IMPERFECT
battant	bats	batte	battisse
BATTU (4)	battons	battes	battisses
	battez	batte	battît
		battions	battissions
		battiez	battissiez
		battent	battissent

Boire (to drink)

INDICATIVE

PRESENT	IMPERFECT	FUTURE	CONDITIONAL	PAST DEFINITE
bois	*buv*ais	*BOIR*ai (2)	*boir*ais	*BU*s (3)
bois	*buv*ais	*boir*as	*boir*ais	*bus*
boit	*buv*ait	*boir*a	*boir*ait	*but*
*BUV*ons (1a)	*buv*ions	*boir*ons	*boir*ions	*bû*mes
*buv*ez	*buv*iez	*boir*ez	*boir*iez	*bû*tes
*BOIV*ent (1b)	*buv*aient	*boir*ont	*boir*aient	*bu*rent

SUBJUNCTIVE

PARTICIPLES	IMPERATIVE	PRESENT	IMPERFECT
*buv*ant	bois	*boiv*e	*bus*se
BU (4)	buvons	*boiv*es	*bus*ses
	buvez	*boiv*e	*bû*t
		*buv*ions	*bus*sions
		*buv*iez	*bus*siez
		*boiv*ent	*bus*sent

Conclure (to conclude)

INDICATIVE

PRESENT	IMPERFECT	FUTURE	CONDITIONAL	PAST DEFINITE
conclus	*concluais*	*CONCLURai* (2)	*conclurais*	*CONCLUs* (3)
conclus	*concluais*	*concluras*	*conclurais*	*conclus*
conclut	*concluait*	*conclura*	*conclurait*	*conclut*
CONCLUons (1)	*concluions*	*conclurons*	*conclurions*	*conclûmes*
concluez	*concluiez*	*conclurez*	*concluriez*	*conclûtes*
concluent	*concluaient*	*concluront*	*concluraient*	*conclurent*

SUBJUNCTIVE

PARTICIPLES	IMPERATIVE	PRESENT	IMPERFECT
concluant	conclus	*conclue*	*conclusse*
CONCLU (4)	concluons	*conclues*	*conclusses*
	concluez	*conclue*	*conclût*
		concluions	*conclussions*
		concluiez	*conclussiez*
		concluent	*conclussent*

Conduire (to lead, to conduct)

INDICATIVE

PRESENT	IMPERFECT	FUTURE	CONDITIONAL	PAST DEFINITE
conduis	conduisais	CONDUIRai (2)	conduirais	CONDUISIs (3)
conduis	conduisais	conduiras	conduirais	conduisis
conduit	conduisait	conduira	conduirait	conduisit
CONDUISons (1)	conduisions	conduirons	conduirions	conduisîmes
conduisez	conduisiez	conduirez	conduiriez	conduisîtes
conduisent	conduisaient	conduiront	conduiraient	conduisirent

SUBJUNCTIVE

PARTICIPLES	IMPERATIVE	PRESENT	IMPERFECT
conduisant	conduis	conduise	conduisisse
CONDUIT (4)	conduisons	conduises	conduisisses
	conduisez	conduise	conduisît
		conduisions	conduisissions
		conduisiez	conduisissiez
		conduisent	conduisissent

Connaître (to know, to be acquainted with)

INDICATIVE

PRESENT	IMPERFECT	FUTURE	CONDITIONAL	PAST DEFINITE
connais	*connaiss*ais	*CONNAÎTR*ai (2)	*connaîtr*ais	*CONNU*s (3)
connais	*connaiss*ais	*connaîtr*as	*connaîtr*ais	*connus*
connaît	*connaiss*ait	*connaîtr*a	*connaîtr*ait	*connut*
CONNAISSons (1)	*connaiss*ions	*connaîtr*ons	*connaîtr*ions	*connûmes*
connaissez	*connaiss*iez	*connaîtr*ez	*connaîtr*iez	*connûtes*
connaissent	*connaiss*aient	*connaîtr*ont	*connaîtr*aient	*connurent*

SUBJUNCTIVE

PARTICIPLES	IMPERATIVE	PRESENT	IMPERFECT
*connaiss*ant	connais	*connaisse*	*connusse*
CONNU (4)	connaissons	*connaisses*	*connusses*
	connaissez	*connaisse*	*connût*
		connaissions	*connussions*
		connaissiez	*connussiez*
		connaissent	*connussent*

Courir (to run)

INDICATIVE

PRESENT	IMPERFECT	FUTURE	CONDITIONAL	PAST DEFINITE
cours	courais	COURRai (2)	courrais	COURUs (3)
cours	courais	courras	courrais	courus
court	courait	courra	courrait	courut
COURons (1)	courions	courrons	courrions	courûmes
courez	couriez	courrez	courriez	courûtes
courent	couraient	courront	courraient	coururent

SUBJUNCTIVE

PARTICIPLES	IMPERATIVE	PRESENT	IMPERFECT
courant	cours	coure	courusse
COURU (4)	courons	coures	courusses
	courez	coure	courût
		courions	courussions
		couriez	courussiez
		courent	courussent

Craindre (to fear)

INDICATIVE

PRESENT	IMPERFECT	FUTURE	CONDITIONAL	PAST DEFINITE
crains	craignais	CRAINDRai (2)	craindrais	CRAIGNIs (3)
crains	craignais	craindras	craindrais	craignis
craint	craignait	craindra	craindrait	craignit
CRAIGNons (1)	craignions	craindrons	craindrions	craignîmes
craignez	craigniez	craindrez	craindriez	craignîtes
craignent	craignaient	craindront	craindraient	craignirent

SUBJUNCTIVE

PARTICIPLES	IMPERATIVE	PRESENT	IMPERFECT
craignant	crains	craigne	craignisse
CRAINT (4)	craignons	craignes	craignisses
	craignez	craigne	craignît
		craignions	craignissions
		craigniez	craignissiez
		craignent	craignissent

Croire (to believe)

INDICATIVE

PRESENT	IMPERFECT	FUTURE	CONDITIONAL	PAST DEFINITE
crois	*croy*ais	*CROIR*ai (2)	*croir*ais	*CRU*s (3)
crois	*croy*ais	*croir*as	*croir*ais	*crus*
croit	*croy*ait	*croir*a	*croir*ait	*crut*
*CROY*ons (1a)	*croy*ions	*croir*ons	*croir*ions	*crû*mes
croyez	*croy*iez	*croir*ez	*croir*iez	*crû*tes
*CROI*ent (1b)	*croy*aient	*croir*ont	*croir*aient	*cru*rent

SUBJUNCTIVE

PARTICIPLES	IMPERATIVE	PRESENT	IMPERFECT
*croy*ant	crois	*croi*e	*cru*sse
CRU (4)	croyons	*croi*es	*cru*sses
	croyez	*croi*e	*crû*t
		*croy*ions	*cru*ssions
		*croy*iez	*cru*ssiez
		*croi*ent	*cru*ssent

Cueillir (to gather, to pick)

INDICATIVE

PRESENT	IMPERFECT	FUTURE	CONDITIONAL	PAST DEFINITE
cueille	*cueill*ais	*CUEILLER*ai (2)	*cueiller*ais	*CUEILLI*s (3)
cueilles	*cueill*ais	*cueiller*as	*cueiller*ais	*cueilli*s
cueille	*cueill*ait	*cueiller*a	*cueiller*ait	*cueilli*t
CUEILLons (1)	*cueill*ions	*cueiller*ons	*cueiller*ions	*cueill*îmes
cueillez	*cueill*iez	*cueiller*ez	*cueiller*iez	*cueill*îtes
cueillent	*cueill*aient	*cueiller*ont	*cueiller*aient	*cueilli*rent

SUBJUNCTIVE

PARTICIPLES	IMPERATIVE	PRESENT	IMPERFECT
*cueill*ant	cueille	*cueille*	*cueilli*sse
CUEILLI (4)	cueillons	*cueilles*	*cueilli*sses
	cueillez	*cueille*	*cueill*ît
		cueillions	*cueilli*ssions
		cueilliez	*cueilli*ssiez
		cueillent	*cueilli*ssent

Devoir (to have to, to be supposed to, must, to owe)

INDICATIVE

PRESENT	IMPERFECT	FUTURE	CONDITIONAL	PAST DEFINITE
dois	*dev*ais	*DEVR*ai (2)	*devr*ais	*DU*s (3)
dois	*dev*ais	*devr*as	*devr*ais	*du*s
doit	*dev*ait	*devr*a	*devr*ait	*du*t
*DEV*ons (1a)	*dev*ions	*devr*ons	*devr*ions	*dû*mes
devez	*dev*iez	*devr*ez	*devr*iez	*dû*tes
*DOIV*ent (1b)	*dev*aient	*devr*ont	*devr*aient	*du*rent

SUBJUNCTIVE

PARTICIPLES	IMPERATIVE	PRESENT	IMPERFECT
*dev*ant	dois	*doiv*e	*du*sse
DÛ (Fem. *DUE*) (4)	devons	*doiv*es	*du*sses
	devez	*doiv*e	*dû*t
		*dev*ions	*du*ssions
		*dev*iez	*du*ssiez
		*doiv*ent	*du*ssent

Dire (to say, to tell)

INDICATIVE

PRESENT	IMPERFECT	FUTURE	CONDITIONAL	PAST DEFINITE
dis	*dis*ais	*DIR*ai (2)	*dir*ais	*DI*s (3)
dis	*dis*ais	*dir*as	*dir*ais	*dis*
dit	*dis*ait	*dir*a	*dir*ait	*dit*
DISons (1)	*dis*ions	*dir*ons	*dir*ions	*d*îmes
dites	*dis*iez	*dir*ez	*dir*iez	*d*îtes
disent	*dis*aient	*dir*ont	*dir*aient	*dir*ent

SUBJUNCTIVE

PARTICIPLES	IMPERATIVE	PRESENT	IMPERFECT
*dis*ant	dis	*dis*e	*d*isse
DIT (4)	disons	*dis*es	*d*isses
	dites	*dis*e	*d*ît
		*dis*ions	*d*issions
		*dis*iez	*d*issiez
		*dis*ent	*dissent*

Dormir (to sleep)

INDICATIVE

PRESENT	IMPERFECT	FUTURE	CONDITIONAL	PAST DEFINITE
dors	dormais	DORMIRai (2)	dormirais	DORMIs (3)
dors	dormais	dormiras	dormirais	dormis
dort	dormait	dormira	dormirait	dormit
DORMons (1)	dormions	dormirons	dormirions	dormîmes
dormez	dormiez	dormirez	dormiriez	dormîtes
dorment	dormaient	dormiront	dormiraient	dormirent

SUBJUNCTIVE

PARTICIPLES	IMPERATIVE	PRESENT	IMPERFECT
dormant	dors	dorme	dormisse
DORMI (4)	dormons	dormes	dormisses
	dormez	dorme	dormît
		dormions	dormissions
		dormiez	dormissiez
		dorment	dormissent

Écrire (to write)

INDICATIVE

PRESENT	IMPERFECT	FUTURE	CONDITIONAL	PAST DEFINITE
écris	écrivais	ÉCRIRai (2)	écrirais	ÉCRIVIs (3)
écris	écrivais	écriras	écrirais	écrivis
écrit	écrivait	écrira	écrirait	écrivit
ÉCRIVons (1)	écrivions	écrirons	écririons	écrivîmes
écrivez	écriviez	écrirez	écririez	écrivîtes
écrivent	écrivaient	écriront	écriraient	écrivirent

SUBJUNCTIVE

PARTICIPLES	IMPERATIVE	PRESENT	IMPERFECT
écrivant	écris	écrive	écrivisse
ÉCRIT (4)	écrivons	écrives	écrivisses
	écrivez	écrive	écrivît
		écrivions	écrivissions
		écriviez	écrivissiez
		écrivent	écrivissent

Envoyer (to send)

INDICATIVE

PRESENT	IMPERFECT	FUTURE	CONDITIONAL	PAST DEFINITE
envoie	*envoy*ais	*ENVERR*ai (2)	*enverr*ais	*ENVOYA*i (3)
envoies	*envoy*ais	*enverr*as	*enverr*ais	*envoyas*
envoie	*envoy*ait	*enverra*	*enverr*ait	*envoya*
ENVOYons (1a)	*envoyi*ons	*enverr*ons	*enverr*ions	*envoyâ*mes
envoyez	*envoyi*ez	*enverr*ez	*enverr*iez	*envoyâ*tes
ENVOIent (1b)	*envoy*aient	*enverr*ont	*enverr*aient	*envoyè*rent

SUBJUNCTIVE

PARTICIPLES	IMPERATIVE	PRESENT	IMPERFECT
*envoy*ant	envoie	*envoie*	*envoy*asse
ENVOYÉ (4)	envoyons	*envoies*	*envoy*asses
	envoyez	*envoie*	*envoyâ*t
		*envoyi*ons	*envoy*assions
		*envoyi*ez	*envoy*assiez
		*envoi*ent	*envoy*assent

Être (to be)

INDICATIVE

PRESENT	IMPERFECT	FUTURE	CONDITIONAL	PAST DEFINITE
	N.B. Special stem: ÉT-			
suis	ÉTais	*SER*ai (2)	*ser*ais	*FU*s (3)
es	ÉTais	*ser*as	*ser*ais	*fus*
est	ÉTait	*ser*a	*ser*ait	*fut*
sommes	ÉTions	*ser*ons	*ser*ions	*fûmes*
êtes	ÉTiez	*ser*ez	*ser*iez	*fûtes*
sont	ÉTaient	*ser*ont	*ser*aient	*furent*

SUBJUNCTIVE

PARTICIPLES	IMPERATIVE	PRESENT	IMPERFECT
N.B. Special stem for Present Participle: ÉT-	N.B. Special Forms:	N.B. Special Forms:	
*ÉT*ant	SOIS	SOIS	*fusse*
ÉTÉ (4)	SOYONS	SOIS	*fusses*
	SOYEZ	SOIT	*fût*
		SOYONS	*fussions*
		SOYEZ	*fussiez*
		SOIENT	*fussent*

Faire (to do, to make)

INDICATIVE

PRESENT	IMPERFECT	FUTURE	CONDITIONAL	PAST DEFINITE
fais	*fais*ais	*FER*ai (2)	*fer*ais	*FIs* (3)
fais	*fais*ais	*fer*as	*fer*ais	*fis*
fait	*fais*ait	*fer*a	*fer*ait	*fit*
FAISons (1a)	*fais*ions	*fer*ons	*fer*ions	*fîmes*
faites	*fais*iez	*fer*ez	*fer*iez	*fîtes*
font	*fais*aient	*fer*ont	*fer*aient	*firent*

SUBJUNCTIVE

PARTICIPLES	IMPERATIVE	PRESENT	IMPERFECT
*fais*ant	fais	N.B. Special stem: FASS-	
FAIT (4)	faisons	FASSe	*fisse*
	faites	FASSes	*fisses*
		FASSe	*fît*
		FASSions	*fissions*
		FASSiez	*fissiez*
		FASSent	*fissent*

Falloir (to be necessary, must)

INDICATIVE

PRESENT	IMPERFECT	FUTURE	CONDITIONAL	PAST DEFINITE
il *faut*	il *fallait*	il *FAUDR*a	il *faudr*ait	il *fallu*t

SUBJUNCTIVE

PARTICIPLE	IMPERATIVE	PRESENT	IMPERFECT
——— FALLU (4)	———	il faille	il fallût

Lire (to read)

INDICATIVE

PRESENT	IMPERFECT	FUTURE	CONDITIONAL	PAST DEFINITE
lis	*lis*ais	*LIR*ai (2)	*lir*ais	*LUs* (3)
lis	*lis*ais	*lir*as	*lir*ais	*lus*
lit	*lis*ait	*lira*	*lir*ait	*lut*
LISons (1)	*lis*ions	*lir*ons	*lir*ions	*lû*mes
lisez	*lis*iez	*lir*ez	*lir*iez	*lû*tes
lisent	*lis*aient	*lir*ont	*lir*aient	*lu*rent

SUBJUNCTIVE

PARTICIPLES	IMPERATIVE	PRESENT	IMPERFECT
*lis*ant	lis	*lis*e	*lu*sse
LU (4)	lisons	*lis*es	*lu*sses
	lisez	*lis*e	*lû*t
		*lis*ions	*lu*ssions
		*lis*iez	*lu*ssiez
		*lis*ent	*lu*ssent

Mettre (to put, to put on)

INDICATIVE

PRESENT	IMPERFECT	FUTURE	CONDITIONAL	PAST DEFINITE
mets	*mett*ais	*METTR*ai (2)	*mettr*ais	*MI*s (3)
mets	*mett*ais	*mettr*as	*mettr*ais	*mi*s
met	*mett*ait	*mettr*a	*mettr*ait	*mî*t
METTons (1)	*mett*ions	*mettr*ons	*mettr*ions	*mî*mes
mettez	*mett*iez	*mettr*ez	*mettr*iez	*mî*tes
mettent	*mett*aient	*mettr*ont	*mettr*aient	*mi*rent

SUBJUNCTIVE

PARTICIPLES	IMPERATIVE	PRESENT	IMPERFECT
*mett*ant	mets	*mett*e	*mi*sse
MIS (4)	mettons	*mett*es	*mi*sses
	mettez	*mett*e	*mî*t
		*mett*ions	*mi*ssions
		*mett*iez	*mi*ssiez
		*mett*ent	*mi*ssent

Mourir (to die), conjugated with *être*. Cf. *aller*.

INDICATIVE

PRESENT	IMPERFECT	FUTURE	CONDITIONAL	PAST DEFINITE
meurs	*mourais*	*MOURRai* (2)	*mourrais*	*MOURUs* (3)
meurs	*mourais*	*mourras*	*mourrais*	*mourus*
meurt	*mourait*	*mourra*	*mourrait*	*mourut*
MOURons (1a)	*mourions*	*mourrons*	*mourrions*	*mourûmes*
mourez	*mouriez*	*mourrez*	*mourriez*	*mourûtes*
MEURent (1b)	*mouraient*	*mourront*	*mourraient*	*moururent*

SUBJUNCTIVE

PARTICIPLES	IMPERATIVE	PRESENT	IMPERFECT
mourant	meurs	*meure*	*mourusse*
MORT (4)	mourons	*meures*	*mourusses*
	mourez	*meure*	*mourût*
		mourions	*mourussions*
		mouriez	*mourussiez*
		meurent	*mourussent*

Naître (to be born), conjugated with *être*. Cf. *aller*.

INDICATIVE

PRESENT	IMPERFECT	FUTURE	CONDITIONAL	PAST DEFINITE
nais	*naissais*	*NAÎTR*ai (2)	*naîtrais*	*NAQUI*s (3)
nais	*naissais*	*naîtras*	*naîtrais*	*naquis*
naît	*naissait*	*naîtra*	*naîtrait*	*naquit*
NAISSons (1)	*naissions*	*naîtrons*	*naîtrions*	*naquîmes*
naissez	*naissiez*	*naîtrez*	*naîtriez*	*naquîtes*
naissent	*naissaient*	*naîtront*	*naîtraient*	*naquirent*

SUBJUNCTIVE

PARTICIPLES	IMPERATIVE	PRESENT	IMPERFECT
naissant	———	*naisse*	*naquisse*
NÉ (4)		*naisses*	*naquisses*
		naisse	*naquît*
		naissions	*naquissions*
		naissiez	*naquissiez*
		naissent	*naquissent*

Ouvrir (to open)

INDICATIVE

PRESENT	IMPERFECT	FUTURE	CONDITIONAL	PAST DEFINITE
ouvre	*ouv*rais	*OUVRIR*ai (2)	*ouvri*rais	*OUVRIs* (3)
ouvres	*ouv*rais	*ouvriras*	*ouvrirais*	*ouvris*
ouvre	*ouv*rait	*ouvrira*	*ouvrirait*	*ouvrit*
OUVRons (1)	*ouv*rions	*ouvri*rons	*ouvri*rions	*ouvrîmes*
ouvrez	*ouv*riez	*ouvrirez*	*ouvririez*	*ouvrîtes*
ouvrent	*ouv*raient	*ouvri*ront	*ouvri*raient	*ouvri*rent

SUBJUNCTIVE

PARTICIPLES	IMPERATIVE	PRESENT	IMPERFECT
*ouv*rant	ouvre	*ouv*re	*ouv*risse
OUVERT (4)	ouvrons	*ouv*res	*ouv*risses
	ouvrez	*ouv*re	*ouv*rît
		*ouv*rions	*ouv*rissions
		*ouv*riez	*ouv*rissiez
		*ouv*rent	*ouv*rissent

Partir (to leave), conjugated with *être*. Cf. *aller*.

INDICATIVE

PRESENT	IMPERFECT	FUTURE	CONDITIONAL	PAST DEFINITE
pars	*partais*	*PARTIRai* (2)	*partirais*	*PARTIs* (3)
pars	*partais*	*partiras*	*partirais*	*partis*
part	*partait*	*partira*	*partirait*	*partit*
PARTons (1)	*partions*	*partirons*	*partirions*	*partîmes*
partez	*partiez*	*partirez*	*partiriez*	*partîtes*
partent	*partaient*	*partiront*	*partiraient*	*partirent*

SUBJUNCTIVE

PARTICIPLES	IMPERATIVE	PRESENT	IMPERFECT
partant	pars	*parte*	*partisse*
PARTI (4)	partons	*partes*	*partisses*
	partez	*parte*	*partît*
		partions	*partissions*
		partiez	*partissiez*
		partent	*partissent*

Plaire (to please)

INDICATIVE

PRESENT	IMPERFECT	FUTURE	CONDITIONAL	PAST DEFINITE
plais	*plaisais*	*PLAIRai* (2)	*plairais*	*PLUs* (3)
plais	*plaisais*	*plairas*	*plairais*	*plus*
plaît	*plaisait*	*plaira*	*plairait*	*plut*
PLAISons (1)	*plaisions*	*plairons*	*plairions*	*plûmes*
plaisez	*plaisiez*	*plairez*	*plairiez*	*plûtes*
plaisent	*plaisaient*	*plairont*	*plairaient*	*plurent*

SUBJUNCTIVE

PARTICIPLES	IMPERATIVE	PRESENT	IMPERFECT
plaisant	plais	*plaise*	*plusse*
PLU (4)	plaisons	*plaises*	*plusses*
	plaisez	*plaise*	*plût*
		plaisions	*plussions*
		plaisiez	*plussiez*
		plaisent	*plussent*

Pleuvoir (to rain)

INDICATIVE				
PRESENT	IMPERFECT	FUTURE	CONDITIONAL	PAST DEFINITE
il *pleut*	il *pleuv*ait	il *PLEUVR*a (2)	il *pleuvr*ait	il *PLU*t (3)

PARTICIPLES	IMPERATIVE	SUBJUNCTIVE PRESENT	SUBJUNCTIVE IMPERFECT
*pleuv*ant *PLU* (4)	———	il *pleuve*	il *plût*

Pouvoir (to be able)

INDICATIVE

PRESENT	IMPERFECT	FUTURE	CONDITIONAL	PAST DEFINITE
*peux**	*pouvais*	*POURR*ai (2)	*pourrais*	*PU*s (3)
peux	*pouvais*	*pourras*	*pourrais*	*pus*
peut	*pouvait*	*pourra*	*pourrait*	*put*
POUVons (1)	*pouvions*	*pourrons*	*pourrions*	*pûmes*
pouvez	*pouviez*	*pourrez*	*pourriez*	*pûtes*
peuvent	*pouvaient*	*pourront*	*pourraient*	*purent*

SUBJUNCTIVE

PARTICIPLES	IMPERATIVE	PRESENT	IMPERFECT
pouvant	———	N.B. Special stem: *PUISS-*	
PU (4)		PUISSe	*pusse*
		PUISSes	*pusses*
		PUISSe	*pût*
		PUISSions	*pussions*
		PUISSiez	*pussiez*
		PUISSent	*pussent*

* *puis:* Alternate form, particularly used in the interrogative (*Puis-je?*).

Prendre (to take)

INDICATIVE

PRESENT	IMPERFECT	FUTURE	CONDITIONAL	PAST DEFINITE
prends	*prenais*	PRENDRai (2)	*prendrais*	PRIs (3)
prends	*prenais*	*prendras*	*prendrais*	*pris*
prend	*prenait*	*prendra*	*prendrait*	*prit*
PRENons (1a)	*prenions*	*prendrons*	*prendrions*	*prîmes*
prenez	*preniez*	*prendrez*	*prendriez*	*prîtes*
PRENNent (1b)	*prenaient*	*prendront*	*prendraient*	*prirent*

SUBJUNCTIVE

PARTICIPLES	IMPERATIVE	PRESENT	IMPERFECT
prenant	prends	*prenne*	*prisse*
PRIS (4)	prenons	*prennes*	*prisses*
	prenez	*prenne*	*prît*
		prenions	*prissions*
		preniez	*prissiez*
		prennent	*prissent*

Recevoir (to receive)

INDICATIVE

PRESENT	IMPERFECT	FUTURE	CONDITIONAL	PAST DEFINITE
reçois	*recevais*	*RECEVR*ai (2)	*recevrais*	*REÇU*s (3)
reçois	*recevais*	*recevras*	*recevrais*	*reçus*
reçoit	*recevait*	*recevra*	*recevrait*	*reçut*
RECEVONS (1a)	*recevions*	*recevrons*	*recevrions*	*reçûmes*
recevez	*receviez*	*recevrez*	*recevriez*	*reçûtes*
REÇOIVent (1b)	*recevaient*	*recevront*	*recevraient*	*reçurent*

SUBJUNCTIVE

PARTICIPLES	IMPERATIVE	PRESENT	IMPERFECT
*recev*ant	reçois	*reçoive*	*reçu*sse
REÇU (4)	recevons	*reçoives*	*reçu*sses
	recevez	*reçoive*	*reçû*t
		recevions	*reçu*ssions
		receviez	*reçu*ssiez
		reçoivent	*reçu*ssent

Rire (to laugh)

INDICATIVE

PRESENT	IMPERFECT	FUTURE	CONDITIONAL	PAST DEFINITE
ris	*ri*ais	*RIR*ai (2)	*rir*ais	*RI*s (3)
ris	*ri*ais	*rir*as	*rir*ais	*ris*
rit	*ri*ait	*rir*a	*rir*ait	*rit*
RIons (1)	*ri*ions	*rir*ons	*rir*ions	*rî*mes
riez	*ri*iez	*rir*ez	*rir*iez	*rî*tes
rient	*ri*aient	*rir*ont	*rir*aient	*rir*ent

SUBJUNCTIVE

PARTICIPLES	IMPERATIVE	PRESENT	IMPERFECT
*ri*ant	ris	*rie*	*ri*sse
RI (4)	rions	*ries*	*ri*sses
	riez	*rie*	*rî*t
		*ri*ions	*ri*ssions
		*ri*iez	*ri*ssiez
		*ri*ent	*ri*ssent

Savoir (to know)

INDICATIVE

PRESENT	IMPERFECT	FUTURE	CONDITIONAL	PAST DEFINITE
sais	*sav*ais	*SAUR*ai (2)	*saur*ais	*SU*s (3)
sais	*sav*ais	*saur*as	*saur*ais	*sus*
sait	*sav*ait	*saur*a	*saur*ait	*sut*
SAVons (1)	*sav*ions	*saur*ons	*saur*ions	*sû*mes
savez	*sav*iez	*saur*ez	*saur*iez	*sû*tes
savent	*sav*aient	*saur*ont	*saur*aient	*sur*ent

SUBJUNCTIVE

PARTICIPLES	IMPERATIVE	PRESENT	IMPERFECT
N.B. Special stem of Present Participle: *SACH-*	N.B. Special stem: *SACH-*	N.B. Special stem: *SACH-*	
*SACH*ant	SACHe	SACHe	*susse*
SU (4)	SACHons	SACHes	*susses*
	SACHez	SACHe	*sû*t
		SACHions	*suss*ions
		SACHiez	*suss*iez
		SACHent	*suss*ent

Suivre (to follow)

INDICATIVE

PRESENT	IMPERFECT	FUTURE	CONDITIONAL	PAST DEFINITE
suis	*suiv*ais	*SUIVR*ai (2)	*suivr*ais	*SUIVI*s (3)
suis	*suiv*ais	*suivr*as	*suivr*ais	*suivi*s
suit	*suiv*ait	*suivr*a	*suivr*ait	*suivi*t
SUIVons (1)	*suiv*ions	*suivr*ons	*suivr*ions	*suivî*mes
suivez	*suiv*iez	*suivr*ez	*suivr*iez	*suivî*tes
suivent	*suiv*aient	*suivr*ont	*suivr*aient	*suivi*rent

SUBJUNCTIVE

PARTICIPLES	IMPERATIVE	PRESENT	IMPERFECT
*suiv*ant	suis	*suive*	*suivi*sse
SUIVI (4)	suivons	*suives*	*suivi*sses
	suivez	*suive*	*suivî*t
		suivions	*suivi*ssions
		suiviez	*suivi*ssiez
		suivent	*suivi*ssent

Vaincre (to conquer)

INDICATIVE

PRESENT	IMPERFECT	FUTURE	CONDITIONAL	PAST DEFINITE
vaincs	*vainquais*	*VAINCR*ai (2)	*vaincrais*	*VAINQUI*s (3)
vaincs	*vainquais*	*vaincras*	*vaincrais*	*vainquis*
vainc	*vainquait*	*vaincra*	*vaincrait*	*vainquit*
VAINQUons (1)	*vainquions*	*vaincrons*	*vaincrions*	*vainquîmes*
vainquez	*vainquiez*	*vaincrez*	*vaincriez*	*vainquîtes*
vainquent	*vainquaient*	*vaincront*	*vaincraient*	*vainquirent*

SUBJUNCTIVE

PARTICIPLES	IMPERATIVE	PRESENT	IMPERFECT
*vainqu*ant	vaincs	*vainque*	*vainquisse*
VAINCU (4)	vainquons	*vainques*	*vainquisses*
	vainquez	*vainque*	*vainquît*
		vainquions	*vainquissions*
		vainquiez	*vainquissiez*
		vainquent	*vainquissent*

Valoir (to be worth)

INDICATIVE

PRESENT	IMPERFECT	FUTURE	CONDITIONAL	PAST DEFINITE
vaux	valais	VAUDRai (2)	vaudrais	VALUs (3)
vaux	valais	vaudras	vaudrais	valus
vaut	valait	vaudra	vaudrait	valut
VALons (1)	valions	vaudrons	vaudrions	valûmes
valez	valiez	vaudrez	vaudriez	valûtes
valent	valaient	vaudront	vaudraient	valurent

SUBJUNCTIVE

PARTICIPLES	IMPERATIVE	PRESENT	IMPERFECT
valant	vaux	N.B. Special stem for all singular and 3rd plural: VAILL-	
VALU (4)	valons		
	valez		
		VAILLe	valusse
		VAILLes	valusses
		VAILLe	valût
		valions	valussions
		valiez	valussiez
		VAILLent	valussent

Venir (to come) conjugated with *être*. Cf. *aller*.

INDICATIVE

PRESENT	IMPERFECT	FUTURE	CONDITIONAL	PAST DEFINITE
viens	*ven*ais	*VIENDR*ai (2)	*viendr*ais	*VIN*s (3)
viens	*ven*ais	*viendr*as	*viendr*ais	*vins*
vient	*ven*ait	*viendr*a	*viendr*ait	*vint*
*VEN*ons (1a)	*ven*ions	*viendr*ons	*viendr*ions	*vînmes*
venez	*ven*iez	*viendr*ez	*viendr*iez	*vîntes*
*VIENN*ent (1b)	*ven*aient	*viendr*ont	*viendr*aient	*vin*rent

SUBJUNCTIVE

PARTICIPLES	IMPERATIVE	PRESENT	IMPERFECT
*ven*ant	viens	*vienne*	*vin*sse
VENU (4)	venons	*viennes*	*vin*sses
	venez	*vienne*	*vînt*
		venions	*vin*ssions
		veniez	*vin*ssiez
		viennent	*vin*ssent

Vivre (to live)

INDICATIVE

PRESENT	IMPERFECT	FUTURE	CONDITIONAL	PAST DEFINITE
vis	*viv*ais	*VIVR*ai (2)	*vivr*ais	*VÉCU*s (3)
vis	*viv*ais	*vivr*as	*vivr*ais	*vécus*
vit	*viv*ait	*vivra*	*vivr*ait	*vécu*t
VIVons (1)	*viv*ions	*vivr*ons	*vivr*ions	*vécû*mes
vivez	*viv*iez	*vivr*ez	*vivr*iez	*vécû*tes
vivent	*viv*aient	*vivr*ont	*vivr*aient	*vécur*ent

SUBJUNCTIVE

PARTICIPLES	IMPERATIVE	PRESENT	IMPERFECT
*viv*ant	vis	*viv*e	*vécu*sse
VÉCU (4)	vivons	*viv*es	*vécu*sses
	vivez	*viv*e	*vécû*t
		*viv*ions	*vécu*ssions
		*viv*iez	*vécu*ssiez
		*viv*ent	*vécu*ssent

Voir (to see)

INDICATIVE

PRESENT	IMPERFECT	FUTURE	CONDITIONAL	PAST DEFINITE
vois	*voy*ais	*VERR*ai (2)	*verr*ais	*VIs* (3)
vois	*voy*ais	*verr*as	*verr*ais	*vis*
voit	*voy*ait	*verr*a	*verr*ait	*vit*
VOYons (1a)	*voy*ions	*verr*ons	*verr*ions	*v*îmes
voyez	*voy*iez	*verr*ez	*verr*iez	*v*îtes
VOIent (1b)	*voy*aient	*verr*ont	*verr*aient	*v*irent

SUBJUNCTIVE

PARTICIPLES	IMPERATIVE	PRESENT	IMPERFECT
*voy*ant	vois	*voi*e	*v*isse
VU (4)	voyons	*voi*es	*v*isses
	voyez	*voi*e	*v*ît
		*voy*ions	*v*issions
		*voy*iez	*v*issiez
		*voi*ent	*v*issent

Vouloir (to want, to wish)

INDICATIVE

PRESENT	IMPERFECT	FUTURE	CONDITIONAL	PAST DEFINITE
veux	*voulais*	*VOUDRai* (2)	*voudrais*	*VOULUs* (3)
veux	*voulais*	*voudras*	*voudrais*	*voulus*
veut	*voulait*	*voudra*	*voudrait*	*voulut*
VOULons (1)	*voulions*	*voudrons*	*voudrions*	*voulûmes*
voulez	*vouliez*	*voudrez*	*voudriez*	*voulûtes*
veulent	*voulaient*	*voudront*	*voudraient*	*voulurent*

SUBJUNCTIVE

PARTICIPLES	IMPERATIVE	PRESENT	IMPERFECT
voulant	Special Form:	N.B. Special stem for all singular and 3rd plural:	
VOULU (4)	VEUILLEZ*	*VEUILL-*	
		VEUILLe	*voulusse*
		VEUILLes	*voulusses*
		VEUILLe	*voulût*
		voulions	*voulussions*
		vouliez	*voulussiez*
		VEUILLent	*voulussent*

* *Veuillez* means "please" and is used at the beginning of the sentence:
Veuillez vous asseoir. (Please be seated.)

FRENCH IDIOMS

In order to make it possible to find the idiom as rapidly as possible, the idiomatic expressions have been listed, not according to key words, the choice of which too often is arbitrary, but rather in strict alphabetical order, which treats the whole expression as a single word. Thus:

servir à
servir de
se sauver
se servir de

Certain elements of some idioms — such as verb, pronoun — have been italicized to indicate that this is the varying part of the idiom.

A

à ______: with (expressing a characteristic)
Ex.: L'étudiant à l'accent français vient de l'Afrique du Nord. (The student with the French accent comes from North Africa.)

à ______: good-by until ______, till ______, see you ______
Ex.: à demain; à dimanche; à tantôt; à bientôt; au revoir (good-by till tomorrow; good-by till Sunday; see you shortly; see you soon; so long)

à cause de: because of
Note: This expression is used only in a phrase. "Because" introducing a clause is translated by *parce que*.
Ex.: L'étudiant a acheté un livre d'occasion à cause du prix. (The student bought a used book because of the price.)

à cheval: on horseback

à demi: half (*adv.*)

adresser la parole à: to speak to (formally)
Note: The main verb is here italicized to show that it will vary.
Ex.: Le président a adressé la parole à la secrétaire. (The president spoke to the secretary.)

à droite: on the (to the) right

à fond: thoroughly

à force de: by dint of, by means of

à gauche: on the (to the) left

à haute voix: aloud, out loud

aimer à la folie: to be crazy about

aimer mieux: to prefer

à jamais: forever

à la ______: ______ style
Note: The adjective used in this expression will always agree in the feminine singular with *mode* (style) understood. The gender and number of the noun being described do not matter.
Ex.: Avez-vous jamais essayé les crêpes à la française? (Have you ever tried pancakes French style?)

à la bonne heure!: good!, fine!
Note: This expression is used only as an exclamation.
Ex.: J'ai trouvé précisément le livre qu'il me fallait. (I found just the book I needed.)
A la bonne heure! (Fine!)

à la campagne: in the country

à la fin: finally

à la fois: at the same time, both

à l'aide de: with the help of

à l'aise: in easy circumstances, well to do

à la main: by hand

à la maison: at home
à la mode: fashionable
à la page ____: on page ____
à l'école: in school
à l'étranger: abroad
à l'heure: on time
à l'instant: at once
aller à: to be becoming, to suit, to fit
Note: The thing that is becoming is the subject of *aller*; the person to whom it is becoming follows *à*.
Ex.: Ces lunettes ne lui vont pas du tout. (Those glasses aren't at all becoming to him.)
aller à la rencontre de: to go and meet
Note: The person to be met is the object of *de*.
Ex.: Ce matin nous sommes allés à la rencontre de Paul. (This morning we went to meet Paul.)
aller au devant de: to go to meet
aller bien: to be well
Note: This expression usually refers to health.
Ex.: Comment va Madame votre mère? Elle va très bien, merci. (How is your mother? She is very well, thank you.)
aller chercher: to go and get
à l'occasion de: on the occasion of
à merveille: admirably
à moitié: half (*adv.*)
à perte de vue: as far as the eye can see
à peu près: almost, nearly, about
à pied: on foot
à plusieurs reprises: repeatedly
apprendre par cœur: to learn, to memorize
à quelle heure?: at what time?
à quoi bon?: what's the use (of)?
à savoir: namely
Note: This expression remains invariable.
à *son* gré: to one's liking
assister à: to attend, to be present at
à temps: in time
à tort et à travers: at random
à tout prix: at any cost
attraper un rhume: to catch a cold
au bas de: at the bottom of
au beau milieu de: in the very middle of
au bout de: at the end of, after
au contraire: on the contrary
au fond: basically, after all
au hasard: at random
au haut de: at the top of
au juste: exactly
au lieu de: instead of
au loin: far away, in the distance
au milieu de: in the middle of
au monde: in the world
au moyen de: by means of
au nom de: in the name of
au premier abord: at first glance, on one's approach
au printemps: in the spring
au revoir: good-by, so long
au sujet de: about, concerning
avoir à: to have to
Ex.: J'ai à me dépêcher; je suis en retard. (I have to hurry; I'm late.)
avoir (dix, vingt, etc.) ans: to be (ten, twenty, etc.) years old
avoir beau ____ (*inf.*): to be useless for someone ____ (*inf.*); to do something in vain
Note: The person involved in this expression always becomes the subject of *avoir*.
Ex.: J'ai beau____ (It is useless for me____)
Vous avez beau____ (It is useless for you____)
Paul a beau____ (It is useless for Paul____)
avoir besoin de: to need, to have need of
avoir bonne mine: to look good
avoir chaud: to be warm (of persons)
avoir de la chance: to be lucky
avoir des nouvelles de: to hear from, have news of
Ex.: Avez-vous des nouvelles de Marguerite? (Have you heard from Margaret?)
avoir envie de: to feel like, to care to, to want to

Ex.: Les étudiants de français ont toujours envie d'aller passer une ou deux heures au laboratoire. (The French students always feel like going to spend an hour or two at the laboratory.)

avoir faim: to be hungry

avoir froid: to be cold (of persons)

avoir honte de: to be ashamed of

avoir la bonté de: to be kind enough to

avoir l'air de: to seem, to appear to, to look like (as though)

Ex.: Ils ont l'air de s'y amuser. (They seem to enjoy themselves there.)

avoir l'habitude de: to be used to, accustomed to

Ex.: Est-ce que vous avez peur de faire un enregistrement? Non, pas du tout, j'en ai l'habitude. (Are you afraid to make a recording? No, not at all, I'm used to it.)

avoir lieu: to take place

avoir l'intention de: to intend to

avoir l'occasion de: to have the opportunity to

avoir mal à ______: to have a ______ache

Note: Wherever one has the ache is expressed *à* ____: avoir mal à la tête (to have a headache); avoir mal aux dents (to have a toothache); etc.

Ex.: Jeannine n'a pu s'enregistrer la voix hier parce qu'elle avait mal à la gorge. (Jeannine couldn't record her voice yesterday because she had a sore throat.)

avoir peine à ______ *(inf.)*: *to find* it hard to ______ *(inf.)*

Ex.: Lorsque l'étudiant va au laboratoire pour la première fois, il a toujours peine à comprendre le français parlé. (When a student goes to the laboratory for the first time, he always finds it hard to understand the spoken French.)

avoir peur: to be afraid

avoir pitié de: to take pity on

avoir quelque chose: to have something the matter with one

avoir raison: to be right

avoir soif: to be thirsty

avoir sommeil: to be sleepy

avoir tort: to be wrong

à voix basse: in a low voice

à vrai dire: to tell the truth

B

bien entendu: of course, naturally

bien sûr: surely, of course

bon gré, mal gré: willy-nilly, willing or unwilling

bon marché: cheap, inexpensive

C

cela m'est égal: it's all the same to me

cela ne fait rien: that does not matter

cela va sans dire (or: cela va de soi): that goes without saying

c'est-à-dire: that is, that is to say

c'est ça (cela): that's right

c'est dommage: it's too bad, it's a pity

c'est entendu: it is agreed

c'est que: the fact is that

Ex.: Cet étudiant a de la peine à comprendre le français parlé. C'est qu'il n'a pas assez de pratique. (That student has difficulty in understanding spoken French. The fact is that he hasn't enough practice.)

changer d'avis: to change one's mind

chemin faisant: on the way

chercher midi à quatorze heures: to look for difficulties where there are none

comme ci, comme ça: so-so

comme il faut: right, proper

Comment *allez-vous*? How are you?

Comment se fait-il que ______? How come ______? How does it happen that ______?

Comment *trouvez-vous* ______? How do you like ______?

Comment *vous portez-vous*? How are you?

D

D'accord!: Agreed! Okay!

d'aujourd'hui en huit: a week from today

d'autant plus que: all the more because
Ex.: Cette partie de football m'intéresse d'autant plus que je connais tous les joueurs. (This football game interests me all the more because I know all the players.)
d'autre part: on the other hand
de bon (grand) cœur: gladly
de bonne heure: early
de ___ en ___: from ___ to ___
Note: This expression usually implies some kind of progressive state.
Ex.: Nous n'avons pas de chance. Les choses vont de mal en pire. (We have no luck. Things are going from bad to worse.)
de la part de: from (a person)
Note: This expression is used only with persons.
Ex.: Marie nous a apporté une invitation de la part de sa mère. (Mary brought us an invitation from her mother.)
de l'autre côté: on the other side
de long en large: up and down
de *mon* côté: for *my* part
de *mon* mieux: as well as *I* can
Ex.: de *son* mieux (as well as he can)
de *notre* mieux (as well as *we* can)
de *votre* (*ton*) mieux (as well as you can)
de *leur* mieux (as well as they can)
de nouveau: again
de parti pris: deliberately
de plus en plus: more and more
See also: de ___ en ___.
de quoi ___ (*inf.*): ___ material, the wherewithal to ___.
Note: Whatever material is involved will appear in the infinitive.
Ex.: *reading* material: de quoi *lire*
writing material: de quoi *écrire*
de rigueur: indispensable, required
de suite: one after another
de temps à autre: from time to time
de temps en temps: from time to time
See also: de ___ en ___
de trop: in the way
dire pis que pendre de quelqu'un: to say the worst of someone
donner la main à quelqu'un: to shake hands with someone
donner sur: to look out on, to face, to front
Ex.: Il y avait deux fenêtres qui donnaient sur l'océan. (There were two windows that looked out on the ocean.)
du côté de: in the direction of, toward
d'un bout à l'autre: from beginning to end
d'un côté: on (the) one hand

E

éclater de ___ (*inf.*): to burst out ___ing
en ___: as a ___
Ex.: En bon élève, il avait fait tous ses devoirs. (As a good pupil, he had done all his homework.)
en automme: in the autumn, in the fall
en avant: forward, ahead
en bas: downstairs
en effet: in fact, indeed
en *être* à: to have reached, to be up to
Ex.: Où en sommes-nous? Nous en sommes à la page 74. (What are we up to? We are up to page 74.)
en face de: opposite, in front of
en famille: at home, as a family
en haut: upstairs, above
en même temps: at the same time
en plein(e) ___ (noun): in the middle of ___ (noun)
en plein air: out of doors, in the open air
en somme: in short
en sursaut: with a start
entendre dire: to hear said
Ex.: Le président du cercle avait entendu dire qu'il y avait une belle collection de disques français à la bibliothèque. (The president of the club had heard that there was a fine collection of French records at the library.)

entendre parler de: to hear about

Ex.: Un des membres du Cercle Français avait entendu parler d'un bon film. (One of the members of the French Club had heard about a good film.)

en tout cas: at any rate

en *venir* à: to come to, to resort to

en *vouloir* à: to have a grudge against, to be angry with, to have it in for

Ex.: Je parie que la bibliothécaire en veut à tous ceux qui sortent cinq ou dix livres et les laissent sur les tables. (I'll wager that the librarian has it in for all those who take out five or ten books and leave them on the tables.)

envoyer chercher: to send for

être à: to belong to

être à même de: to be in a position to, to be able to

Ex.: Marianne était bien aise d'être à même d'aider son amie. (Marianne was very glad to be able to help her friend.)

être à quelqu'un de faire quelque chose: to be up to someone to do something

Ex.: C'est à Marie d'aller chercher les billets. (It is up to Mary to go and get the tickets.)

être ______ (*adj.*) à quelqu'un de faire quelque chose: to be ______ (*adj.*) of someone to do something

Ex.: C'était très gentil à Marianne de prêter sa carte à Hélène. (It was very nice of Marianne to lend her card to Helen.)

être à son aise: to be comfortable, to be well off

être au courant de: to be informed about

être bien: to be comfortable

Note: This is said of the person. *Être confortable* is used of the thing conducive to comfort.

Ex.:Mon père était toujours bien dans son fauteuil. (My father was always comfortable in his armchair.)

Ce fauteuil est très confortable. (This armchair is very comfortable.)

être bien aise (de): to be glad (to)

être d'accord avec: to agree with

être de retour: to be back

être des nôtres: to be one of our party

être en train de: to be busy (doing something), to be in the act of (doing something)

être hors de soi: to be beside oneself

être la peine de: to be worthwhile to

être le (la) bienvenu(e): to be welcome

être on ne peut plus ______: to be as ______ as can be

Ex.: Les Desjardins étaient on ne peut plus hospitaliers envers leur hôte. (The Desjardins were as hospitable as could be to their guest.)

être sur le point de: to be about to

F

faillir ______ (*inf.*): nearly, almost ______ (*verb*)

Ex.: Le patineur a failli tomber. (The skater almost fell.)

faire à *sa* tête: to have one's own way

faire attention à: to pay attention to

faire beau: to be fine weather

Note: Il is subject in all weather expressions.

Ex.: Il a fait beau toute la journée. (The weather was fine all day.)

faire bon: to be nice weather; to be comfortable (conducive to comfort)

Note: This expression applies usually to places.

Ex.: Il faisait si bon dans le petit restaurant que nous avons commandé deux cafés seulement pour y rester et bavarder. (It was so comfortable in the little restaurant that we ordered two coffees just to stay there and chat.)

faire bonne chère: to eat well

faire cadeau de: to give as a gift

faire cas de: to esteem

faire chaud: to be warm weather

faire de la peine à: to hurt (someone), to grieve (someone) *faire* des économies: to save, to economize

faire des emplettes: to make purchases, to shop

faire de *son* mieux: to do one's best

faire des progrès: to make progress

faire du ski: to go skiing, to go in for skiing

faire du vent: to be windy

faire exprès: to do on purpose

faire faire: to get done, to have done, to make ______ (*verb*)

Note: Faire is used with an infinitive to indicate that the speaker causes the action to be carried out by another person.

Ex.: Laurent nous a fait attendre deux heures à l'aérodrome. (Laurence made us wait two hours at the airport.)

faire frais: to be cool (weather)

faire froid: to be cold (weather)

faire grand cas de: to attach great importance to

faire la connaissance de: to become acquainted with

faire la queue: to stand in line

faire la sourde oreille: to pretend not to hear

faire le tour de: to go around

faire le (la, les) ______(s): to play the ______(s)

Ex.: Cet élève fait le malade lorsqu'il a un examen à passer. (This pupil plays sick when he has an examination to take.)

faire lourd: to be sultry (weather)

faire mal à: to hurt (someone)

faire mine de: to pretend

faire part à quelqu'un de quelque chose: to let someone know about something

faire partie de: to belong to, to be a member of

faire peur à: to frighten

faire plaisir à: to please

faire savoir: to let know

faire semblant de: to pretend to

faire ses adieux à: to say good-by to

faire ses amitiés à: to give one's regards to

faire son affaire: to answer (someone's) purpose

Ex.: Je n'ai pas de stylo, mais ce crayon fera mon affaire. (I haven't any pen, but this pencil will answer my purpose.)

faire son marché: to do one's shopping

faire son possible: to do one's best

faire une malle: to pack a trunk

faire une promenade: to take a walk

faire une question: to ask a question

faire un voyage: to take a trip

faire venir: to send for

faire visite à: to pay a visit to

faire voir: to show

faute de: for lack of

finir par: to end up by, finally to

G

gagner sa vie: to earn one's living

I

il est trois (neuf, etc.) heures: it is three (nine, etc.) o'clock

il n'y a pas de quoi (*also:* pas de quoi): you're welcome, don't mention it

il y a: ago

Ex.: La lettre nous est parvenue il y a trois jours. (The letter reached us three days ago.)

il y a: for (with expression of time)

Note: This expression is interchangeable with *ça fait, voilà, depuis.*

Ex.: Il y a un quart d'heure que nous attendons le facteur. (We've been waiting for the postman for a quarter of an hour.)

il y a: there is, there are

Ex.: Il n'y aura pas de courrier lundi prochain; c'est jour de fête. (There won't be any mail next Monday; it's a holiday.)

il y a: the trouble is, the matter is

Ex.: Qu'est-ce qu'il y a? (What's the matter?)

Il y a que le courrier arrive en retard à cause de la neige. (The trouble is that the mail arrives late because of the snow.)

il y va de ______: it is a question of ______; ______ is at stake

Note: Whatever is at stake is the object of *de*.

Ex.: Il faudra que la lettre de recommendation leur parvienne avant lundi. Il y va de mon poste. (The letter of recommendation will have to reach them by Monday. My position is at stake.)

J

jamais de la vie: never on your life

je crois que oui (non): I think so (not)

je n'y *manquerai* pas: I shall not fail to do so

jeter un coup d'œil sur: to glance over

je vous en *prie*: I beg of you, you're welcome, please

jouer le rôle: to play the part

L

la plupart du temps: most of the time

l'*échapper* belle: to have a narrow escape

Ex.: Lorsque la voiture qui faisait du quatre-vingts à l'heure a heurté le taxi, les passagers du taxi l'ont échappé belle. Heureusement j'en ai été quitte pour une égratignure. (When the car that was doing eighty miles an hour struck the taxi, the passengers of the taxi had a narrow escape. Fortunately I got off with a scratch.)

l'*emporter* sur: to prevail over, to win out over

Ex.: Les deux équipes étaient très fortes, mais la nôtre, étant plus expérimentée, n'a pas tardé à l'emporter sur l'adversaire. (The two teams were very strong, but ours, being more experienced, didn't take long in winning out over the opponent.)

le plus tôt possible: as soon as possible

M

manquer à: to be lacking, to miss

Note: If "miss" is changed into terms of "to be missing to", this expression will be easily used in French. Thus: "Armand misses his friends" becomes "His friends are missing to Armand," or "*Ses amis manquent à Armand.*"

manquer de: nearly to, to fail to; to lack

Note: This expression is synonymous with *faillir*.

Ex.: Le patineur a manqué de tomber. (The skater almost fell.)

Ce garçon manque de sens commun. (That boy lacks common sense.)

mener grand train (*also: vivre* sur un grand pied): to live on an elaborate scale

mettre (a certain amount of time) à faire quelque chose: to take (a certain amount of time) to do something

Ex.: On a mis deux semaines à répondre à ma lettre. (They took two weeks to answer my letter.)

mettre au courant de: to inform about

mettre fin à: to put an end to

mettre le couvert: to set the table

monter à cheval: to ride horseback

N

n'en pas *revenir:* not to be able to get over it

Ex.: Quelle surprise! Je n'en reviens pas. (What a surprise! I can't get over it.)

n'en *pouvoir* plus: to be exhausted

Ex.: Après avoir passé l'après-midi à faire des emplettes en bas de la ville, les deux dames n'en pouvaient plus. (After having spent the afternoon shopping downtown, the two ladies were exhausted.

n'est-ce pas?: isn't it so?

Note: This expression can be translated in a variety of ways, such as: "don't you?", "didn't she?", "won't they?", "hadn't it?", "weren't you?", etc. It simply calls for confirmation of the statement that has been made.

Ex.: Si le libraire avait l'anthologie, vous l'achèteriez, n'est-ce pas? (If the bookseller had the anthology, you would buy it, wouldn't you?)

ni moi non plus: nor I either

n'y *pouvoir* rien: not to be able to do anything about it

P

par: on (with weather expressions); per, a (with wages, times, etc.)

Ex.: Par une belle journée d'été, les Desjardins s'embarquèrent pour la France. (On a fine summer day, the Desjardins embarked for France.)

Cet étudiant gagne cinq dollars par jour. (That student earns five dollars a day.)

par-ci, par-là: here and there

par conséquent: therefore

par-dessus le marché: into the bargain

par exemple: for example, for instance

par hasard: by chance

par ici: this way (direction)

par jour: per day, a day

par là: that way (direction)

parler à tort et à travers: to speak without knowing what one is talking about

par terre: on the ground

pas grand'chose: not much

passer par: to pass by, to call on

passer une nuit blanche: to spend a sleepless night

passer un examen: to take an examination

Note: This expression means to "take," not to "pass" an examination. "To pass an examination" is either *réussir à un examen* or *être reçu à un examen.*

Ex.: Mardi dernier j'ai passé deux examens mais je ne sais pas encore si j'y ai réussi. (Last Tuesday I took two examinations, but I don't yet know whether I passed them.)

petit à petit: little by little

peu à peu: little by little

plaît-il?: I beg your pardon?

pleuvoir à verse: to pour rain

poser une question: to put (ask) a question

pour ainsi dire: so to speak

pour de bon: in earnest, for good

pour la plupart: for the most part

prendre des renseignements: to get information

prendre en grippe: to take a dislike to

Ex.: Il arrive quelquefois que les gens que nous prenons en grippe au début deviennent plus tard de bons amis. (It sometimes happens that the people we take a dislike to in the beginning later become good friends.)

prendre froid: to take cold

prendre garde (de + *inf.*): to take care (not to ______), to be careful (not to ______)

Note: The negative element "not to" is already contained in *prendre garde de* and therefore is not to be expressed.

Ex.: Prenez *garde de tomber* en descendant cet escalier. (Be careful not to fall going down that staircase.)

prendre le parti de: to decide, to determine to

prendre l'habitude de: to get into the habit of

prendre un billet: to buy a ticket

profiter de: to profit by, to take advantage of

Q

quand même: even so, anyhow, just the same

qu'*avez-vous*?: what's the matter with you?, what's wrong with you?

que de ______!: what a lot of ______!

quel âge *avez-vous*?: how old are you?

quelle date sommes-nous?: what day of the month is it?, what's today's date?

quelle heure est-il?: what time is it?

qu'il faut: the right

Ex.: Ce n'est pas le billet qu'il faut. (That isn't the right ticket.)

R

rappelez-*moi* au bon souvenir de: remember *me* to
rebrousser chemin: to retrace one's steps
rendre visite à: to pay a visit to
rien du tout: nothing at all

S

s'*agir* de: to be a question of, to be a matter of
Note: This expression, being impersonal, is used only in the third person singular with *il* as subject.
Ex.: Lorsque le récepteur de télévision est détraqué, il s'agit généralement du tube cathodique. (When the television set is out of order, it is usually a question of the picture tube.)
s'*amuser:* to have a good time, to enjoy oneself
sans doute: of course
s'*appeler:* to be called, to be named
s'*attendre* à: to expect
sauter aux yeux: to be evident
savoir bon gré à: to be grateful to
se *charger* de: to take charge of
se *connaître* en: to be an authority on, to know all about
se *débarrasser* de: to get rid of
se *donner* des airs: to put on airs
se *donner* la peine de: to take the trouble to
se *douter* de: to suspect
se *fâcher* contre: to be angry with
se *faire* à: to get accustomed to
se *faire* entendre: to make oneself understood
se *faire* mal: to hurt oneself
se *faire* tard: to grow late
se *faire* un plaisir de: to take pleasure in
se *garder* de + *inf.:* to beware of ______ing
se *mettre* à: to begin to
se *mettre* à table: to sit down at the table
se *mettre* en rapport avec: to get in contact with
se *mettre* en route: to set out
s'en *aller:* to go away, to leave
Note: S'en aller is used when no destination is mentioned.
Ex.: Si Paul n'arrive pas dans un quart d'heure, Marianne s'en ira. (If Paul doesn't arrive in a quarter of an hour, Marianne will leave.)
s'en *prendre* à: to lay the blame on
Ex.: Quand Marianne est en retard, elle s'en prend à sa montre. (When Marianne is late, she blames her watch.)
s'en *remettre* à: to rely on, to leave it up to
Ex.: Lorsqu'il s'agit d'actions, je m'en remets à l'agent de change. (When it's a matter of stocks, I leave it up to the stockbroker.)
sens dessus dessous: topsy-turvy, upside down
s'*entendre* avec: to get along with, to understand someone
s'en *tenir* à: to stick to, to keep to
Ex.: Henri a proposé un second projet mais les membres du cercle s'en sont tenus au premier. (Henry proposed a second plan, but the members of the club stuck to the first.)
s'en *tirer:* to get along
s'en *vouloir* de: not to forgive oneself for
Ex.: Jeannine s'en voulait d'avoir oublié les gâteaux qu'elle avait préparés pour le pique-nique. (Jeannine didn't forgive herself for having forgotten the cakes that she had prepared for the picnic.)
se *passer* de: to do without
se *piquer* de: to pride oneself on
se *plaire* à: to take pleasure in
se *porter* (bien, mal): to be (well, ill — of health)
se *prendre* à: to begin to
se *rapporter* à: to refer back to
se *rendre* à: to go to
se *rendre* compte de: to realize
serrer la main à quelqu'un: to shake

someone's hand
servir à: to be useful (good) for
servir de: to serve as
se sauver: to run away, to run along
se servir de: to make use of, to use
se tenir debout: to be standing (up), to remain standing
se tirer d'affaire: to get along, to manage
se tromper de: to make a mistake in, to be mistaken about
se trouver: to be (located)
s'il vous plaît: please
s'informer de: to inquire about
s'occuper à: to be busy with
s'occuper de: to look after
sur-le-champ: immediately

T

tant bien que mal: fairly well
tant mieux: so much the better
tantôt . . . tantôt: now . . . now; sometimes . . . at other times

Note: This is used to express contrast. Ex.: Il y avait tant de choses à faire pendant la traversée. Tantôt nous nous promenions sur le pont, tantôt nous nagions dans la piscine. (There were so many things to do during the crossing. Sometimes we strolled on the deck, other times we swam in the pool.)

tant pis: so much the worse
tant que: as long as, so long as

Ex.: Nous resterons à la campagne tant que vous voudrez. (We'll stay in the country as long as you wish.)

tarder à + *inf.*: to be slow or long in _____ing

Ex.: Laurent n'a pas tardé à chercher une situation pour l'été. (Laurence wasn't long in looking for a position for the summer.)

tenir à: to be anxious to
tenir compte de: to take into consideration, to keep in mind
tenir de: to resemble
tenir parole: to keep one's word
tirer parti de: to profit by
tôt ou tard: sooner or later
tour à tour: in turn, by turns
tout à coup: suddenly
tout à fait: entirely
tout à l'heure: in a little while, a little while ago
tout de même: all the same, just the same
tout de suite: immediately, at once, right away
tout droit: straight ahead
tout d'un coup: all of a sudden
tout en _____ant: while _____ing
tout le long du chemin: all along the way
tout le monde: everyone
trouver à redire à: to find fault with

U

un je ne sais quoi de _____ (*adj.*): something indescribably _____ (*adj.*)

V

valoir la peine (de): to be worth while (to)
valoir mieux: to be better
venir à: to happen to
venir à bout de + *inf.*: to succeed in _____ing
venir chercher: to come and get
venir de: to have just
veuillez + *inf.*: please _____, be kind enough _____ (*inf.*)
vis-à-vis (de): opposite; with respect (to)
vouloir bien: to be willing
vouloir dire: to mean
voyons!: come now!

Y

y *être:* to catch on, to understand

LIST OF ABBREVIATIONS USED IN THIS VOCABULARY

abbrev., abbreviation
adj., adjective
adv., adverb
art., article
aux., auxiliary
comp., compound
conj., conjunction
def., definite
demon., demonstrative
f., feminine
indef., indefinite
interj., interjection
interr., interrogative
m., masculine
m. plu., masculine plural
n., noun
past part., past participle
pl., plural
poss., possessive
prep., preposition
pres. part., present participle
pron., pronoun
rel., relative
sing., singular
v.i., verb intransitive
v.t., verb transitive

Explanation of phonetic symbols will be found in the Pronunciation Guide.

VOCABULARY

English – French

A

a, *indef. art.*, un, une
abandon, *v.t.*, abandonner
able, *adj.*, capable
  to be ——, pouvoir
aboard, *adv.*, à bord
about, *prep.*, de, sur, au sujet de; *adv.*, à peu près, -aine (suffix expressing approximation of numbers)
accompany, *v.t.*, accompagner
acquaintance, *n.*, connaissance, *f.*
across, *prep.*, à travers
acting, *n.*, jeu, *m.*
actor, *n.*, acteur, *m.*
ad, *n.*, annonce, *f.*
  classified ——, petite annonce
add, *v.t.*, ajouter
admire, *v.t.*, admirer
aerial, *n.*, antenne (*f.*) aérienne
afraid, *adj.*, peureux, -se
  to be ——, avoir peur
after, *prep.*, après; *conj.*, après que
afternoon, *n.*, après-midi, *m.* or *f.*
ago, *adv.*, il y a
  half an hour ——, il y a une demi-heure
algebra, *n.*, algèbre, *f.*
  —— class, classe d'algèbre
all, *adj.*, tout, *m.*, toute, *f.*, tous, *m.plu.*, toutes *f.plu.*; *n.*, tout (everything), *m.*; tous (everybody), *m.plu.*
  —— that (which), tout ce qui, tout ce que
  —— the while, tout en (+ *pres. part.*)
almost, *adv.*, presque
alone, *adj.*, seul, -e
already, *adv.*, déjà
also, *adv.*, aussi
although, *conj.*, bien que, quoique
always, *adv.*, toujours
amazing, *adj.*, étonnant, -e
ambitious, *adj.*, ambitieux, -se
American, *adj.*, américain, -e; *n.*, Américain, -e (person)
among, *prep.*, parmi
analysis, *n.*, analyse, *f.*
ancient, *adj.*, ancien, -ne
and, *conj.*, et
announce, *v.t.*, annoncer
annoying, *adj.*, embêtant, -e; ennuyeux, -se
another, *adj.*, un(e) autre, encore un(e)
  one ——, se, l'un(e) l'autre, les un(e)s les autres
answer, *v.t.*, répondre (à); *n.*, réponse, *f.*
anthology, *n.*, anthologie, *f.*
any, *adj.*, du, de la, des, de; *pron.*, en
anyhow, *adv.*, n'importe comment
anyone, *pron.*, n'importe qui
anyway, *adv.*, quand même
anywhere, *adv.*, n'importe où
applaud, *v.t.*, applaudir
apple, *n.*, pomme, *f.*
  —— pie, tarte (*f.*) aux pommes
applicant, *n.*, candidat, *m.*
arrive, *v.i.*, arriver
as, *adv.*, comme
  —— you wish, comme vous voulez
  —— soon ——, aussitôt que, dès que
  —— much, autant (de + a noun)
  —— many, autant (de + a noun)
  —— (+ adj. or adv.) ——, aussi (si) —— que
Asia, *n.*, Asie, *f.*
ask, *v.t.*, demander
  to —— someone for something, demander quelque chose à quelqu'un
  to —— a question, faire une question, poser une question
assignment, *n.*, devoir, *m.*
astonish, *v.t.*, étonner
  to be ——ed, s'étonner

at, *prep.*, à, chez
attentive, *adj.*, attentif, -ve
attentively, *adv.*, attentivement
attic, *n.*, grenier, *m.*
attract, *v.t.*, attirer
author, *n.*, auteur, *m.*
authority, *n.*, autorité, *f.*
to be an _____ on (planes), se connaître en (avions)
avoid, *v.t.*, éviter

B

bad, *adj.*, mauvais, -e; méchant, -e
badly, *adv.*, mal
bag, *n.*, sac, *m.*
hand_____, sac à main
ball, *n.*, balle, *f.*; ballon, *m.* (football)
bank, *n.*, banque, *f.*
bathroom, *n.*, salle (*f.*) de bain
be, *v.i.*, être
beautiful, *adj.*, beau, *m.*, belle, *f.*
beauty, *n.*, beauté, *f.*
because, *conj.*, parce que
become, *v.i.*, devenir
bed, *n.*, lit, *m.*
before, *prep.*, avant (time), devant (place), avant de (+ *inf.*); *conj.*, avant que
begin, *v.t.*, commencer, se mettre à
beginning, *n.*, commencement, *m.*, début, *m.*
behind, *prep.*, derrière
believe, *v.t.*, croire
belong, *v.i.*, appartenir (à), être (à)
best, *adj.*, le (la) meilleur, -e; *adv.*, le mieux
better, *adj.*, meilleur, -e; *adv.*, mieux
between, *prep.*, entre
big, *adj.*, grand, -e; gros, -sse
bilingual, *adj.*, bilingue
billion, *n.*, milliard, *m.*
one _____ books, un milliard de livres
black, *adj.*, noir, -e
blessing, *n.*, bénédiction, *f.*
blue, *adj.*, bleu, -e
blush, *v.i.*, rougir
body, *n.*, corps, *m.*
book, *n.*, livre, *m.*
bookkeeper, *n.*, comptable, *m.*
bookstore, *n.*, librairie, *f.*
booth, *n.*, cabine, *f.*
born, *past part.*, né, -e
to be _____, naître
borrow, *v.t.*, emprunter
boy, *n.*, garçon, *m.*
Brazil, *n.*, Brésil, *m.*
bread, *n.*, pain, *m.*
break, *v.t.*, casser, rompre
bring, *v.t.*, apporter
broadcast, *n.*, émission, *f.*
brother, *n.*, frère, *m.*
burst, *v.t.*, *v.i.*, éclater
busy, *adj.*, affairé, occupé
but, *conj.*, mais
buy, *v.t.*, acheter
by, *prep.*, par

C

cabin, *n.*, cabine, *f.*
cabin boy, *n.*, mousse, *m.*
cake, *n.*, gâteau, *m.*; petit four (little frosted cake) *m.*
call, *v.t.*, appeler
to be _____ed, s'appeler
Canada, *n.*, Canada, *m.*
car, *n.*, voiture, *f.*, automobile, *f.*
care, *n.*, soin, *m.*
to _____ for, to take _____ of, soigner
carefully, *adv.*, soigneusement
carnival, *n.*, carnaval, *m.*
carrot, *n.*, carotte, *f.*
carry, *v.t.*, porter
case, *n.*, cas, *m.*
catch, *v.t.*, attraper
to _____ cold, prendre froid
cathedral, *n.*, cathédrale, *f.*
cauliflower, *n.*, chou-fleur, *m.*
celebrate, *v.t.*, fêter, célébrer
certainly, *adv.*, certainement
chair, *n.*, chaise, *f.*
change, *n.*, monnaie, *f.*; *v.t.*, changer
chat, *v.i.*, bavarder, causer
cheap, *adj.*, bon marché
check, *v.t.*, vérifier; *n.m.*, chèque
child, *n.*, enfant, *m. and f.*
China, *n.*, Chine, *f.*
choose, *v.t.*, choisir
chop, *n.*, côtelette, *f.*
lamb _____, côtelette d'agneau
Christmas, *n.*, Noël, *m.*
_____ gift, étrenne, *f.*
church, *n.*, église, *f.*
city, *n.*, ville, *f.*
class, *n.*, classe, *f.*
history _____, classe d'histoire

classic, *n.*, classique, *m.*
classified, *adj.*, classé, -e
_____ ad, petite annonce, *f.*
classroom, *n.*, salle (*f.*) de classe
clean, *v.t.*, nettoyer
clear, *adj.*, clair, -e
clerk, *n.*, employé, *m.*
clock, *n.*, pendule, *f.*, horloge, *f.*
It is ten o'_____. Il est dix heures.
clue, *n.*, piste, *f.*
coffee, *n.*, café, *m.*
cold, *adj.*, froid, -e; *n.*, froid, *m.*
to be _____ (person), avoir froid
to be _____ (weather), faire froid
to be _____ (thing), être froid
collection, *n.*, collection, *f.*
color, *n.*, couleur, *f.*
come, *v.i.*, venir
_____ back, revenir
_____ in, entrer
commercial, *adj.*, commercial, -e; *n.*, réclame, *f.*
company, *n.*, compagnie, *f.*; maison, *f.* (commercial)
complain, *v.i.*, se plaindre
complete, *adj.*, complet, -ète, entier, -ère, total, -e; *v.t.*, compléter, finir, achever
completely, *adv.*, complètement, tout à fait
congress, *n.*, congrès, *m.*
construct, *v.t.*, construire
consult, *v.t.*, consulter
contact, *v.t.*, contacter
contain, *v.t.*, contenir
contribute, *v.t.*, contribuer
cool, *adj.*, frais, *m.*, fraîche, *f.*
copy, *n.*, exemplaire, *m.*
correct, *v.t.*, corriger
cough, *v.i.*, tousser
country, *n.*, pays (nation), *m.*; campagne (countryside), *f.*; patrie (fatherland), *f.*
course, *n.*, cours, *m.*
cross, *v.t.*, traverser, franchir; *n.*, croix, *f.*
crowded, *adj.*, bondé, -e
custard, *n.*, flan, *m.*

D

dancing, *n.*, danse, *f.*
dare, *v.i.*, oser
darkness, *n.*, obscurité, *f.*
date, *n.*, date, *f.*
What is today's _____? Quel jour du mois sommes-nous aujourd'hui?
daughter, *n.*, fille, *f.*
day, *n.*, jour, *m.*; journée (whole day), *f.*
death, *n.*, mort, *f.*
December, *n.*, décembre, *m.*
decide, *v.t.*, décider (de), se décider (à)
deck, *n.*, pont, *m.*
decoration, *n.*, décor, *m.*
defend, *v.t.*, défendre
delighted, *adj.*, enchanté, -e
demanding, *adj.*, exigeant, -e
dentist, *n.*, dentiste, *m.*
department, *n.*, département, *m.*
descend, *v.i.*, descendre
desire, *v.t.*, désirer, vouloir, souhaiter
desk, *n.*, bureau, *m.*
dessert, *n.*, dessert, *m.*
detective, *n.*, détective, *m.*
_____ story, roman policier
dial, *v.t.*, composer
diction, *n.*, diction, *f.*
die, *v.i.*, mourir
diet, *n.*, régime, *m.*
to be on a _____, être au régime
difference, *n.*, différence, *f.*
difficult, *adj.*, difficile
dinner, *n.*, dîner, *m.*
director, *n.*, directeur; (directress, *n.*, directrice, *f.*)
dirty, *adj.*, sale
disc, *n.*, disque, *m.*
disgraceful, *adj.*, honteux, -se
display, *n.*, étalage, *m.*
do, *v.t.*, faire
doctor, *n.*, médecin, *m.*
doll, *n.*, poupée, *f.*
door, *n.*, porte, *f.*
doubt, *n.*, doute, *m.*; *v.t.*, douter
dozen, *n.*, douzaine, *f.*
draw, *v.t.*, tirer (a prize), dessiner (a picture)
dream, *n.*, rêve, *m.*; *v.t.*, rêver
dress, *n.*, robe, *f.*
drill, *v.t.*, creuser
drink, *v.t.*, boire; *n.*, boisson, *f.*
soft _____, boisson non-alcoolique
dry, *v.t.*, essuyer

E

each, *adj.*, chaque; *pron.*, chacun, *m.*, chacune, *f.*,
_____ other, se, l'un(e) l'autre

ear, *n.*, oreille, *f.*
early, *adv.*, de bonne heure
earn, *v.t.*, gagner
easily, *adv.*, facilement
easy, *adj.*, facile
eat, *v.t.*, manger
egg, *n.*, oeuf, *m.*
eight, *adj.*, huit
eighteen, *adj.*, dix-huit
elective, *adj.*, facultatif, -ve
eleven, *adj.*, onze
elsewhere, *adv.*, ailleurs
empty, *adj.*, vide
end, *n.*, fin, *f.*; bout (limit), *m.*; *v.t.*, terminer, finir
to ——— up by, finir par
ending, *n.*, fin, *f.*
engineer, *n.*, ingénieur, *m.*
England, *n.*, Angleterre, *f.*
English, *adj.*, anglais, -e
enjoy, *v.t.*, jouir de, prendre plaisir à
to ——— oneself, se divertir, s'amuser
enough, *adv.*, assez (de + noun)
enrich, *v.t.*, enrichir
enter, *v.i.*, entrer (dans + noun)
erase, *v.t.*, effacer
especially, *adv.*, surtout
establish, *v.t.*, établir
Europe, *n.*, Europe, *f.*
European, *adj.*, européen, -ne
even, *adv.*, même; *adj.*, égal, -e
evening, *n.*, soir, *m.*; soirée (whole evening), *f.*
ever, *adv.*, jamais
every, *adj.*, chaque, tout, -e; tous (toutes) les
everybody, *pron.*, tout le monde
everywhere, *adv.*, partout
examine, *v.t.*, examiner
excellent, *adj.*, excellent, -e
exclaim, *v.t.*, s'écrier
exercise, *n.*, exercice, *m.*
expensive, *adj.*, cher, -ère; coûteux, -se
to be ———, coûter cher
experienced, *adj.*, expérimenté
explain, *v.t.*, expliquer
extract, *v.t.*, arracher
eye, *n.*, oeil (*plu.*, les yeux), *m.*

F

face, *n.*, figure, *f.*, visage, *m.*
fact, *n.*, fait, *m.*
in ———, en effet
faithful, *adj.*, fidèle
fall, *v.i.*, tomber
family, *n.*, famille, *f.*
famous, *adj.*, fameux, -se
far, *adv.*, loin
fascinating, *adj.*, fascinant, passionnant
fast, *adj.*, rapide; *adv.*, vite
father, *n.*, père, *m.*
fear, *n.*, crainte, *f.*, peur, *f.*; *v.t.*, craindre, avoir peur
February, *n.*, février, *m.*
few, *adj.*, quelques
fifteen, *adj.*, quinze
fifty, *adj.*, cinquante
fill, *v.t.*, remplir; plomber (of teeth)
finally, *adv.*, enfin, finalement
find, *v.t.*, trouver
to ——— out about, se renseigner sur
fine, *adj.*, beau (bel), *m.*, belle, *f.*
finish, *v.t.*, finir, terminer, achever
fireworks, *n.*, feu d'artifice, *m.*
firm, *n.*, maison, *f.*; *adj.*, ferme, solide
first, *adj.*, premier, -ère
fitting, *adj.*, convenable
five, *adj.*, cinq
floor, *n.*, étage (story), *m.*
flower, *n.*, fleur, *f.*
fly, *v.i.*, voler
folder, *n.*, chemise, *f.*
foot, *n.*, pied, *m.*
three feet long by two feet wide, trois pieds de long sur deux pieds de large
football, *n.*, football (the game); *m.*, ballon (the ball), *m.*
for, *prep.*, pour, depuis (with time expressions); *conj.*, car
forbid, *v.t.*, défendre
forget, *v.t.*, oublier
forty, *adj.*, quarante
found, *v.t.*, fonder, établir
fountain, *n.*, fontaine, *f.*
four, *adj.*, quatre
fourteen, *adj.*, quatorze
France, *n.*, France, *f.*
free, *adj.*, libre
freedom, *n.*, liberté, *f.*
French, *adj.*, français, -e; ——— (language), *n.*, français, *m.*
Frenchman, *n.*, français, *m.*; ———-woman, *n.*, Française, *f.*
fresh, *adj.*, frais, *m.*, fraîche, *f.*
friend, *n.*, ami, *m.*, amie, *f.*

front, *n.*, façade, *f.*, devant, *m.*
  in _____ of, devant
fulfill, *v.t.*, remplir, accomplir, exécuter
  to be _____ed, se réaliser
furious, *adj.*, furieux, -se
  to be _____, enrager
furnish, *v.t.*, fournir (provide); meubler (a room, etc.)

G

gain, *v.t.*, gagner
  _____ weight, prendre du poids
game, *n.*, jeu, *m.*, partie (match), *f.*
gangplank, *n.*, passerelle, *f.*
gargle, *v.i.*, se gargariser
gentleman, *n.*, monsieur (*plu.*, messieurs), *m.*
geometry, *n.*, géométrie, *f.*
German, *adj.*, allemand, -e; *n.m. and f.* Allemand, -e; *n.*, allemand (langage), *m.*
Germany, *n.*, Allemagne, *f.*
get, *v.t.*, obtenir, se procurer, devenir
  to _____ thin, maigrir
  to _____ a ticket, prendre un billet
  to _____ over, se rendre à
  to _____ up, se lever
  to _____ there, y parvenir
  to _____ out (of a conveyance), descendre
  to _____ something done, faire faire quelque chose
gift, *n.*, cadeau, *m.*
  Christmas _____, étrenne, *f.*
girl, *n.*, jeune fille, *f.*
  little _____, petite fille, *f.*, fillette, *f.*
give, *v.t.*, donner
  _____ back, rendre
  _____ up, renoncer à
  _____ an injection, faire une injection
  _____ a course, faire un cours
glad, *adj.*, content, -e, heureux, -se, joyeux, -se
glass, *n.*, verre, *m.*
go, *v.i.*, aller
  to _____ by, passer
  to _____ with, accompagner
  to _____ down, descendre
  to _____ out, sortir
  to _____ along, marcher
  to _____ back, retourner
  to _____ up, monter
God, *n.*, Dieu, *m.*
good, *adj.*, bon, -ne
  _____-by, au revoir
  _____ day, bonjour
  _____ evening, bonsoir
  _____ luck, bonne chance
  _____ morning, bonjour
grant, *v.t.*, accorder
great, *adj.*, grand, -e
green, *adj.*, vert, -e
guess, *v.t.*, deviner
guest, *n.*, invité, *m.*, invitée, *f.*

H

half, *adj.*, demi, -e; *n.*, moitié, *f.*
  a _____ hour, une demi-heure
hand, *n.*, main, *f.*
hang, *v.t.*, suspendre
happen, *v.i.*, arriver, se passer
happy, *adj.*, content, -e, heureux, -se
hard, *adj.*, dur, difficile
hardly, *adv.*, ne _____ guère, à peine
hat, *n.*, chapeau, *m.*
have, *v.t.*, avoir, posséder
  to _____ something done, faire + inf.
  to _____ to, avoir à, être obligé de, devoir, falloir (impersonal verb)
  to _____ a good time, se divertir, s'amuser
  to _____ dinner, dîner
  to _____ the tooth examined, faire examiner la dent
  to _____ just, venir de (+ *inf.*)
he, *pron.*, il, lui
head, *n.*, tête, *f.*
  to have a _____ache, avoir mal à la tête
health, *n.*, santé, *f.*
hear, *v.t.*, entendre
  to _____ (of), entendre parler de
heart, *n.*, coeur, *m.*
heat, *n.*, chaleur, *f.*
help, *v.t.*, aider
her, *poss. adj.*, son, sa, ses; *pron.*, elle, la
here, *adv.*, ici
  _____ is, voici
hers, *pron.*, le sien, la sienne, les siens, les siennes
him, *pron.*, le, lui
  to _____, lui
his, *poss. adj.*, son, sa, ses; *pron.*, le sien, la sienne, les siens, les siennes
history, *n.*, histoire, *f.*
hold, *v.t.*, tenir

hope, *v.t.*, espérer
hospital, *n.*, hôpital, *m.*
hot, *adj.*, chaud, -e
hour, *n.*, heure, *f.*
house, *n.*, maison, *f.*
how, *adv.*, comment
_____ long, depuis quand
_____ many, combien (de + noun)
_____ much, combien (de + noun)
however, *conj.*, cependant, pourtant; *adv.*, si _____ que, quelque _____ que
hundred, *adj. and n.*, cent, *m.*
hungry, *adj.*, affamé, -e
to be _____, avoir faim
hurry, *v.i.*, se dépêcher
husband, *n.*, mari, *m.*

I

I, *pron.*, je, moi
ice cream, *n.*, glace, *f.*
icicle, *n.*, glaçon, *m.*
idea, *n.*, idée, *f.*
if, *conj.*, si
imagine, *v.t.*, imaginer, s'imaginer, se faire une idée, se figurer
immediately, *adv.*, immédiatement, tout de suite
important, *adj.*, important, -e
impossible, *adj.*, impossible
in, *prep.*, en (within a certain time), dans (at the end of a certain time), à (located at)
_____ order to, pour
_____ front of, devant
indication, *n.*, indication, *f.*
injection, *n.*, injection, *f.*
inn, *n.*, auberge, *f.*
institution, *n.*, institution, *f.*
intelligent, *adj.*, intelligent, -e
intend, *v.i.*, avoir l'intention (de), compter
interesting, *adj.*, intéressant, -e
interpreter, *n.*, interprète, *m.*
interrupt, *v.t.*, interrompre
interruption, *n.*, interruption, *f.*
introduce, *v.t.*, présenter
invite, *v.t.*, inviter (à)
it, *pron.*, il, elle, le, la
Italian, *adj.*, italien, -ne; *n.m. and f.*, Italien, -ne; *n.*, italien (language), *m.*

J

January, *n.*, janvier, *m.*
Japan, *n.*, Japon, *m.*
jet, *n.*, jet, *m.*
joy, *n.*, joie, *f.*

K

keep, *v.t.*, garder
kick, *v.t.*, lancer (of a football)
kill, *v.t.*, tuer
kind, *adj.*, gentil, -le; aimable; bon, -ne; *n.*, sorte, *f.*, espèce, *f.*, genre, *m.*
know, *v.t.*, savoir (facts), connaître (to be acquainted with)
knowledge, *n.*, connaissance, *f.*, savoir, *m.*, science, *f.*

L

laboratory, *n.*, laboratoire, *m.*
lady, *n.*, dame, *f.*
lamb, *n.*, agneau, *m.*
_____ chop, côtelette (*f.*) d'agneau
lamp, *n.*, lampe, *f.*
land, *v.i.*, atterrir; *n.*, terre, *f.*
landing, *n.*, atterrissage, *m.*
language, *n.*, langue, *f.*
lantern, *n.*, lanterne, *f.*
large, *adj.*, grand, -e
last, *adj.*, dernier, -ère, passé,-e
late, *adv.*, en retard (for an appointment), tard (at an advanced hour)
laugh, *v.i.*, rire
lay, *v.t.*, mettre, poser
to _____ a hand on, mettre la main sur
lazy, *adj.*, paresseux, -se
learn, *v.t.*, apprendre
leave, *v.i.*, partir (to depart, go away), sortir (to go out), s'en aller (to go away); *v.t.*, quitter
lecturer, *n.*, conférencier, *m.*, conférencière, *f.*
left, *n.*, gauche, *f.*
on the _____, à gauche
lend, *v.t.*, prêter
less, *adv.*, moins
lesson, *n.*, leçon, *f.*
let, *v.t.*, laisser, permettre
to _____ know, faire savoir
letter, *n.*, lettre, *f.*
library, *n.*, bibliothèque, *f.*
life, *n.*, vie, *f.*

light, *v.t.*, allumer (to turn on light), illuminer (to light up); *n.*, lumière, *f.*; *adj.*, léger, -ère (in weight), clair (of colors)
like, *v.t.*, aimer, plaire à; *conj.*, comme
line, *n.*, ligne, *f.*
list, *n.*, liste, *f.*
listen, *v.t.*, écouter
literature, *n.*, littérature, *f.*
little, *adj.*, petit, -e
live, *v.i.*, habiter, demeurer, vivre
London, *n.*, Londres
long, *adj.*, long, -ue; *adv.*, longtemps
look, *n.*, regard, *m.*, air, *m.*
to ——— at, regarder
to ——— for, chercher
to ——— out on, donner sur
to ——— like, ressembler à
to ——— (to appear), avoir l'air (de)
loosen, *v.t.*, desserrer
lose, *v.t.*, perdre
to ——— weight, maigrir
lot, *n.*, tas, *m.*
a ——— of, pas mal de
love, *v.t.*, aimer
luck, *n.*, chance, *f.*
to be in ———, avoir de la chance
bad ———, guignon, *m.*

M

magnetic, *adj.*, magnétique
magnificent, *adj.*, magnifique
mail, *n.*, courrier, *m.*; *v.t.*, jeter dans la boîte aux lettres
major, *v.i.*, se spécialiser
——— in, se spécialiser en
make, *v.t.*, faire
man, *n.*, homme, *m.*
many, *adj.*, beaucoup de, pas mal de
March, *n.*, mars, *m.*
mathematics, *n.*, mathématiques, *f.pl.*
matter, *n.*, affaire, *f.*
to be a ——— of, s'agir de
What is the ——— with her?, Qu'a-t-elle?
no ———, n'importe
no ——— how, n'importe comment
no ——— where, n'importe où
no ——— who, n'importe qui
no ——— how (*adj. or adv.*), si (or quelque) (*adj. or adv.*) que
no ——— when, n'importe quand
May, *n.*, mai, *m.*
may, *aux. v.*, pouvoir
it ——— be that, il se peut que
me, *pron.*, me, moi
meal, *n.*, repas, *m.*
meet, *v.t.*, rencontrer (by chance); retrouver, se réunir (by previous appointment)
to go and ———, aller à la rencontre de, aller au devant de
menu, *n.*, carte, *f.*
merchant, *n.*, marchand, *m.*
Mexico, *n.*, Mexique, *m.*
middle, *n.*, milieu, *m.*
milk, *n.*, lait, *m.*
million, *n.*, million, *m.*
one ——— books, un million de livres
mine, *pron.*, le mien, la mienne, les miens, les miennes
minute, *n.*, minute, *f.*
miserable, *adj.*, misérable
Miss, *n.*, Mademoiselle (*abbrev.* Mlle) *f.*
mistake, *n.*, faute, *f.*
molar, *n.*, molaire, *f.*
moment, *n.*, moment, *m.*, instant, *m.*
Monday, *n.*, lundi, *m.*
money, *n.*, argent, *m.*, monnaie (currency, change), *f.*
month, *n.*, mois, *m.*
more, *adv.*, plus (de + *noun*), davantage
morning, *n.*, matin, *m.*
Moscow, *n.*, Moscou
most, *n.*, plupart (de), *f.*; *adv.*, plus
the ——— beautiful book, le plus beau livre
a ——— beautiful book, un livre des plus beaux
mother, *n.*, mère, *f.*
motive, *n.*, mobile, *m.*
mountain, *n.*, montagne, *f.*
Mr., *n.*, Monsieur (*abbrev.*, M.), *m.*
Mrs., *n.*, Madame (*abbrev.*, Mme), *f.*
much, *adv.*, beaucoup
murder, *n.*, meurtre, *m.*; *v.t.*, assassiner
museum, *n.*, musée, *m.*
music, *n.*, musique, *f.*
must, *aux. v.*, devoir, falloir, avoir à, être obligé de (obligation), devoir (conjecture and obligation)
my, *poss. adj.*, mon, ma, mes

N

name, *n.*, nom, *m.*; *v.t.*, nommer
my ——— is, je m'appelle

native, *adj.*, natal, -e
natural, *adj.*, naturel, -le
naturally, *adv.*, naturellement
near, *adv.*, près; *prep.*, près de
nearly, *adv.*, presque, à peu près
necessary, *adj.*, nécessaire
to be ______, falloir, être nécessaire
need, *v.t.*, avoir besoin de, falloir à, manquer à
neighborhood, *n.*, voisinage, *m.*
neither, *conj.*, ni, non plus; *pron.*, ni l'un(e) ni l'autre
never, *adv.*, ne ______ jamais
new, *adj.*, nouveau (nouvel), -nouvelle
newspaper, *n.*, journal, *m.*
next, *adj.*, prochain, -e, suivant, -e, d'à côté; *adv.*, à côté
night, *n.*, nuit, *f.*
nine, *adj.*, neuf
nineteen, *adj.*, dix-neuf
ninety, *adj.*, quatre-vingt-dix
no, *adv.*, non
nobody, *pron.*, personne
noise, *n.*, bruit, *m.*
no longer, *adv.*, ne ______ plus
noon, *n.*, midi, *m.*
not, *adv.*, ne ______ pas, pas
______ at all, ne ______ point
______ anything, ne ______ rien
nothing, *n.*, rien, *m.*
novel, *n.*, roman, *m.*
now, *adv.*, maintenant, à présent
number, *n.*, numéro, *m.*, nombre, *m.*, chiffre (figure), *m.*

O

obey, *v.t.*, obéir (à)
observe, *v.t.*, observer
obtain, *v.t.*, obtenir, se procurer
occasion, *n.*, occasion, *f.*
of, *prep.*, de
______ course, bien entendu
offer, *v.t.*, offrir
office, *n.*, bureau, *m.*
often, *adv.*, souvent
old, *adj.*, vieux (vieil), *m.*, vieille, *f.*; ancien, -ne, âgé, -e
He is ten years ______. Il a dix ans.
on, *prep.*, sur
once, *adv.*, une fois
one, *adj.*, un, -e; *pron.*, on
______ another, se; l'un(e) l'autre; les un(e)s les autres
the ______, celui (celle)
the ______s, ceux (celles)
only, *adv.*, seulement, ne ______ que; *adj.*, seul, -e
open, *v.t.*, ouvrir; *adj.*, ouvert, -e
or, *conj.*, ou
order, *v.t.*, commander; *n.*, ordre, *m.*, commande, *f.*
original, *adj.*, original, -e
other, *adj.*, autre
our, *poss. adj.*, notre (*sing.*), nos (*plu.*)
ours, *pron.*, le nôtre, la nôtre, les nôtres
owe, *v.t.*, devoir
own, *adj.*, propre; *v.t.*, posséder, avoir

P

page, *n.*, page, *f.*
paper, *n.*, papier, *m.*, journal (newspaper), *m.*
______bound, broché
______ clip, trombone, *m.*
carbon ______, papier carbone, *m.*
typing ______, papier pour machine à écrire
parent, *n.*, parent, *m.*
part, *n.*, partie, *f.*
pass, *v.t.*, passer
passenger, *n.*, voyageur, *m.*
pay, *v.t.*, payer
peace, *n.*, paix, *f.*
peak, *n.*, pic, *m.*, sommet, *m.*
pen, *n.*, stylo, *m.*
pencil, *n.*, crayon, *m.*
pension, *n.*, pension, *f.*
people, *n.*, gens, *m.pl.*
perfect, *adj.*, parfait, -e
perhaps, *adv.*, peut-être
permit, *v.t.*, permettre
pie, *n.*, tarte, *f.*
apple ______, tarte aux pommes
piece, *n.*, morceau, *m.*
______ of furniture, meuble, *m.*
pilot, *n.*, pilote, *m.*
place, *n.*, endroit, *m.*, lieu, *m.*
plane, *n.*, avion, *m.*
play, *n.*, pièce, *f.*; *v.t.*, jouer (à + game; de + instrument)
player, *n.*, joueur, *m.*
pleasant, *adj.*, agréable
pleasantly, *adv.*, agréablement
please, *v.t.*, plaire à
if you ______, s'il vous plaît

pleasure, *n.*, plaisir, *m.*
plot, *n.*, intrigue, *f.*
pocket, *n.*, poche, *f.*
poetry, *n.*, poésie, *f.*
police, *n.*, police, *f.*
poor, *adj.*, pauvre
Portugal, *n.*, Portugal, *m.*
position, *n.*, poste, *m.*
possible, *adj.*, possible
post office, *n.*, bureau (*m.*) de poste
pray, *v.t.*, prier
precious, *adj.*, précieux, -se
prefer, *v.t.*, préférer
prepare, *v.t.*, préparer
pretty, *adj.*, joli, -e
prevent, *v.t.*, empêcher
prize, *v.t.*, estimer; *n.*, prix, *m.*
professor, *n.*, professeur, *m.*
program, *n.*, programme, *m.*
promenade, *n.*, promenade, *f.*
promise, *v.t.*, promettre; *n.*, promesse, *f.*
promote, *v.t.*, promouvoir
pronounce, *v.t.*, prononcer
pronunciation, *n.*, prononciation, *f.*
provided that, *conj.*, pourvu que
put, *v.t.*, mettre, placer
 ——— off, remettre

Q

question, *n.*, question, *f.*; *v.t.*, interroger
quiet, *adj.*, tranquille
quite, *adv.*, tout, tout à fait
 ——— a few, pas mal de

R

rain, *n.*, pluie, *f.*
rainbow, *n.*, arc-en-ciel, *m.*
rapid, *adj.*, rapide
rapidly, *adv.*, rapidement
reach, *v.t.*, arriver à, parvenir à
read, *v.t.*, lire
reading, *n.*, lecture, *f.*
ready, *adj.*, prêt, -e
realize, *v.t.*, se rendre compte de (to comprehend), réaliser (to cause to materialize)
really, *adv.*, vraiment
ream, *n.*, rame, *f.*
rear, *adj.*, (d')arrière
 in the ———, en arrière
reason, *n.*, raison, *f.*
receive, *v.t.*, recevoir
recognize, *v.t.*, reconnaître
recommend, *v.t.*, recommander
record, *n.*, disque, *m.*; *v.t.*, enregistrer
recording, *n.*, enregistrement, *m.*
recover, *v.i.*, se remettre
red, *adj.*, rouge
reflect, *v.i.*, réfléchir (to ponder); *v.t.*, refléter (to throw back light)
refreshments, *n.*, rafraîchissements, *m.*
refuge, *n.*, refuge, *m.*
 to take ———, se réfugier
refuse, *v.t.*, refuser
relative, *n.*, parent, *m.*
remember, *v.t.*, se souvenir de, se rappeler
remind, *v.t.*, rappeler, faire penser à
 That ———s me of my country. Cela me rappelle (fait penser) à mon pays.
repair, *v.t.*, réparer; *n.*, réparation, *f.*
repairman, *n.*, dépanneur, *m.*
report, *n.*, rapport, *m.*
reputation, *n.*, réputation, *f.*
required, *adj.*, obligatoire, requis, -e
respond, *v.t.*, répondre (à + *noun*)
rest, *v.i.*, se reposer; *n.m.*, repos
 to ——— one's voice, se reposer la voix
restaurant, *n.*, restaurant, *m.*
return, *v.i.*, retourner (go back), revenir (come back); *v.t.*, rendre (give back)
ribbon, *n.*, ruban, *m.*
 typewriter ———, ruban de machine à écrire
rich, *adj.*, riche
right, *n.*, droite, *f.*; droit, *m.*
 on the ———, à droite
 to be ———, avoir raison
ring, *v.i.*, sonner; *n.*, anneau, *m.*
room, *n.*, chambre (bedroom), *f.*; salle (room for community living), *f.*; pièce (division of a house or apartment), *f.*
 class———, salle de classe
 dining ———, salle à manger
 double ———, chambre à deux personnes
 waiting ———, salle d'attente
rug, *n.*, tapis, *m.*
run, *v.i.*, courir
runway, *n.*, piste (*f.*) de décollage
Russia, *n.*, Russie, *f.*
Russian, *adj.*, russe; *n.m. and f.*, Russe; *n.*, russe (language), *m.*

S

sad, *adj.*, triste
salary, *n.*, salaire, *m.*
save, *v.t.*, sauver (preserve), économiser (economize)
say, *v.t.*, dire
scarcely, *adv.*, à peine, ne _____ guère
scene, *n.*, scène, *f.*
seat, *v.t.*, asseoir; *n.*, place, *f.*
to be _____ed (to sit down), s'asseoir
to be _____ed (to be sitting down), être assis
secretary, *n.*, secrétaire, *m. and f.*
see, *v.t.*, voir
seem, *v.i.*, sembler, paraître, avoir l'air (de)
seize, *v.t.*, saisir
select, *v.t.*, choisir
sell, *v.t.*, vendre
send, *v.t.*, envoyer, expédier
to _____ for, envoyer chercher, faire venir
sentence, *n.*, phrase, *f.*
September, *n.*, septembre, *m.*
serve, *v.t.*, servir
set, *n.*, appareil, *m.*
seven, *adj.*, sept
seventeen, *adj.*, dix-sept
seventy, *adj.*, soixante-dix
several, *adj.*, plusieurs
she, *pron.*, elle
short, *adj.*, court, -e
show, *v.t.*, montrer, faire voir, indiquer, faire remarquer
shut, *v.t.*, fermer
sick, *adj.*, malade, souffrant, -e
simple, *adj.*, simple, facile
since, *prep.*, depuis (time); *conj.*, puisque (reason)
sing, *v.t.*, chanter
sir, *n.*, monsieur, *m.*
sister, *n.*, soeur, *f.*
six, *adj.*, six
sixteen, *adj.*, seize
sixty, *adj.*, soixante
skate, *v.i.*, patiner; *n.*, patin, *m.*
sketch, *n.*, dessin, *m.*
sky, *n.*, ciel, *m.*
sleep, *v.i.*, dormir
slope, *n.*, pente, *f.*
small, *adj.*, petit, -e
smart, *adj.*, calé, -e (clever), chic (stylish)
smile, *v.i.*, sourire; *n.*, sourire, *m.*
snow, *v.i.*, neiger; *n.*, neige, *f.*
snowy, *adj.*, neigeux, -se
so, *adv.*, si, tellement; alors, donc
_____ as to, afin de, de façon à
_____ that, afin que, de sorte que, de façon que
_____ much, tant, tellement
soil, *v.t.*, salir
solve, *v.t.*, résoudre
some, *adj.*, du, de la, des, de, quelques; *pron.*, quelques-un(e)s
_____day, un jour
_____ holiday or other, une fête quelconque
something, *pron.*, quelquechose
_____ good, quelquechose de bon
_____ to eat, quelquechose à manger
sometimes, *adv.*, quelquefois, parfois
somewhere, *adv.*, quelque part
soon, *adv.*, bientôt
sorry, *adj.*, fâché, -e, triste
to be _____, regretter
soul, *n.*, âme, *f.*
sound, *n.*, son, *m.*; *adj.*, sain, -e
South America, *n.*, Amérique du Sud, *f.*
southern, *adj.*, méridional, -e
Spain, *n.*, Espagne, *f.*
Spaniard, *n.*, Espagnol, -e
Spanish, *adj.*, espagnol, -e; *n.*, espagnol (language), *m.*
speak, *v.t. and i.*, parler
spend, *v.t.*, passer (time), dépenser (money)
spinach, *n.*, épinards, *m.pl.*
spread, *v.t.*, répandre; *v.i.*, se répandre
spring, *n.*, printemps, *m.*
stab, *v.t.*, poignarder
stain, *n.*, tache, *f.*
start, *v.t.*, commencer, se mettre à
stay, *v.i.*, rester
to _____ at home, rester à la maison
steep, *adj.*, raide
still, *adv.*, encore, toujours
stop, *v.t.*, arrêter, cesser
to _____, s'arrêter
store, *n.*, magasin, *m.*
stationery _____, papeterie, *f.*
storm, *n.*, tempête, *f.*
story, *n.*, histoire, *f.*

strong, *adj.*, fort, -e
student, *n.*, étudiant, *m.*, étudiante, *f.*
study, *v.t.*, étudier
succeed, *v.i.*, réussir (à); succéder (to follow in succession)
succumb, *v.i.*, succomber
such, *adj.*, tel, -le
 ——— a story, une telle histoire
 ——— a short story, une si courte histoire
sudden, *adj.*, soudain, -e, brusque, subit, -e
suddenly, *adv.*, subitement, soudainement, tout à coup
summer, *n.*, été, *m.*
sun, *n.*, soleil, *m.*
sure, *adj.*, sûr, -e, certain, -e
sweet, *adj.*, doux, *m.*, douce, *f.*
swim, *v.t. and i.*, nager
 ———ming pool, piscine, *f.*
Switzerland, *n.*, Suisse, *f.*

T

table, *n.*, table, *f.*
take, *v.t.*, prendre, occuper, falloir (time)
 to ——— out, sortir
 to ——— refuge, se réfugier
 to ——— one's bearings, s'orienter
 to ——— off (aviation), décoller
taken, *adj.*, occupé, -e
take-off, *n.*, décollage, *m.*; *v.i.*, décoller
tape, *n.*, bande, *f.*
tea, *n.*, thé, *m.*
teach, *v.t.*, enseigner
team, *n.*, équipe, *f.*
tease, *v.t.*, taquiner
telephone, *n.*, téléphone, *m.*; *v.t.*, téléphoner
 ——— booth, cabine téléphonique
 ——— call, coup (*m.*) de téléphone
tell, *v.t.*, dire, raconter (to narrate)
 to ——— someone all about it, en dire les nouvelles à
ten, *adj.*, dix
tenant, *n.*, locataire, *m.*
tent, *n.*, tente, *f.*
term paper *n.*, travail, *m.*
than, *conj.*, que
thank, *v.t.*, remercier
 ——— you, merci
Thanksgiving Day, *n.*, Jour (*m.*) d'Actions de grâces
that, *conj.*, que; *rel. pron.*, qui, que; *demon. adj.*, ce, cet, cette; *demon. pron.*, celui, celle, (*neuter form*) cela (familiar, ça)
the, *def. art.*, le, la, l', les
theater, *n.*, théâtre, *m.*
their, *poss. adj.*, leur, leurs
theirs, *pron.*, le leur, la leur, les leurs
them, *pron.*, les
 to ———, leur
then, *adv.*, puis, ensuite, alors
there, *adv.*, là, y
 ——— is, voilà, il y a
 ——— are, voilà, il y a
 ——— it is, le voilà
 ——— they are, les voilà
therefore, *adv.*, alors, donc
these, *adj.*, ces; *pron.*, ceux-ci, celles-ci
they, *pron.*, ils, elles, eux
thing, *n.*, chose, *f.*
think, *v.i.*, penser, croire
 to ——— of one's vacation, penser à ses vacances (to turn attention to)
 to ——— of the criminal, penser du criminel (judgment)
thirst, *n.*, soif, *f.*
 to be thirsty, avoir soif
thirteen, *adj.*, treize
thirty, *adj.*, trente
this, *adj.*, ce, cet, cette; *pron.*, celui-ci, celle-ci, ceci (*neuter*)
those, *adj.*, ces; *pron.*, ceux-là, celles-là
thousand, *adj.*, mille, mil (in dates)
three, *adj.*, trois
thrilling, *adj.*, palpitant, -e, émouvant, -e
throw, *v.t.*, jeter, lancer
Thursday, *n.*, jeudi, *m.*
ticket, *n.*, billet, *m.*
 ——— window, guichet, *m.*
 to get a ———, prendre un billet
 round-trip ———, billet d'aller et retour
time, *n.*, temps (duration), *m.*; fois (occasion), *f.*; heure (clock time), *f.*; époque (period), *f.*
 What ——— is it? Quelle heure est-il?
tip, *n.*, pourboire (gratuity), *m.*
to, *prep.*, à
today, *adv.*, aujourd'hui
 ——— is February 11, c'est aujourd'hui le 11 février
together, *adv.*, ensemble
tomorrow, *adv.*, demain

too, *adv.*, aussi
_____ many, trop (de)
_____ much, trop (de)
It's _____ bad. C'est dommage.
tooth, *n.*, dent, *f.*
to have a _____ache, avoir mal aux dents
toward, *prep.*, vers, envers
travel, *v.t.*, voyager
trip, *n.*, voyage, *m.*, trajet (short trip), *m.*
trouble, *n.*, peine, *f.*, difficulté, *f.*; *v.t.*, inquiéter, troubler
troupe, *n.*, troupe, *f.*
true, *adj.*, vrai, -e
truth, *n.*, vérité, *f.*
try, *v.t.*, essayer (de), tâcher (de)
Tuesday, *n.*, mardi, *m.*
turkey, *n.*, dinde, *f.*
turn, *v.t.*, tourner
to _____ around, se retourner
to _____ over, renverser
twelve, *adj.*, douze
twenty, *adj.*, vingt
two, *adj.*, deux
type, *v.t.*, taper (à la machine)
typing, *n.*, dactylographie, *f.*

U

ugly, *adj.*, laid, -e
understand, *v.t.*, comprendre
to _____ about, comprendre à
undertake, *v.t.*, entreprendre
unhappy, *adj.*, malheureux, -se, triste
United States, *n.*, États-Unis, *m.plu.*
university, *n.*, université, *f.*; *adj.*, universitaire
unless, *prep.*, à moins de; *conj.*, à moins que
until, *prep.*, jusqu'à; *conj.*, jusqu'à ce que
upset, *v.t.*, renverser
us, *pron.*, nous
use, *v.t.*, employer, se servir de, utiliser
used, *adj.*, d'occasion; *past part.*, servi, employé
useful, *adj.*, utile
useless, *adj.*, inutile
usually, *adv.*, d'habitude, d'ordinaire

V

valise, *n.*, valise, *f.*
very, *adv.*, très, fort, bien
viewer, *n.*, téléspectateur, *m.*, téléspectatrice, *f.*
village, *n.*, village, *m.*
visit, *v.t.*, visiter
voice, *n.*, voix, *f.*
vowel, *n.*, voyelle, *f.*

W

wait (for), *v.t.*, attendre
waiter, *n.*, garçon, *m.*
want, *v.t.*, vouloir, désirer
war, *n.*, guerre, *f.*
warm, *adj.*, chaud, -e
wash, *v.t.*, laver
water, *n.*, eau, *f.*
wave, *n.*, vague, *f.*, onde, *f.*; *v.i.*, faire signe de la main
way, *n.*, chemin, *m.*, route, *f.*; moyen (means), *m.*, façon (means), *f.*
we, *pron.*, nous
weapon, *n.*, arme, *f.*
wear, *v.t.*, porter
Wednesday, *n.*, mercredi, *m.*
week, *n.*, semaine, *f.*
welcome, *v.t.*, accueillir; *n.*, accueil, *m.*, bienvenue, *f.*; *adj.*, bienvenu, -e
well, *adv.*, bien
_____ known, bien connu, -e
what, *adj.*, quel(le), quel(le)s; *interr. pron.*, que, qu'est-ce qui, qu'est-ce que, quoi; *comp. pron.*, ce qui, ce que
whatever, *pron.*, quoi que; *adj.*, quel(le)(s) que, quelconque
when, *conj.*, quand, lorsque; *adv.*, quand
where, *adv.*, où
whereas, *conj.*, tandis que
which, *rel. pron.*, qui, que, lequel (laquelle, lesquels, lesquelles); *interr. pron.*, lequel (laquelle, lesquels, lesquelles); *interr. adj.*, quel (quelle, quels, quelles)
while, *conj.*, pendant que (time), tandis que (whereas)
white, *adj.*, blanc, -blanche
who, *rel. pron.*, qui, lequel (laquelle, lesquels, lesquelles); *interr. pron.*, qui, qui est-ce qui
whoever, *pron.*, quiconque, qui que
whole, *adj.*, tout, -e, entier, -ère; *n.*, tout, *m.*
whom, *rel. pron.*, que, lequel (laquelle,

lesquels, lesquelles); *interr. pron.*, qui, qui est-ce que
whose, *pron.*, dont, de qui, duquel (de laquelle, desquels, desquelles)
why, *adv.*, pourquoi
wide, *adj.*, large
wife, *n.*, femme, *f.*, épouse, *f.*
wine, *n.*, vin, *m.*
wing, *n.*, aile, *f.*
winter, *n.*, hiver, *m.*
wish, *v.t.*, souhaiter, désirer, vouloir
with, *prep.*, avec (accompaniment), à (characteristic)
without, *prep.*, sans; *conj.*, sans que
woman, *n.*, femme, *f.*
wonder, *v.i.*, se demander
word, *n.*, mot, *m.*, parole, *f.*
work, *v.i.*, travailler; *n.* travail, *m.*
world, *n.*, monde, *m.*
worse, *adj.*, pire; *adv.*, pis
worth, *n.*, valeur, *f.*; *adj.*, qui vaut
 to be ____ the trouble, valoir la peine (de)
write, *v.t.*, écrire
writer, *n.*, écrivain, *m.*
written, *past. part.*, écrit, -e
wrong, *n.*, tort, *m.*
 to be ____, avoir tort

X

X-ray, *v.t.*, radiographier; *n.*, radiographie, *f.*

Y

year, *n.*, an, *m.*; année, *f.*
yellow, *adj.*, jaune
yes, *adv.*, oui, si
yesterday, *adv.*, hier
yet, *adv.*, encore, cependant (however)
you, *pron.*, vous, tu, te, toi
young, *adj.*, jeune
your, *adj.*, votre, vos, ton, ta, tes
yours, *pron.*, le vôtre, la vôtre, les vôtres; le tien, les tiens, la tienne, les tiennes
yourself, *pron.*, vous, vous - même
youth, *n.*, jeunesse, *f.*

VOCABULARY

French – English

A

à [a], *prep.*, at, to, in; with (to express a characteristic)
abandonné, -e [abɑ̃dɔne], *adj.*, abandoned
abord [abɔ:r], *n.m.*, approach
  d'______, first, at first
  tout d'______, first of all
absent [apsɑ̃], absente [apsɑ̃:t], *adj.*, absent, away
absolu, -e [apsɔly], *adj.*, absolute
absolument [apsɔlymɑ̃], *adv.*, absolutely
accompagner [akɔ̃paɲe], *v.t.*, to accompany
accorder [akɔrde], *v.t.*, to grant
  s'______, to agree
achat [aʃa], *n.m.*, purchase
  faire des ______, to go shopping
acheter [aʃte], *v.t.*, to buy
acquérir [akeri:r], *v.t.*, to acquire
acteur [aktœ:r], *n.m.*, actor
action [aksjɔ̃], *n.f.*, action
actrice [aktris], *n.f.*, actress
actualité [aktyalite], *n.f.*, actuality (event of the moment)
actuel, -le [aktyɛl], *adj.*, present
admiration [admirasjɔ̃], *n.f.*, admiration
admirer [admire], *v.t.*, to admire
adopter [adɔpte], *v.t.*, to adopt
adresse [adrɛs], *n.f.*, address
adversaire [advɛrsɛ:r], *n.m.*, opponent
affaire [afɛ:r], *n.f.*, affair, matter; *pl.*, business
  faire l'______, to do, to serve the purpose, to do the trick
affecté, -e [afɛkte], *adj.*, affected, conceited
affiler [afile], *v.t.*, to sharpen
afin de [afɛ̃ də], *prep.*, in order to; afin que, *conj.*, in order that
Afrique [afrik], *n.f.*, Africa
âge [ɑ:ʒ], *n.m.*, age
  Quel ______ avez-vous? How old are you?
âgé, -e [ɑʒe], *adj.*, old
agilité [aʒilite], *n.f.*, agility
agir [aʒi:r], *v.i.*, to act
  il s'agit de, it is a question of
agréable [agreabl], *adj.*, pleasant
aider [ɛde], *v.t.*, to help
aile [ɛl], *n.f.*, wing
aimable [ɛmabl], *adj.*, kind
aimer [ɛme], *v.t.*, to like, to love
ainsi [ɛ̃si], *adv.*, thus, so
air [ɛ:r], *n.m.*, air, appearance
  en plein ______, in the open air
  dans l'______, in the air
ajuster [aʒyste], *v.t.*, to adjust
algèbre [alʒɛbr], *n.f.*, algebra
Allemagne [almaɲ], *n.f.*, Germany
allemand [almɑ̃], allemande [almɑ̃:d], *adj.*, German; *n.m.*, German (language)
Allemand [almɑ̃], Allemande [almɑ̃:d], *n.m. and f.*, German (person)
aller [ale], *v.i.*, to go; to suit; to fit
  Comment allez-vous? How are you?
  Comment ça va? How goes it?
  Ça va. Everything is all right.
  ______ chercher, to go and get
  s'en ______, to go away, to be off
allumer [alyme], *v.t.*, to light (up)
alors [alɔ:r], *adv.*, then, therefore
alpenstock [alpɛnstɔk], *n.m.*, alpenstock (climbing stick used in the Alps)
alpestre [alpɛstr], *adj.*, alpine
alpiniste [alpinist], *n.m.*, alpine climber
amateur [amatœ:r], *n.m.*, amateur, devotee, enthusiast, fan
  ______ de sports, sports enthusiast
âme [ɑ:m], *n.f.*, soul
améliorer [ameljɔre], *v.t.*, to improve
américain [amerikɛ̃], américaine [amerikɛn], *adj.*, American
Américain [amerikɛ̃], Américaine [amerikɛn], *n.m. and f.*, American (person)
Amérique [amerik], *n.f.*, America

Amérique du Sud [amerik dy syd], *n.f.*, South America
ami, -e [ami], *n.m. and f.*, friend
à moins de [a mwɛ̃ də], *prep.*, unless; à moins que, *conj.*, unless
amusant [amyzɑ̃], amusante [amyzɑ̃:t], *adj.*, amusing, funny
amuser [amyze], *v.t.*, to amuse
s'_____, to have a good time
an [ɑ̃], *n.m.*, year
ancien [ɑ̃sjɛ̃], ancienne [ɑ̃sjɛn], *adj.*, old, ancient, former
ange [ɑ̃:ʒ], *n.m.*, angel
anglais [ɑ̃glɛ], anglaise [ɑ̃glɛ:z], *adj.*, English; *n.m.*, English (language)
Anglais [ɑ̃glɛ], Anglaise [ɑ̃glɛ:z], *n.m. and f.*, Englishman, Englishwoman
Angleterre [ɑ̃glətɛ:r], *n.f.*, England
année [ane], *n.f.*, year
annonce [anɔ̃:s], *n.f.*, advertisement
les petites _____s, the classified ads
annoncer [anɔ̃se], *v.t.*, to announce
antenne [ɑ̃tɛn], *n.f.*, antenna
anthologie [ɑ̃tɔlɔʒi], *n.f.*, anthology
août [u], *n.m.*, August
appareil [aparɛ:j], *n.m.*, apparatus, set
_____ photographique, camera
appeler [aple], *v.t.*, to call
s'_____ to be called, named
apporter [apɔrte], *v.t.*, to bring
apprécier [apresje], *v.t.*, to appreciate
apprêter [aprɛte], *v.t.*, to make ready, to prepare
apprendre [aprɑ̃:dr], *v.t.*, to learn
appuyer [apyije], *v.t.*, to support; to second (parliamentary procedure)
après [aprɛ], *prep.*, after; *adv.*, afterward
après-midi [aprɛmidi], *n.m. or f.*, afternoon
argent [arʒɑ̃], *n.m.*, money
arracher [araʃe], *v.t.*, to extract
arranger [arɑ̃ʒe], *v.t.*, to arrange
s'_____, to be arranged
arrêter [arɛte], *v.t.*, to stop
s'_____, to stop
arrière [arjɛ:r], *adv.*, backward
en _____, behind, back
arriver [arive], *v.i.*, to arrive, to happen
art [a:r], *n.m.*, art
article [artikl], *n.m.*, article
artificiel, -le [artifisjɛl], *adj.*, artificial
Asie [azi], *n.f.*, Asia
aspirine [aspirin], *n.f.*, aspirin
asseoir [aswa:r], *v.t.*, to seat
s'_____, to sit down
assez [ase], *adv.*, enough (with de + a noun); rather
assiette [asjɛ:t], *n.f.*, plate
assister [asiste], *v.t.*, to assist
_____ à, to attend
assurer [asyre], *v.t.*, to assure
s'_____, to make sure
atmosphère [atmɔsfɛ:r], *n.f.*, atmosphere
attabler [atable], *v.t.*, to seat at a table
s'_____, to sit down at a table
attaquer [atake], *v.t.*, to attack, to assault
attendre [atɑ̃:dr], *v.t.*, to wait (for)
en attendant, meanwhile, while waiting
attente [atɑ̃:t], *n.f.*, wait, waiting
attention [atɑ̃sjɔ̃], *n.f.*, attention
faire _____, to pay attention
atterrir [atɛri:r], *v.i.*, to land (aviation)
atterrissage [atɛrisa:ʒ], *n.m.*, landing (aviation)
attirer [atire], *v.t.*, to attract
attraper [atrape], *v.t.*, to catch
au [o] (contraction of *à le*), to the, at the
aubaine [obɛn], *n.f.*, windfall
auberge [obɛ:rʒ], *n.f.*, inn
aucun [okœ̃], aucune [okyn], *pron.*, none, no one, not any; *adj.*, no, not any
aujourd'hui (oʒurdyi], *adv.*, today
auspices [ɔspis], *n.m.pl.*, auspices, sponsorship
aussi [osi], *adv.*, also, too
_____ grand que, as tall as
aussitôt [osito], *adv.*, at once, immediately
_____ que, as soon as
autant [otɑ̃], *adv.*, as much, so much, as many, so many (with de + a noun)
d'_____ plus que, all the more since
auteur [otœ:r], *n.m.*, author
autour [otu:r], *adv.*, around
_____ de, *prep.*, around
autre [o:tr], *adj. and pron.*, other
autrefois [otrəfwa], *adv.*, formerly
autrui [otrɥi], *pron.*, others, other people
aux [o] (contraction of *à les*), to the, at the

avant [avɑ̃], *prep.*, before
  ——— de (+ *inf.*), before (———ing)
  ——— que, *conj.*, before
  en ———, forward
avare [ava:r], *n.m.*, miser
avec [avɛk], *prep.*, with
avertir [avɛrti:r], *v.t.*, to warn, to give notice of
avion [avjɔ̃], *n.m.*, airplane
  l'——— de six heures, the six-o'clock plane
  par ———, by plane, air mail
avoir [avwa:r], *v.t.*, to have
  ——— à, to have to
  ——— (dix, vingt, etc.) ans, to be (ten, twenty, etc.) years old
  ——— beau (+ *inf.*), to be useless for someone (+ *inf.*), to do something in vain
  ——— besoin de, to need, to have need of
  ——— bonne mine, to look good
  ——— chaud, to be warm (of persons)
  ——— de la chance, to be lucky
  ——— des nouvelles de, to hear from, have news of
  ——— envie de, to feel like, to care to, to want to
  ——— faim, to be hungry
  ——— froid, to be cold (of persons)
  ——— honte de, to be ashamed of
  ——— la bonté de, to be kind enough to
  ——— l'air de, to seem, to appear to, to look like (as though)
  ——— l'habitude de, to be used to, to be accustomed to
  ——— lieu, to take place
  ——— l'intention de, to intend to
  ——— l'occasion de, to have the opportunity to
  ——— mal à, to have a ———ache
  ——— peine à, to find it hard to
  ——— peur, to be afraid
  ——— pitié de, to take pity on
  ——— quelque chose, to have something the matter with one
  ——— raison, to be right
  ——— soif, to be thirsty
  ——— sommeil, to be sleepy
avouer [avwe], *v.t.*, to admit, to confess
avril [avril], *n.m.*, April

B

balbutier [balbysje], *v.i.*, to stammer, to stutter
baliverne [balivɛrn], *n.f.*, nonsense, humbug
ballet [balɛ], *n.m.*, ballet
ballon [balɔ̃], *n.m.*, football
bande [bɑ̃:d], *n.f.*, tape
bandit [bɑ̃di], *n.m.*, bandit
banquet [bɑ̃kɛ], *n.m.*, banquet
bâtir [bɑti:r], *v.t.*, to build
beau [bo], belle [bɛl], *adj.*, beautiful
beaucoup [boku], *adv.*, much, many (with de + a noun)
beauté [bote], *n.f.*, beauty
bénédiction [benediksjɔ̃], *n.f.*, blessing
besoin [bəzwɛ̃], *n.m.*, need
  avoir ——— de, to need
bêtise [beti:z], *n.f.*, stupidity, absurdity
bibliographie [bibliɔgrafi], *n.f.*, bibliography
bibliothécaire [bibliɔtekɛ:r], *n.m. and f.*, librarian
bibliothèque [bibliɔtɛk], *n.f.*, library, bookcase
bien [bjɛ̃], *adv.*, well, very, quite, indeed, much, many; *n.m.*, property, wealth
  ——— du (de la, des), much, many
  ——— que, although
  c'est ———, that's right
  très ———, very well, fine
bientôt [bjɛ̃to], *adv.*, soon
  à ———, see you soon
bijou [biʒu], *n.m.*, jewel
bijouterie [biʒutri], *n.f.*, jewelry
bilingue [bilɛ̃:g], *adj.*, bilingual
billet [bijɛ], *n.m.*, ticket, bill (monetary)
  prendre un ———, to get a ticket
  ——— d'aller et retour, round-trip ticket
  ——— de dix dollars, ten-dollar bill
blanc [blɑ̃], blanche [blɑ̃:ʃ], *adj.*, white
blancheur [blɑ̃ʃœ:r], *n.f.*, whiteness
bleu, -e [blø], *adj.*, blue
bloqué, -e [blɔke], *adj.*, blocked
boire [bwa:r], *v.t.*, to drink
boisson [bwasɔ̃], *n.f.*, drink, beverage
  une ——— non-alcoolique, a soft drink
boîte [bwat], *n.f.*, box
  ——— aux lettres, letter box

bol [bɔl], *n.m.*, bowl
bon [bɔ̃], bonne [bɔn], *adj.*, good, kind; *interj.*, all right, okay, fine, very well
bondé, -e [bɔ̃de], *adj.*, crowded, packed
bonjour [bɔ̃ʒu:r], *n.m. and interj.*, good day, good morning, good afternoon
bonsoir [bɔ̃swa:r], *n.m. and interj.*, good evening, good night
bonté [bɔ̃te], *n.f.*, kindness, goodness
bord [bɔ:r], *n.m.*, edge, brink, border
à ——, on board
bouillabaisse [bujabɛs], *n.f.*, fish soup
bourgeois [burʒwa], bourgeoise [burʒwaz], *adj.*, middle class, bourgeois
bout [bu], *n.m.*, end
au —— de, at the end of, after
boutique [butik], *n.f.*, shop
bras [brɑ], *n.m.*, arm
bref [brɛf], brève [brɛ:v], *adj.*, brief
Brésil [brezil], *n.m.*, Brazil
bridge [bridʒ], *n.m.*, bridge (dental)
brosser [brɔse], *v.t.*, to brush
se —— les dents, to brush one's teeth
buffet [byfɛ], *n.m.*, buffet
bureau [byro], *n.m.*, office, desk
—— de poste, post office
but [by, byt], *n.m.*, goal, aim, purpose

C

ça [sa], *dem. pron.* (familiar form of cela), that
cabine [kabin], *n.f.*, booth, cabin
—— téléphonique, telephone booth
cadeau [kado], *n.m.*, gift
café [kafe], *n.m.*, coffee
cahier [kaje], *n.m.*, notebook
caisse [kɛ:s], *n.f.*, case
caissier [kɛsje], *n.m.*, cashier
campagne [kɑ̃paɲ], *n.f.*, country (rural)
à la ——, in the country
Canada [kanada], *n.m.*, Canada
canal [kanal], *n.m.*, channel, canal
candidat [kɑ̃dida], *n.m.*, applicant, candidate
capable [kapabl], *adj.*, capable, able
capitale [kapital], *n.f.*, capital
car [ka:r], *conj.*, for, because
caractère [karaktɛ:r], *n.m.*, character
caractérisé, -e [karakterize], *adj.*, characterized
carié, -e [karje], *adj.*, decayed
carillon [karijɔ̃], *n.m.*, carillon, chimes
carnaval [karnaval], *n.m.*, carnival
carnet [karnɛ], *n.m.*, small notebook
carotte [karɔt], *n.f.*, carrot
carrière [karjɛ:r], *n.f.*, career
carte [kart], *n.f.*, card
cas [kɑ], *n.m.*, case
en tout ——, anyway, in any case
casser [kase], *v.t.*, to break
catastrophe [katastrɔf], *n.f.*, disaster, catastrophe
catégorie [kategɔri], *n.f.*, category
ce [sə], cet [sɛt], cette [sɛt], *adj.*, this, that; ces [se], *adj.*, these, those
cela [səla, sla], *pron.*, that
—— ne fait rien, that's nothing
celui [səlɥi], celle [sɛl], ceux [sø], celles [sɛl], *pron.*, he, she, the one(s), those
——-ci, the latter
——-là, the former
cent [sɑ̃], *adj. and n.m.*, hundred
cependant [spɑ̃dɑ̃], *conj.*, still, yet, nevertheless
ce que [səkə, skə], *pron.*, what (that which)
ce qui [səki, ski], *pron.*, what (that which)
cercle [sɛrkl], *n.m.*, circle, club
cérémonie [seremɔni], *n.f.*, ceremony
certain [sɛrtɛ̃], certaine [sɛrtɛn], *adj.*, certain, sure
certainement [sɛrtɛnmɑ̃], *adv.*, certainly
cesser [sɛse], *v.t.*, to stop
chacun [ʃakœ̃], chacune [ʃakyn], *pron.*, each, each one
chaise [ʃɛ:z], *n.f.*, chair
chaleur [ʃalœ:r], *n.f.*, heat
chambre [ʃɑ̃:br], *n.f.*, room
—— à deux personnes, double room
champagne [ʃɑ̃paɲ], *n.m.*, champagne
chance [ʃɑ̃:s], *n.f.*, luck
avoir de la ——, to be lucky
bonne ——, good luck
changer [ʃɑ̃ʒe], *v.t.*, to change
chanter [ʃɑ̃te], *v.t.*, to sing
chaque [ʃak], *adj.*, each, every
char [ʃa:r], *n.m.*, float
châteaubriant [ʃɑtobriɑ̃], *n.m.*, grilled steak
chaud [ʃo], chaude [ʃo:d], *adj.*, hot, warm
chef [ʃɛf], *n.m.*, head, leader

chef-d'œuvre [ʃɛdœ:vr], *n.m.*, masterpiece
chemin [ʃmɛ̃], *n.m.*, road, way
chemise [ʃəmi:z], *n.f.*, shirt; folder
chèque [ʃɛk], *n.m.*, check
cher, -ère [ʃɛ:r], *adj.*, dear, expensive
chercher [ʃɛrʃe], *v.t.*, to look for
chéri, -e [ʃeri], *n.m. and f.*, dear, darling
chez [ʃe], *prep.*, at the home of, at the office or place of business of, with
chic [ʃik], *adj.*, elegant, swell
chien [ʃjɛ̃], *n.m.*, dog
choisir [ʃwazi:r], *v.t.*, to select
choix [ʃwa], *n.m.*, choice
chose [ʃo:z], *n.f.*, thing
chou-fleur [ʃuflœ:r], *n.m.*, cauliflower
chute [ʃyt], *n.f.*, fall
ciel [sjɛl], *n.m.*, the sky, heaven
cieux [sjø], *n.m.* (*pl.* of *ciel*) the heavens
cinq [sɛ̃:k], *adj.*, five
cinquante [sɛ̃kɑ̃:t], *adj.*, fifty
classe [klɑ:s], *n.f.*, class
la ______ d'anglais, the English class
classique [klasik], *n.m.*, classic; *adj.*, classic
clôturer [klotyre], *v.t.*, to enclose, to close down
coeur [kœ:r], *n.m.*, heart
à ______ joie, to one's heart's content
cognac [kɔɲak], *n.m.*, cognac, brandy
coin [kwɛ̃], *n.m.*, corner
colis [kɔli], *n.m.*, package
collier [kɔlje], *n.m.*, necklace
______ de perles, pearl necklace
colline [kɔlin], *n.f.*, hill
combien [kɔ̃bjɛ̃], *adv.*, how much, how many (de + a noun)
comédie [kɔmedi], *n.f.*, comedy
comique [kɔmik], *adj.*, comic; *n.m.*, comedy
commander [kɔmɑ̃de], *v.t.*, to order
comme [kɔm], *conj.*, as, like, how
______ ça, that way
______ ci, ______ ça, so-so
commencer [kɔmɑ̃se], *v.t.*, to begin
comment [kɔmɑ̃], *adv.*, how
______ ça se fait-il que, how is it that
compagnie [kɔ̃paɲi], *n.f.*, company
complet [kɔ̃plɛ], complète [kɔ̃plɛt], *adj.*, complete
complètement [kɔ̃plɛtmɑ̃], *adv.*, completely
comporter [kɔ̃pɔrte], *v.t.*, to comprise
composer [kɔ̃poze], *v.t.*, to compose, to dial
comprendre [kɔ̃prɑ̃:dr], *v.t.*, to understand
comptabilité [kɔ̃tabilite], *n.f.*, bookkeeping, accountancy
comptable [kɔ̃tabl], *n.m.*, accountant, bookkeeper
compter [kɔ̃te], *v.t.*, to count, to intend
comptoir [kɔ̃twa:r], *n.m.*, counter
concierge [kɔ̃sjɛrʒ], *n.m. and f.*, concierge (kind of superintendent of an apartment building)
conduire [kɔ̃dɥi:r], *v.t.*, to conduct, take, lead, drive
conférence [kɔ̃ferɑ̃:s], *n.f.*, conference, lecture
conférencier [kɔ̃ferɑ̃sje], *n.m.*, lecturer
connaissance [kɔnɛsɑ̃:s], *n.f.*, knowledge, acquaintance
faire la ______ de, to meet, to make the acquaintance of
connaître [kɔnɛ:tr], *v.t.*, to know, to be acquainted
se ______ en (avions), to be an authority on (planes)
conseiller [kɔ̃sɛje], *v.t.*, to advise
consolateur [kɔ̃sɔlatœ:r], consolatrice [kɔ̃sɔlatris], *adj.*, consoling
consulter [kɔ̃sylte], *v.t.*, to consult
conte [kɔ̃:t], *n.m.*, tale
______ de fées, fairytale
contempler [kɔ̃tɑ̃ple], *v.t.*, to think about, to contemplate
contenant [kɔ̃tnɑ̃] (*pres. part.* of contenir), containing
contenir [kɔ̃tni:r], *v.t.*, to contain
content [kɔ̃tɑ̃], contente [kɔ̃tɑ̃:t], *adj.*, happy, pleased
continuer [kɔ̃tinɥe], *v.t.*, continue
contre [kɔ̃:tr], *prep.*, against
contretemps [kɔ̃trətɑ̃], *n.m.*, disappointment
convenable [kɔ̃vnabl], *adj.*, suitable, fitting, proper
convenir [kɔ̃vni:r], *v.i.*, to agree, to suit, to be advisable, to be fitting
corps [kɔ:r], *n.m.*, body
côte [ko:t], *n.f.*, shore, coast
la Côte d'Azur, the Riviera
côté [kote], *n.m.*, side, direction
à ______, alongside

du ____ de, in the direction of
côtelette [kɔtlɛt], *n.f.*, chop
____ d'agneau, lamb chop
couleur [kulœ:r], *n.f.*, color
____ de vin, wine-colored
coup [ku], *n.m.*, blow
____ de téléphone, telephone call
tout à ____, suddenly
tout d'un ____, all at once
coupe-papier [kup papje], *n.m.*, paper knife
courage [kura:ʒ], *n.m.*, courage
couramment [kuramɑ̃], *adv.*, fluently
courant [kurɑ̃], courante [kurɑ̃:t], *adj.*, current; *n.m.*, current, course
courir [kuri:r], *v.i.*, to run
couronné, -e [kurɔne], *adj.*, crowned
couronnement [kurɔnmɑ̃], *n.m.*, crowning
courrier [kurje], *n.m.*, mail
cours [ku:r], *n.m.*, course
court [ku:r], courte [kurt], *adj.*, short
coûter [kute], *v.i.*, to cost
____ cher, to be expensive
coûteux [kutø], coûteuse [kutø:z], *adj.*, expensive
craindre [krɛ̃:dr], *v.t.*, to fear
crainte [krɛ̃:t], *n.f.*, fear
cravate [kravat], *n.f.*, necktie
crèche [krɛ:ʃ], *n.f.*, crib, manger
crime [krim], *n.m.*, crime
croire [krwa:r], *v.t.*, to believe
cruel, -lle [kryɛl], *adj.*, cruel
cueillir [kœji:r], *v.t.*, to gather
curieux [kyrjø], curieuse [kyrjø:z], *adj.*, strange, curious, odd

D

dactylographie [daktilɔgrafi], *n.f.*, typing
dame [dam], *n.f.*, lady
dans [dɑ̃], *prep.*, in, into
davantage [davɑ̃ta:ʒ], *adv.*, more
décembre [desɑ̃:br], *n.m.*, December
décider [deside], *v.t.*, to decide, to settle
se ____ à, to make up one's mind to
décollage [dekɔla:ʒ], *n.m.*, take-off (of a plane)
décoller [dekɔle], *v.i.*, to take off (of a plane
décor [dekɔ:r], *n.m.*, decoration, scenery, setting
décorum [dekɔrɔm], *n.m.*, decorum, propriety
découper [dekupe], *v.t.*, to cut out
découvrir [dekuvri:r], *v.t.*, to discover, to find out
défendre [defɑ̃:dr], *v.t.*, to defend; to forbid
défi [defi], *n.m.*, defiance, challenge
définitif [definitif], définitive [definiti:v], *adj.*, definitive, definite
déformé, -e [defɔrme], *adj.*, out of shape
déjà [deʒa], *adv.*, already
déjeuner [deʒœne], *n.m.*, lunch; *v.i.*, to have lunch
le petit ____, the breakfast
délicieux [delisjø], délicieuse [delisjø:z], *adj.*, delicious, delightful
demain [dəmɛ̃], *adv.*, tomorrow
à ____, good-by until tomorrow, see you tomorrow
____ matin, tomorrow morning
demande [dəmɑ̃:d], *n.f.*, request, application
demander [dəmɑ̃de], *v.t.*, to ask
____ quelquechose à quelqu'un, to ask someone for something
____ de parler (chanter, etc.), to ask to speak (sing, etc.)
se ____, to wonder
demi, -e [dəmi], *adj.*, half; *n.m.*, one half
dent [dɑ̃], *n.f.*, tooth
____ de sagesse, wisdom tooth
dentiste [dɑ̃tist], *n.m.*, dentist
dépanneur [depanœ:r], *n.m.*, repairman
département [departəmɑ̃], *n.m.*, department
dépêcher [depɛʃe], *v.t.*, to dispatch
se ____, to hurry, to hasten
depuis [dəpɥi], *prep.*, since, for (with expressions of time)
____ quand, how long
dernier [dɛrnje], dernière [dɛrnjɛ:r], *adj.*, last
dérouler [derule], *v.t.*, to unroll, to unfold
se ____, to unfold, to happen
derrière [dɛrjɛ:r], *prep.*, behind, back of
des [de] (contraction of *de les*), some, of the, from the, any
dès [dɛ], *prep.*, since, from
____ que, as soon as

descendre [desɑ̃:dr], *v.i.*, to get out (of a conveyance), to descend, to go (or come) down; *v.t.*, to take down, to bring down
description [deskripsjɔ̃], *n.f.*, description
désirer [dezire], *v.t.*, to wish
desserrer [desɛre], *v.t.*, to loosen
dessert [desɛ:r], *n.m.*, dessert
dessin [desɛ̃], *n.m.*, sketch, design, drawing
destinataire [dɛstinatɛ:r], *n.m. and f.*, addressee
détective [detɛkti:v], *n.m.*, detective
détente [detɑ̃:t], *n.f.*, relaxation
détester [detɛste], *v.t.*, to detest
détraqué, -e [detrake], *adj.*, out of order
deux [dø], *adj.*, two
  tous les ——, both
deuxième [døzjɛ:m], *adj.*, second
devant [dəvɑ̃], *prep.*, in front of, before
devenir [dəvni:r], *v.i.*, to become, to get
deviner [dəvine], *v.t.*, to guess
devoir [dəvwa:r], *v.t.*, to have to, to owe, to be (supposed) to
différence [diferɑ̃:s], *n.f.*, difference
différent [diferɑ̃], différente [diferɑ̃:t], *adj.*, different
difficile [difisil], *adj.*, difficult
difficulté [difikylte], *n.f.*, difficulty, trouble
dimanche [dimɑ̃:ʃ], *n.m.*, Sunday
dinde [dɛ̃:d], *n.f.*, turkey
dîner [dine], *n.m.*, dinner
dire [di:r], *v.t.*, to say, to tell
directeur [dirɛktœ:r], directrice [dirɛktris], *n.m. and f.*, director, directress
disque [disk], *n.m.*, record
distraire [distrɛ:r], *v.t.*, to distract, to take one's mind off
divertir [divɛrti:r], *v.t.*, to entertain
  se ——, to amuse oneself, to enjoy oneself
divertissement [divɛrtismɑ̃], *n.m.*, entertainment
dix [dis, di, diz], *adj.*, ten
dix-huit [dizyit], *adj.*, eighteen
dix-neuf [diznœf], *adj.*, nineteen
dix-sept [disɛt], *adj.*, seventeen
docteur [dɔktœ:r], *n.m.*, doctor
dollar [dɔlar], *n.m.*, dollar
dommage [dɔma:ʒ], *n.m.*, harm, pity
  c'est ——, it's too bad, it's a pity
don [dɔ̃], *n.m.*, gift
donc [dɔ̃:k, dɔ̃], *conj.*, so, therefore, then
donner [dɔne], *v.t.*, to give
  —— un rendez-vous à, to make an appointment with
dont [dɔ̃], *pron.*, whose, of whom, from whom, of which, from which
dormir [dɔrmi:r], *v.i.*, to sleep
dortoir [dɔrtwa:r], *n.m.*, dormitory
doute [dut], *n.m.*, doubt
douter [dute], *v.t.*, to doubt
  se —— (de), to suspect
doux [du], douce [dus], *adj.*, sweet, gentle
douzaine [duzɛn], *n.f.*, dozen
douze [du:z], *adj.*, twelve
droit [drwa], *n.m.*, law
droit [drwa], droite [drwat], *adj.*, right
  à droite, to the right, on the right
du [dy] (contraction of *de le*), of the, from the, some, any
dur, -e [dy:r], *adj.*, hard

E

eau [o], *n.f.*, water
échange [eʃɑ̃:ʒ], *n.m.*, exchange
échapper [eʃape], *v.t.*, to escape
  l'—— belle, to have a narrow escape
éclaircir [eklɛrsi:r], *v.t.*, to clear up, to enlighten
école [ekɔl], *n.f.*, school
écouter [ekute], *v.t.*, to listen (to)
écrire [ekri:r], *v.t.*, to write
écriteau [ekrito], *n.m.*, sign
écritoire [ekritwa:r], *n.f.*, desk
écrivain [ekrivɛ̃], *n.m.*, writer
édelweiss [edɛlvajs], *n.m.*, edelweiss
édition [edisjɔ̃], *n.f.*, edition, publication
effacer [efase], *v.t.*, to erase
effet [efɛ], *n.m.*, effect
  en ——, in fact, indeed
égal, -e [egal], *adj.*, equal
égalé, -e [egale], *adj.*, equaled
également [egalmɑ̃], *adv.*, equally, also, too
égarer [egare], *v.t.*, to mislead;
  s'——, to get lost, to go astray
église [egli:z], *n.f.*, church
élancer [elɑ̃se], *v. t.*, to launch, to emit forcibly
  s'——, to rush forth, to soar
élargir [elarʒi:r], *v.t.*, to broaden, to widen

elle [ɛl], *pron.*, she, her, it, *f.*
embarquer [ɑ̃barke], *v.t.*, to embark
s'_____, to go on board
embellir [ɑ̃bɛli:r], *v.t.*, to embellish, to make beautiful
embêtant [ɑ̃bɛtɑ̃], embêtante [ɑ̃bɛtɑ̃:t], *adj.*, annoying
émission [emisjɔ̃], *n.f.*, broadcast
_____ en direct, live broadcast
émouvant [emuvɑ̃], émouvante [emuvɑ̃:t], *adj.*, thrilling, moving
empêcher [ɑ̃pɛʃe], *v.t.*, prevent
employé, -e [ɑ̃plwaje], *n.m. and f.*, clerk, employee
emprunter [ɑ̃prœ̃te], *v.t.*, to borrow
en [ɑ̃], *pron.*, some, some of it, some of them, from it, from them; *prep.*, in, into, to (before feminine names of countries)
enchanté, -e [ɑ̃ʃɑ̃te], *adj.*, delighted
enchanter [ɑ̃ʃɑ̃te], *v.t.*, to delight
encore [ɑ̃kɔ:r], *adv.*, still, yet
_____ de, some more
encourager [ɑ̃kuraʒe], *v.t.*, to encourage
encourageant [ɑ̃kuraʒɑ̃], encourageante [ɑ̃kuraʒɑ̃:t], *adj.*, encouraging
encre [ɑ̃:kr], *n.f.*, ink
endroit [ɑ̃drwa], *n.m.*, place, spot
enfance [ɑ̃fɑ̃:s], *n.f.*, childhood
enfant [ɑ̃fɑ̃], *n.m. and f.*, child
enfin [ɑ̃fɛ̃], *adv.*, finally
engager [ɑ̃gaʒe], *v.t.*, to engage
ennuyeux [ɑ̃nyijø], ennuyeuse [ɑ̃nyijø:z], *adj.*, boring, annoying
énorme [enɔrm], *adj.*, enormous, huge
énormément [enɔrmemɑ̃], *adv.*, enormously
_____ de, a great deal of
enrager [ɑ̃raʒe], *v.i.*, to be in a rage
enregistrer [ɑ̃rəʒistre], *v.t.*, to record
enrichir [ɑ̃riʃi:r], *v.t.*, to enrich
enseigner [ɑ̃sɛɲe], *v.t.*, to teach
ensemble [ɑ̃sɑ̃:bl], *adv.*, together
ensuite [ɑ̃sɥit], *adv.*, then, afterward, next
entendre [ɑ̃tɑ̃:dr], *v.t.*, to hear, to understand
_____ parler de, to hear of
entendu [ɑ̃tɑ̃dy], *past part.* of *entendre*, understood
enthousiasmé, -e [ɑ̃tuzjasme], *adj.*, enthusiastic, filled with enthusiasm
entier [ɑ̃tje], entière [ɑ̃tjɛ:r], *adj.*, whole, entire
des heures entières, hours on end
entouré, -e [ɑ̃ture], *adj.*, surrounded
entre [ɑ̃:tr], *prep.*, between
entrer [ɑ̃tre], *v.i.*, to enter, to go (or come) in
enveloppe [ɑ̃vlɔp], *n.f.*, envelope
envie [ɑ̃vi], *n.f.*, desire, longing, envy
avoir _____ de, to want to, to feel like
envoyer [ɑ̃vwaje], *v.t.*, to send
épatant [epatɑ̃], épatante [epatɑ̃:t], *adj.*, wonderful
épinards [epina:r], *n.m.pl.*, spinach
époque [epɔk], *n.f.*, era, age, time
à l'_____ de, at the time of
équipe [ekip], *n.f.*, team, crew
esclave [ɛsklɑ:v], *n.m.*, slave
espagnol, -e [ɛspaɲɔl], *adj.*, Spanish; *n.m.*, Spanish (language)
Espagnol, -e [ɛspaɲɔl], *n.m. and f.*, Spaniard
espèce [ɛspɛs], *n.f.*, kind
espérer [ɛspere], *v.i.*, to hope
essayer [esɛje], *v.t.*, to try
essentiel, -le [ɛsɑ̃sjɛl], *adj.*, essential
essuyer [esɥije], *v.t.*, to dry
estimer [ɛstime], *v.t.*, to esteem, to prize
et [e], *conj.*, and
établir [etabli:r], *v.t.*, to establish
étage [eta:ʒ], *n.m.*, floor, story (in a building)
étalage [etala:ʒ], *n.m.*, display
étaler [etale], *v.t.*, to spread out
s'_____, to be displayed
États-Unis [etazyni], *n.m.pl.*, United States
été [ete], *n.m.*, summer
éteindre [etɛ̃:dr], *v.t.*, to extinguish, to put out
étonner [etɔne], *v.t.*, to astonish
s'_____, to be astonished
étranger [etrɑ̃ʒe], étrangère [etrɑ̃ʒɛ:r], *adj.*, foreign
être [ɛ:tr], *v.i.*, to be
étrenne [etrɛn], *n.f.*, Christmas gift
étudiant [etydjɑ̃], étudiante [etydjɑ̃:t], *n.m. and f.*, student
étudier [etydje], *v.t.*, to study
Europe [œrɔp], *n.f.*, Europe
européen [œrɔpeɛ̃], européenne [œrɔpeɛn], *adj.*, European
eux [ø], *pron.*, them, *m.*

éveil [evɛ:j], *n.m.*, awakening, alarm
en ——, on the watch, on the alert
évidemment [evidamɑ̃], *adv.*, evidently
évident [evidɑ̃], évidente [evidɑ̃:t], *adj.*, evident
éviter [evite], *v.t.*, to avoid
examen [egzamɛ̃], *n.m.*, examination
examiner [egzamine], *v.t.*, to examine
excellent [ɛksɛlɑ̃], excellente [ɛksɛlɑ̃:t], *adj.*, excellent
exceptionnel, -lle [ɛksepsjɔnel], *adj.*, exceptional
excuser [ɛkskyze], *v.t.*, to excuse, to pardon
exécuté, -e [egzekyte], *adj.*, executed, performed
exemplaire [egzɑ̃plɛ:r], *n.m.*, copy
exemple [egzɑ̃:pl], *n.m.*, example
par ——, for example
exercice [egzɛrsis], *n.m.*, exercise
exigeant [egziʒɑ̃], exigeante [egziʒɑ̃:t], *adj.*, demanding
exiger [egziʒe], *v.t.*, to exact, to demand
expéditeur [ɛkspeditœ:r], *fem.* expéditrice [ɛkspeditri:s], *n.m. and f.*, sender
expérience [ɛksperjɑ̃:s], *n.f.*, experience
expérimenté, -e [ɛksperimɑ̃te], *adj.*, experienced
expliquer [ɛksplike], *v.t.*, to explain
exposé, -e [ɛkspoze], *adj.*, exposed

F

facile [fasil], *adj.*, easy
façon [fasɔ̃], *n.f.*, way, manner, means
de —— à, *prep.*, so as to
de —— que, *conj.*, so that
de cette ——, in this (that) way
facteur [faktœ:r], *n.m.*, mailman
facultatif [fakyltatif], facultative [fakyltati:v], *adj.*, elective, optional
faim [fɛ̃], *n.f.*, hunger
avoir ——, to be hungry
faire [fɛ:r], *v.t.*, to make, to do
—— à sa guise, to do as one likes
—— à sa tête, to have one's own way
—— attention à, to pay attention to
—— beau, to be fine weather
—— bon, to be nice weather; to be comfortable (used of places)
—— bonne chère, to eat well
—— cadeau de, to give as a gift
—— cas de, to esteem
—— chaud, to be warm weather
—— de la peine à, to hurt someone
—— des achats (or: des emplettes), to make purchases, to shop
—— des économies, to save, to economize
—— de son mieux, to do one's best
—— des progrès, to make progress
—— du bien, to do good, to be beneficial
—— du ski, to go skiing
—— du vent, to be windy
—— exprès, to do on purpose
—— faire, to get done, to have (something) done
—— frais, to be cool weather
—— froid, to be cold weather
—— grand cas de, to attach great importance to
—— la connaissance de, to become acquainted with
—— la joie de, to be the delight of
—— la queue, to stand in line
—— la sourde oreille, to pretend not to hear
—— le ——, to play the ——
—— le tour de, to go around
—— lourd, to be sultry weather
—— mal à, to hurt someone
—— mine de, to pretend
—— part à quelqu'un de quelque chose, to let someone know about something
—— partie de, to belong to, to be a member of
—— peur à, to frighten
—— plaisir à, to please
—— savoir, to let know
—— semblant de, to pretend to
—— ses adieux à, to say good-by to
—— ses amitiés à, to give one's regards to
—— son affaire, to answer one's purpose
—— son marché, to do one's shopping
—— son possible, to do one's best
—— une injection, to give an injection
—— une malle, to pack a trunk
—— une promenade, to take a walk
—— une question, to ask a question
—— un voyage, to take a trip

_____ venir, to send for
_____ visite à, to pay a visit to
_____ voir, to show
fait [fɛ, fɛt], *n.m.*, fact; *past part.* of *faire*, did, made
falloir [falwa:r], *v. impersonal*, to be necessary, must, to need, to take (of time, etc.), to require
fameux [famø], fameuse [famø:z], *adj.*, famous
famille [fami:j], *n.f.*, family
farce [fars], *n.f.*, farce
fatigué, -e [fatige], *adj.*, tired
faute [fo:t], *n.f.*, fault, mistake
faux [fo], fausse [fo:s], *adj.*, false
favori [favɔri], favorite [favɔrit], *adj.*, favorite
féerique [ferik], *adj.*, fairy
félicitations [felisitɑsjɔ̃], *n.f.pl.*, congratulations
fenêtre [fənɛ:tr], *n.f.*, window
fermer [fɛrme], *v.t.*, to close, to turn off
festivité [fɛstivite], *n.f.*, festivity
fête [fɛ:t], *n.f.*, feast, holiday, festivity
fêter [fɛte], *v.t.*, to celebrate
feu [fø], *n.m.*, fire
feux (*pl.*) d'artifice, fireworks
feuille [fœ:j], *n.f.*, sheet, leaf
février [fevrie], *n.m.*, February
fidèle [fidɛl], *adj.*, faithful
fièvre [fjɛ:vr], *n.f.*, fever
figurer [figyre], *v.t.*, to represent
se _____, to imagine
fillette [fijɛt], *n.f.*, little girl
fin [fɛ̃], *n.f.*, end
final, -e [final], *adj.*, final
finalement [finalmɑ̃], *adv.*, finally
fini, -e [fini], *adj.*, finished, over
finir [fini:r], *v.t.*, to finish
flamme [flɑ:m], *n.f.*, flame
flan [flɑ̃], *n.m.*, custard
flatteur [flatœ:r], flatteuse [flatø:z], *adj.*, flattering
fleur [flœ:r], *n.f.*, flower
flotter [flɔte], *v.i.*, to float
fois [fwa], *n.f.*, time
deux _____ trois font six, two times three is six
à la _____, at the same time
foncé [fɔ̃se], *adj.*, dark (of colors)
fond [fɔ̃], *n.m.*, bottom, back, far end
au _____, at the back, at the bottom, at heart
fonder [fɔ̃de], *v.t.*, to found, to establish
fontaine [fɔ̃tɛn], *n.f.*, fountain
forger [fɔrʒe], *v.t.*, to forge
forgeron [fɔrʒrɔ̃], *n.m.*, blacksmith
forme [fɔrm], *n.f.*, shape, form
en _____ de, in the shape of
fort [fɔr], forte [fɔrt], *adj.*, strong, solid; *n.m.*, strong point, forte
fortifier [fɔrtifje], *v.t.*, to fortify
se _____, to fortify oneself, to make oneself strong
fou [fu], folle [fɔl], *adj.*, foolish
fouler [fule], *v.t.*, to trample
se _____ la cheville, to sprain one's ankle
four [fu:r], *n.m.*, oven
petit _____, fancy small cake
frais [frɛ], fraîche [frɛ:ʃ], *adj.*, fresh
franc [frɑ̃], franche [frɑ̃:ʃ], *adj.*, frank, candid
français [frɑ̃sɛ], française [frɑ̃sɛ:z], *adj.*, French; *n.m.*, French (language)
Français [frɑ̃sɛ], Française [frɑ̃sɛ:z], *n.m. and f.*, Frenchman, Frenchwoman
France [frɑ̃:s], *n.f.*, France
franchir [frɑ̃ʃi:r], *v.t.*, to cross
frapper [frape], *v.t.*, to strike
frère [frɛ:r], *n.m.*, brother
frisson [frisɔ̃], *n.m.*, chill
froid [frwa], *n.m.*, cold; *adj.*, cold
avoir _____, to be cold (persons)
être _____, to be cold (things)
faire _____, to be cold (weather)
prendre _____, to take cold
fruit [frɥi], *n.m.*, fruit

G

gagner [gaɲe], *v.t.*, to win
galant [galɑ̃], galante [galɑ̃:t], *adj.*, gallant
gant [gɑ̃], *n.m.*, glove
garanti, -e [garɑ̃ti], *adj.*, guaranteed
garçon [garsɔ̃], *n.m.*, boy, waiter
garder [garde], *v.t.*, to keep
gargariser [gargarize], *v.t.*, to gargle
se _____, to gargle
gâteau [gɑto], *n.m.*, cake
gauche [go:ʃ], *adj.*, clumsy, awkward, left
à _____, to the left, on the left
gelée [ʒəle], *n.f.*, frost, jelly
_____ d'airelles, cranberry jelly

gens [ʒɑ̃], *n.pl.*, people
gentil [ʒɑ̃ti], gentille [ʒɑ̃ti:j], *adj.*, nice
  c'est très ______ à vous, it's very nice of you
gentilhomme [ʒɑ̃tijɔm], *n.m.*, nobleman
géometrie [ʒeɔmetri], *n.f.*, geometry
glace [glas], *n.f.*, ice, mirror, ice cream
glisser [glise], *v.i.*, to glide, to slide, to slip; *v.t.*, to slip
gloire [glwa:r], *n.f.*, glory
goûter [gute], *n.m.*, snack, light meal; *v.t.*, to taste
gouvernement [guvɛrnəmɑ̃], *n.m.*, government
grand [grɑ̃], grande [grɑ̃:d], *adj.*, big, great, large
grenier [grənje], *n.m.*, attic
grimper [grɛ̃pe], *v.t.*, to climb
grippe [grip], *n.f.*, grippe, flu, virus
gros [gro], grosse [grɔs], *adj.*, big, large
guichet [giʃɛ], *n.m.*, ticket window
  au ______ d'en face, at the opposite window
guignon [giɲɔ̃], *n.m.*, bad luck

H

Note: An asterisk before the word indicates that the initial *h* is aspirate, allowing no elision or liaison. (Ex: le hangar, les hangars [leɑ̃ga:r]).
habileté [abilte], *n.f.*, cleverness, skill
habituer [abitye], *v.t.*, to accustom
  s'______ à, to get used to
*hangar [ɑ̃ga:r], *n.m.*, hangar
*haricot [ariko], *n.m.*, bean
  ______s verts, string beans
*haut [o], haute [o:t], *adj.*, high
*haut-parleur [oparlœ:r], *n.m.*, loudspeaker
hélice [elis], *n.f.*, propeller
hésiter [ezite], *v.i.*, to hesitate
heure [œ:r], *n.f.*, hour
  de bonne ______, early
heureusement [œrøzmɑ̃], *adv.*, fortunately, happily
heureux [œrø], heureuse [œrø:z], *adj.*, happy, fortunate
hier [jɛ:r], *adv.*, yesterday
  ______ soir, last night
histoire [istwa:r], *n.f.*, history, story
hiver [ivɛ:r], *n.m.*, winter
hommage [ɔma:ʒ], *n.m.*, homage, tribute; *pl.*, respects
  faire ses ______s, to pay one's respects
honneur [ɔnœ:r], *n.m.*, honor
*honteux [ɔ̃tø], honteuse [ɔ̃tø:z], *adj.*, shameful
horaire [ɔrɛ:r], *n.m.*, schedule, timetable
horizon [ɔrizɔ̃], *n.m.*, horizon
horizontal, -e [ɔrizɔ̃tal], *adj.*, horizontal
horreur [ɔrœ:r], *n.f.*, horror
*hors-d'œuvre [ɔrdœ:vr], *n.m.*, hors-d'œuvre
*huit [yit, yi], *adj.*, eight
humain [ymɛ̃], humaine [ymɛ:n], *adj.*, human
hypocrite [ipɔkrit], *n.m.*, hypocrite

I

ici [isi], *adv.*, here
  par ______, through here, this way
idée [ide], *n.f.*, idea
il [il], *pron.*, he, it (*m.*)
illustre [ilystr], *adj.*, illustrious
ils [il], *pron.*, they (*m.*)
image [ima:ʒ], *n.f.*, picture
imaginaire [imaʒinɛ:r], *adj.*, imaginary
imagination [imaʒinasjɔ̃], *n.f.*, imagination
immédiatement [imedjatmɑ̃], *adj.*, immediately
important [ɛ̃pɔrtɑ̃], importante [ɛ̃pɔrtɑ̃:t], *adj.*, important
importer [ɛ̃pɔrte], *v.t.*, to import; *v.i.*, to be important, to matter
  n'importe, never mind, it does not matter
  n'importe comment, anyhow
  n'importe où, anywhere
  n'importe quand, any time
  n'importe qui, anyone
incomparable [ɛ̃kɔ̃parabl], *adj.*, incomparable
indiquer [ɛ̃dike], *v.t.*, to indicate
indiscrétion [ɛ̃diskresjɔ̃], *n.f.*, indiscretion
infini, -e [ɛ̃fini], *adj.*, infinite
infiniment [ɛ̃finimɑ̃], *adv.*, infinitely
infirmière [ɛ̃firmjɛ:r], *n.f.*, nurse
information [ɛ̃fɔrmɑsjɔ̃], *n.f.*, information
ingénieur [ɛ̃ʒenjœ:r], *n.m.*, engineer
injection [ɛ̃ʒɛksjɔ̃], *n.f.*, injection
  faire une ______, to give an injection
innovation [inɔvasjɔ̃], *n.f.*, innovation

inquiéter [ɛ̃kjete], *v.t.*, to make anxious, to disturb
s'——, to worry, to be anxious
inspiration [ɛ̃spirasjɔ̃], *n.f.*, inspiration
inspirer [ɛ̃spire], *v.t.*, to inspire
instant [ɛ̃stɑ̃], *n.m.*, moment, second
instruire [ɛ̃strɥi:r], *v.t.*, to instruct, to teach
intellectuel, -le [ɛ̃tɛlɛktyɛl], *adj.*, intellectual
intéressant [ɛ̃terɛsɑ̃], intéressante [ɛ̃terɛsɑ̃:t], *adj.*, interesting
interprète [ɛ̃tɛrprɛt], *n.m.*, interpreter
inutile [inytil], *adj.*, useless
inviter [ɛ̃vite], *v.t.*, to invite
Irlande [irlɑ̃:d], *n.f.*, Ireland
irréel, -le [ireɛl], *adj.*, unreal
italien [italjɛ̃], italienne [italjɛn], *adj.*, Italian

J

jamais [ʒamɛ], *adv.*, ever, never
ne——, never
japonais [ʒapɔnɛ], japonaise [ʒapɔnɛ:z], *adj.*, Japanese; *n.m.*, Japanese (language)
Japonais [ʒapɔnɛ], Japonaise [ʒapɔnɛ:z], *n.m. and f.*, Japanese (man, woman)
je [ʒə], *pron.*, I
jet [ʒɛt], *n.m.*, jet plane
jeter [ʒəte], *v.t.*, to throw, to hurl
—— dans la boîte aux lettres, to mail
se ——, to throw oneself
—— un coup d'œil sur, to glance over
jeu [ʒø], *n.m.*, game
jeudi [ʒødi], *n.m.*, Thursday
joie [ʒwɑ], *n.f.*, joy, gladness
joli, -e [ʒɔli], *adj.*, pretty
—— comme tout, as pretty as can be
jouer [ʒwe], *v.t.*, to play
—— à la balle, to play ball
—— du piano, to play the piano
jouet [ʒwɛ], *n.m.*, toy
joueur [ʒwœ:r], *n.m.*, player
jouir [ʒwi:r], *v.i.*, to enjoy (with *de* + a noun)
joujou [ʒuʒu], *n.m.*, toy
jour [ʒu:r], *n.m.*, day
—— d'Actions de grâces, Thanksgiving
journal [ʒurnal], *n.m.*, newspaper
journée [ʒurne], *n.f.*, day (the full day)
jusqu'à ce que [ʒyskaskə], *conj.*, until
jusque [ʒysk], *prep.*, until, up to, as far as
jusqu'ici, up to now
juste [ʒyst], *adj.*, just, fair, exact, right
au ——, exactly
c'est ——, that's right

K

kilomètre [kilɔmɛtr], *n.m.*, kilometer
kiosque [kjɔsk], *n.m.*, newsstand

L

la [la], *def. art., f. sing.*, the; *pron.*, her, it (*f.*)
là [la], *adv.*, there
——-bas, over there
laboratoire [labɔratwa:r], *n.m.*, laboratory
—— de langues, language laboratory
lac [lak], *n.m.*, lake
laid [lɛ], laide [lɛd], *adj.*, ugly
laisser [lɛse], *v.t.*, to leave
lampe [lɑ̃:p], *n.f.*, lamp
lancer [lɑ̃se], *v.t.*, to throw, to launch
langage [lɑ̃ga:ʒ], *n.m.*, language
langue [lɑ̃:g], *n.f.*, language, tongue
—— maternelle, native tongue
lanterne [lɑ̃tɛrn], *n.f.*, lantern
large [larʒ], *adj.*, wide
largement [larʒmɑ̃], *adv.*, largely, abundantly, fully
largeur [larʒœ:r], *n.f.*, width
laryngite [larɛ̃ʒit], *n.f.*, laryngitis
las [la], lasse [la:s], *adj.*, weary, tired
le [lə], *def. art., m. sing.*, the; *pron.*, him, it (*m.*)
lecture [lɛkty:r], *n.f.*, reading
lendemain [lɑ̃dmɛ̃], *n.m.*, the following day
lequel [ləkɛl] (laquelle [lakɛl], lesquels [lekɛl], lesquelles [lekɛl]), *rel. pron.*, which, who, whom; *interr. pron.*, which (one[s])
les [lɛ], *def. art., m. and f. pl.*, the; *pron.*, them (*m. and f.*)
lettre [lɛtr], *n.f.*, letter
leur [lœ:r], *poss. adj.*, their; *pron.*, to them
le (la, les) ——(s), theirs
leurs [lœ:r], *opss. adj.*, their

lever [ləve], *v.t.*, to raise
se ———, to get up
libraire [librɛ:r], *n.m.*, bookseller
librairie [librɛri], *n.f.*, bookstore
licence [lisɑ̃:s], *n.f.*, university degree following the baccalaureate, similar to M.A.
——— en droit, law degree
lieu [ljø], *n.m.*, place
ligne [liɲ], *n.f.*, line
lire [li:r], *v.t.*, to read
liste [list], *n.f.*, list
littérature [literaty:r], *n.f.*, literature
livre [li:vr], *n.m.*, book; *f.*, pound
——— broché, paperbound book
locataire [lɔkatɛ:r], *n.m.*, tenant
locomotive [lɔkɔmɔti:v], *n.f.*, locomotive
loin [lwɛ̃], *adv.*, far
loisir [lwazi:r], *n.m.*, leisure
à ———, leisurely
Londres [lɔ̃:dr], *n.*, London
long [lɔ̃], longue [lɔ̃:g], *adj.*, long
longtemps [lɔ̃tɑ̃], *adv.*, long, a long time
lorsque [lɔrskə], *conj.*, when
lourd [lu:r], lourde [lu:rd], *adj.*, heavy
loyer [lwaje], *n.m.*, rent
lui [lɥi], *pron.*, he, him, to him, to her
lumière [lymjɛ:r], *n.f.*, light
lundi [lœ̃di], *n.m.*, Monday
lutte [lyt], *n.f.*, struggle, wrestling
luxueux [lyksyø], luxueuse [lyksyø:z], *adj.*, luxurious

M

ma [ma], *poss. adj.*, my
machine [maʃin], *n.f.*, machine
——— à écrire, typewriter
madame [madam], *n.f.*, madam; Madame, Mrs.
mademoiselle [madmwazɛl], *n.f.*, Miss
magasin [magazɛ̃], *n.m.*, store
magnétique [maɲetik], *adj.*, magnetic
magnétophone [maɲetɔfɔn], *n.m.*, tape recorder
magnifique [maɲifik], *adj.*, magnificent, splendid, wonderful
maigrir [mɛgri:r], *v.i.*, to lose weight
main [mɛ̃], *n.f.*, hand
maintenant [mɛ̃tnɑ̃], *adv.*, now
mais [mɛ], *conj.*, but
maison [mezɔ̃], *n.f.*, house, firm (commercial)
à la ———, home, at home

mal [mal], *n.m.*, evil, harm, trouble, ache
avoir ——— à la tête, to have a headache
avoir ——— aux dents, to have a toothache
mal [mal], *adv.*, badly
pas ———, quite
pas ——— de, quite a few, quite a lot of
malade [malad], *adj.*, sick, ill; *n.m. and f.*, patient
maladresse [maladrɛs], *n.f.*, clumsiness
malgré [malgre], *prep.*, in spite of
malheureux [malœrø], malheureuse [malœrø:z], *adj.*, unhappy
maman [mamɑ̃], *n.f.*, mamma, mother
mandat-poste [mɑ̃dapɔst], *n.m.*, postal money order
manger [mɑ̃ʒe], *v.t.*, to eat
manquer [mɑ̃ke], *v.t.*, to miss
marcher [marʃe], *v.i.*, to walk, to get along
mardi [mardi], *n.m.*, Tuesday
mari [mari], *n.m.*, husband
mathématiques, [matematik], *n.f.pl.*, mathematics
matière [matjɛ:r], *n.f.*, material
matin [matɛ̃], *n.m.*, morning
le ———, in the morning
mauvais [mɔvɛ], mauvaise [mɔvɛ:z], *adj.*, bad
me [mə], *pron.*, me, to me
méchant [meʃɑ̃], méchante [meʃɑ̃:t], *adj.*, naughty, mean
médecin [mɛtsɛ̃], *n.m.*, doctor
meilleur, -e [mɛjœ:r], *adj.*, better, best
membre [mɑ̃:br], *n.m. and f.*, member
même [mɛ:m], *adj.*, same; *adv.*, even
tout de ———, all the same, even so
mener [məne], *v.t.*, to lead
mensonge [mɑ̃sɔ̃:ʒ], *n.m.*, lie, untruth
mercerie [mɛrsəri], *n.f.*, haberdashery
merci [mɛrsi], *n.m.*, thank you, thanks
mercredi [mɛrkrədi], *n.m.*, Wednesday
méridional, -e, [meridjɔnal], *adj.*, southern
mes [mɛ], *poss. adj.*, my
mésaventure [mezavɑ̃ty:r], *n.f.*, mishap
messieurs [mesjø], *n.m.*, sirs, gentlemen
métro [metro], *n.m.*, subway
métropole [metrɔpɔl], *n.f.*, metropolis

mettre [mɛ:tr], *v.t.*, to put, to put on
se ______ à, to begin to
meuble [mœbl], *n.m.*, piece of furniture; *pl.* furniture
Mexique [mɛksik], *n.m.*, Mexico
midi [midi], *n.m.*, noon
mien(s) [mjɛ̃], mienne(s) [mjɛn], *pron.* (used with the *def. art.*), mine
mieux [mjø], *adv.*, better
mignon [miɲɔ̃], mignonne [miɲɔn], *adj.*, cute
milieu [miljø], *n.m.*, middle, milieu, atmosphere
au ______, in the middle
mille [mil], *adj.*, thousand
milliard [milja:r], *n.m.*, billion
un ______ de livres, a billion books
million [miljɔ̃], *n.m.*, million
un ______ de livres, a million books
mince [mɛ̃s], *adj.*, thin
minuit [minɥi], *n.m.*, midnight
minute [minyt], *n.f.*, minute
mis [mi], (*past part.* of *mettre*), put
misanthrope [mizɑ̃trɔp], *n.m.*, misanthrope
misérable [mizerabl], *adj.*, miserable, wretched
mi-temps [mitɑ̃], *adv.*, part time
mode [mɔd], *n.f.*, fashion
mœurs [mœrs], *n.f.pl.*, customs, habits, morals, manners
moi [mwa], *pron.*, me, to me, I
moins [mwɛ̃], *adv.*, less
du ______, at least
mois [mwa], *n.m.*, month
molaire [mɔlɛ:r], *n.f.*, molar
moment [mɔmɑ̃], *n.m.*, moment
momerie [momri], *n.f.*, mummery
mon [mɔ̃], *poss. adj.*, my
monde [mɔ̃:d], *n.m.*, world, people
tout le ______, everybody, everyone
monnaie [mɔnɛ], *n.f.*, money, currency, change
monsieur [məsjø], *n.m.*, sir, gentleman; Mr.
montagne [mɔ̃taɲ], *n.f.*, mountain
monter [mɔ̃te], *v.i.*, to go up; *v.t.*, to take up, to carry up
moquer [mɔke], *v.t.*, to ridicule
se ______ de, to make fun of
mou [mu], molle [mɔl], *adj.*, soft
mourir [muri:r], *v.i.*, to die
mousse [mus], *n.m.*, cabin boy
moyen [mwajɛ̃], *n.m.*, way, means
muni, -e [myni], (de) *adj.*, fortified (with), armed (with)
musique [myzik], *n.f.*, music

N

nain [nɛ̃], *n.m.*, dwarf
naissance [nɛsɑ̃:s], *n.f.*, birth
naître [nɛ:tr], *v.i.*, to be born (*past part.*, né, born)
nappe [nap], *n.f.*, tablecloth
nature [naty:r], *n.f.*, nature
naturel, -le [natyrɛl], *adj.*, natural
naturellement [natyrɛlmɑ̃], *adv.*, naturally
nécessaire [nesɛsɛ:r], *adj.*, necessary
ne ______ guère [nə gɛ:r], *adv.*, scarcely, hardly
neige [nɛ:ʒ], *n.f.*, snow
ne ______ jamais [nə ʒamɛ], *adv.*, never
ne ______ pas [nə pɑ], *adv.*, not
ne ______ personne [nə pɛrsɔn], *adv.*, no one, not anyone
ne ______ plus [nə ply], *adv.*, no longer, not any more
ne ______ point [nə pwɛ̃], *adv.*, not at all
ne ______ que [nə kə], *adv.*, only
nerf [nɛ:r], *n.m.*, nerve
ne ______ rien [nə rjɛ̃], *adv.*, nothing, not anything
n'est-ce pas? [nɛspɑ], isn't it so?, aren't you?, doesn't it?, etc. (Any similar expression that suits the sense of confirming what has been said.)
net [nɛt], nette [nɛt], *adj.*, clear, clean, distinct
nettoyer [nɛtwaje], *v.t.*, to clean
neuf [nœf, nœ], *adj.*, nine
neuf [nœf], neuve [nœv], *adj.*, new (brand new)
nez [ne], *n.m.*, nose
ni [ni], *conj.*, neither
______ vous ______ moi, neither you nor I
Noël [nɔɛl], *n.m.*, Christmas
noël [nɔɛl], *n.m.*, carol
noir, -e [nwa:r], *adj.*, black
nom [nɔ̃], *n.m.*, name, noun
nommer [nɔme], *v.t.*, to name
non [nɔ̃], *adv.*, no, not
nos [no], *adj.*, our
nostalgique [nɔstalʒik], *adj.*, nostalgic

note [nɔt], *n.f.*, note, grade (in school)
notre [nɔtr], *adj.*, our
nôtre(s) [no:tr], *pron.* (used with the *def. art.*), ours
nous [nu], *pron.*, we, us, to us, ourselves
nouveau [nuvo], nouvelle [nuvɛl], *adj.*, new
de ——, again
nouvelle [nuvɛl], *n.f.*, piece of news; *pl.*, news
nuage [nɥa:ʒ], *n.m.*, cloud
nuit [nɥi], *n.f.*, night
la ——, at night
numéro [nymero], *n.m.*, number

O

obligatoire, [ɔbligatwa:r], *adj.*, obligatory, required
obligé, -e [ɔbliʒe], *adj.*, obliged
obliger [ɔbliʒe], *v.t.*, to force, to oblige
observer [ɔpsɛrve], *v.t.*, to observe
obstacle [ɔpstakl], *n.m.*, obstacle
obtenir [ɔptəni:r], *v.t.*, to obtain
occasion [ɔkɑzjɔ̃], *n.f.*, occasion
d'—— secondhand, used
occupé, -e [ɔkype], *adj.*, occupied, taken, busy
octobre [ɔktɔbr], *n.m.*, October
œil [œ:j], *n.m.*, eye
œuf [œf], *n.m.*, egg
œuvre [œ:vr], *n.f.*, work
offrir [ɔfri:r], *v.t.*, to offer
on [ɔ̃], *pron.*, one, you, they, people
onze [ɔ̃:z], *adj.*, eleven
orchestre [ɔrkɛstr], *n.m.*, orchestra
ordre [ɔrdr], *n.m.*, order
orienter [ɔrjɑ̃te], *v.t.*, to orient
s'——, to get one's bearings
orné (de) [ɔrne], *adj.*, decorated (with)
oser [oze], *v.i.*, to dare
ou [u], *conj.*, or
—— bien, or else
où [u], *adv.*, where
oublier [ublie], *v.t.*, to forget
oui [wi], *adv.*, yes
je crois que ——, I think so
ouvert [uvɛ:r], ouverte [uvɛ:rt] (*past part. of ouvrir*), opened; *adj.*, open
ouvrir [uvri:r], *v.t.*, to open, to turn on

P

paix [pɛ], *n.f.*, peace
pantomime [pɑ̃tɔmim], *n.f.*, pantomime
papeterie [paptri], *n.f.*, stationery store
papier [papje], *n.m.*, paper
—— carbone, carbon paper
paquebot [pakbo], *n.m.*, ship
paquet [pakɛ], *n.m.*, package
par [pa:r], *prep.*, by, per, through
—— an (jour, semaine), a year (a day, a week)
paradis [paradi], *n.m.*, paradise
paraître [parɛ:tr], *v.i.*, to appear, to seem, to be published
parce que [parskə], *conj.*, because
pardon [pardɔ̃], *n.m.*, pardon, forgiveness; *interj.* excuse me
pardonner [pardɔne], *v.t.*, to excuse, to pardon
pareil, -lle [parɛ:j], *adj.*, similar
parent [parɑ̃], *n.m.*, parent, relative
parfait [parfɛ], parfaite [parfɛt], *adj.*, perfect
parfaitement [parfɛtmɑ̃], *adv.*, perfectly
parfumerie [parfymri], *n.f.*, perfumery
parisien [parizjɛ̃], parisienne [parizjɛn], *adj.*, Parisian
Parisien [parizjɛ̃], Parisienne [parizjɛn], *n.m. and f.*, Parisian (person)
parler [parle], *v.i.*, to speak
parmi [parmi], *prep.*, among
parole [parɔl], *n.f.*, word, speech (the faculty of speech)
particulier [partikylje], particulière [partikyljɛ:r], *adj.*, particular, special, private
partie [parti], *n.f.*, game, match
—— de football, football game
partir [parti:r], *v.i.*, to leave, to go away
à —— de, from
partout [partu], *adv.*, everywhere
parvenir [parvəni:r], *v.i.*, to reach, to succeed
pas [pɑ], *adv.*, not; *n.m.*, step, pace
—— mal de, quite a few, quite a lot of
—— du tout, not at all
passage [pɑsa:ʒ], *n.m.*, passage
passé, -e [pɑse], *adj.*, past, last
passer [pɑse], *v.t. and v.i.*, to pass, to spend
se ——, to happen, to take place
passerelle [pɑsrɛl], *n.f.*, gangplank
passion [pɑsjɔ̃], *n.f.*, passion
patate [patat], *n.f.*, sweet potato

patience [pasjɑ̃:s], *n.f.*, patience
patin [patɛ̃], *n.m.*, skate
patinage [patina:ʒ], *n.m.*, skating
patiner [patine], *v.i.*, to skate
patineur [patinœ:r], *n.m.*, skater
pauvre [po:vr], *adj.*, poor
payer [pɛje], *v.t.*, to pay (for)
pays [pei], *n.m.*, country
paysage [peiza:ʒ], *n.m.*, landscape
peine [pɛn], *n.f.*, trouble, sorrow
valoir la _____, to be worth the trouble
à _____, scarcely, hardly
pendant [pɑ̃dɑ̃], *prep.*, during
_____ que, while
pensée [pɑ̃se], *n.f.*, thought
penser [pɑ̃se], *v.i.*, to think
faire _____ à, to remind of
_____ à, to think of (to turn the attention to)
_____ de, to think of (to form a judgment upon)
pension [pɑ̃sjɔ̃], *n.f.*, pension, board and room
pente [pɑ̃:t], *n.f.*, slope
perdre [pɛrdr], *v.t.*, to lose
père [pɛ:r], *n.m.*, father
le _____ Noël, Santa Claus
pérégrination [peregrinɑsjɔ̃], *n.f.*, peregrination
perle [pɛrl], *n.f.*, pearl
permettre [pɛrmɛtr], *v.t.*, to permit
permis [pɛrmi], permise [pɛrmiz], *adj.*, (*past part.* of *permettre*), permitted
personne [pɛrsɔn], *n.f.*, person
petit [pəti], petite [pətit], *adj.*, little, small
peu [pø], *adv.*, little, not much, few, not very, not many
un _____, a little, rather
_____ à _____, little by little
à _____ près, almost
peur [pœ:r], *n.f.*, fear
de _____ de, *prep.*, for fear of
de _____ que, *conj.*, for fear that
avoir _____ de, to be afraid of
peut-être [pøtɛ:tr], *adv.*, perhaps, maybe
philatéliste [filatelist], *n.m.*, philatelist, stamp collector
phonétique [fɔnetik], *n.f.*, phonetics
phtisie [ftizi], *n.f.*, tuberculosis, consumption
pic [pik], *n.m.*, peak
pied [pje], *n.m.*, foot
pilote [pilɔt], *n.m.*, pilot
pilule [pilyl], *n.f.*, pill
pipe [pip], *n.f.*, pipe
piscine [pisin], *n.f.*, pool
piste [pist], *n.f.*, track, trail
_____ de décollage, runway
pittoresque [pitɔrɛsk], *adj.*, picturesque
placard [plaka:r], *n.m.*, closet
place [plas], *n.f.*, place, seat, job, room, public square
placer [plase], *v.t.*, to place
plaindre [plɛ̃:dr], *v.t.*, to pity
se _____ de, to complain
plaire [plɛ:r], *v.i.*, to please
s'il vous plaît, please
plaisir [plɛzi:r], *n.m.*, pleasure
prendre _____ à, to take pleasure in
plan [plɑ̃], *n.m.*, outline
pleuvoir [plœvwa:r], *v.i.*, to rain
plomber [plɔ̃be], *v.t.*, to fill (of a tooth)
plu [ply] (*past part.* of *pleuvoir* and of *plaire*), rained, pleased
pluie [plɥi], *n.f.*, rain
plupart [plypa:r], *n.f.*, most, the majority, the greater part
la _____ des voyageurs, the majority of the travelers
plus [ply], *adv.*, more
de _____ en _____, more and more
un jour de _____, one day more
plusieurs [plyzjœ:r], *adj. and pron.*, several
plutôt [plyto], *adv.*, rather
poche [pɔʃ], *n.f.*, pocket
poésie [pɔezi], *n.f.*, poetry
point [pwɛ̃], *n.m.*, point, period
être sur le _____ de, to be about to
police [pɔlis], *n.f.*, police
pomme [pɔm], *n.f.*, apple
_____ de terre, potato
pont [pɔ̃], *n.m.*, bridge, deck
porte [pɔrt], *n.f.*, door
porte-monnaie [pɔrtmɔnɛ], *n.m.*, wallet
porter [pɔrte], *v.t.*, to carry, to wear
se _____ à merveille, to feel great
_____ sur, to have a bearing on, to have to do with
portugais [pɔrtygɛ], portugaise [pɔrtygɛ:z], *adj.*, Portuguese; *n.m.*, Portuguese (language)

Portugal [pɔrtygal], *n.m.*, Portugal
possible [pɔsibl], *adj.*, possible
postal, -e [pɔstal], *adj.*, postal
poste [pɔst], *n.m.*, post, job, station; *n.f.*, post, post office
mettre une lettre à la ——, to mail a letter
pouding [pudiɲ], *n.m.*, pudding
—— aux fruits, fruit pudding
poulet [pulɛ], *n.m.*, chicken
poupée [pupe], *n.f.*, doll
pour [pu:r], *prep.*, for, in order to
—— que, *conj.*, in order that
pourboire [purbwa:r], *n.m.*, tip (gratuity)
pourquoi [purkwa], *adv.*, why
poursuivre [pursɥi:vr], *v.t.*, to pursue
pourtant [purtɑ̃], *adv.*, yet, however
pourvu que [purvykə], *conj.*, provided that
pouvoir [puvwa:r], *v.i.*, to be able
il se peut que, it may be that
on ne peut plus, *adv.*, most
précieux [presjø], précieuse [presjø:z], *adj.*, precious, valuable; *n.m. and f.*, affected person (one who followed the ideas of "préciosité," a seventeenth-century movement of refinement in expression, manners, and dress)
précisément [presizemɑ̃], *adv.*, precisely, just
précision [presizjɔ̃], *n.f.*, precision
préférer [prefere], *v.t.*, to prefer
premier [prəmje], première [prəmjɛ:r], *adj.*, first
prendre [prɑ̃:dr], *v.t.*, to take
—— froid, to take cold
préoccuper [preɔkype], *v.t.*, to preoccupy
se —— de, to worry about
préparatif [preparatif], *n.m.*, preparation
préparation [preparɑsjɔ̃], *n.f.*, preparation
préparer [prepare], *v.t.*, to prepare
près [prɛ], *adv.*, near
—— de, *prep.*, near
présence [prezɑ̃:s], *n.f.*, presence
en —— de, in the presence of
présent [prezɑ̃], *n.m.*, present
à ——, now
présenter [prezɑ̃te], *v.t.*, to introduce, to present
président [prezidɑ̃], *n.m.*, president
presque [prɛsk], *adv.*, nearly, almost
prêt [prɛ], prête [prɛt], *adj.*, ready
prétentieux [pretɑ̃sjø], prétentieuse [pretɑ̃sjø:z], *adj.*, pretentious, elaborate
prêter [prɛte], *v.t.*, to lend
prier [prie], *v.t.*, to pray, to request, to ask
je vous en prie, please, you're welcome
principal, -e [prɛ̃sipal], *adj.*, principal
printemps [prɛ̃tɑ̃], *n.m.*, spring
au ——, in the spring
prix [pri], *n.m.*, prize, price
probable [prɔbabl], *adj.*, probable
probablement [prɔbabləmɑ̃], *adv.*, probably
problème [prɔblɛ:m], *n.m.*, problem
procès-verbal [prɔsɛvɛrbal], *n.m.*, minutes (parliamentary procedure)
prochain [prɔʃɛ̃], prochaine [prɔʃɛn], *adj.*, next
professeur [prɔfɛsœ:r], *n.m.*, professor
profiter (de) [prɔfite], *v.i.*, to take advantage of
profondeur [prɔfɔ̃dœ:r], *n.f.*, depth, profundity
programme [prɔgram], *n.m.*, program
progrès [prɔgrɛ], *n.m.*, progress
promenade [prɔmnad], *n.f.*, walk, promenade
promesse [prɔmɛs], *n.f.*, promise
promettre [prɔmɛ:tr], *v.t.*, to promise
prononcer [prɔnɔ̃se], *v.t.*, to pronounce
prononciation [prɔnɔ̃sjɑsjɔ̃], *n.f.*, pronunciation
proposer [prɔpoze], *v.t.*, to propose, to suggest; to move (parliamentary procedure)
proposition [prɔpozisjɔ̃], *n.f.*, proposal, clause; motion (parliamentary procedure)
propre [prɔpr], *adj.*, own (preceding noun); clean (following noun)
propriétaire [prɔprietɛ:r], *n.m. and f.*, owner
protégé, -e [prɔteʒe], *adj.*, protected
protéger [prɔteʒe], *v.t.*, to protect
province [prɔvɛ̃:s], *n.f.*, province
psychologique [psikɔlɔʒik], *adj.*, psychological

public [pyblik], *n.m.*, public
le grand ____, the public at large, the masses
public, -que [pyblik], *adj.*, public
publicité [pyblisite], *n.f.*, advertising
puis [pɥi], *adv.*, then
puisque [pɥiskə], *conj.*, as, since
punir [pyni:r], *v.t.*, to punish

Q

quai [ke], *n.m.*, pier
quand [kɑ̃], *conj.*, when
quantité [kɑ̃tite], *n.f.*, quantity, a great number
quarante [karɑ̃:t], *adj.*, forty
quart [ka:r], *n.m.*, quarter
____ d'heure, quarter of an hour
trois heures et ____, a quarter-past three
sept heures moins un ____, a quarter to seven
quatorze [katɔrz], *adj.*, fourteen
quatre [katr], *adj.*, four
quatre-vingt-dix [katrəvɛ̃dis], *adj.*, ninety
quatre-vingts [katrəvɛ̃], *adj.*, eighty
que [kə], *conj.*, that; *interr. pron.*, what; *rel. pron.*, that, which, whom
ne ____, only
quel, quelle, quels, quelles [kɛl], *adj.*, what, which
quelconque [kɛlkɔ̃:k], *adj.*, some or other, mediocre
quel (quelle, quels, quelles) que [kɛl kə], *adj.*, whatever, whichever
quelque [kɛlkə], *adj.*, some
____ peu, somewhat
____ (adj. or adv.) que, however (adj. or adv.)
quelquefois [kɛlkəfwa], *adv.*, sometimes
quelques-uns [kɛlkəzœ̃], quelques-unes [kɛlkəzyn], *pron.*, a few, some
quelqu'un [kɛlkœ̃], quelqu'une [kɛlkyn], *pron.*, someone; quelques-un(e)s, some (ones)
qu'est-ce que [kɛskə], *interr. pron.*, what (object of verb)
qu'est-ce que c'est que [kɛskəsɛkə], *interr. pron.*, what (used in asking definitions)
qu'est-ce qui [kɛski], *interr. pron.*, what (subject of verb)
question [kɛstjɔ̃], *n.f.*, question
il est ____ de, it is a question of
queue [kø], *n.f.*, tail
faire la ____, to stand in line
qui [ki], *rel. pron.*, who, whom, which, that; *interr. pron.*, who, whom
quiconque [kikɔ̃:k], *pron.*, whoever
qui est-ce que [kiɛskə], *interr. pron.*, whom
qui est-ce qui [kiɛski], *interr. pron.*, who
quinze [kɛ̃:z], *adj.*, fifteen
qui que [kikə], *pron.*, whoever, whomever
quoi [kwa], *interr. pron.*, what (standing alone or after a prep.); *interj.*, what!
quoi que [kwakə], *pron.*, whatever
quoique [kwakə], *conj.*, although

R

raccrocher [racrɔʃe], *v.t.*, to hang up
raconter [rakɔ̃te], *v.t.*, to tell, to relate
radiographie [radjɔgrafi], *n.f.*, X-ray
radiographier [radjɔgrafje], *v.t.*, to X-ray
rafraîchissement [rafrɛʃismɑ̃], *n.m.pl.*, refreshments
raide [rɛd], *adj.*, steep
raison [rɛzɔ̃], *n.f.*, reason
ramasser [ramɑse], *v.t.*, to gather
rame [ram], *n.f.*, ream
rappeler [raple], *v.t.*, to recall, to remind, to call back
se ____, to remember
rayé, -e [rɛje], *adj.*, striped
rayon [rɛjɔ̃], *n.m.*, department, shelf
rayure [rɛjy:r], *n.f.*, stripe, line
réaction [reaksjɔ̃], *n.f.*, reaction
réaliser [realize], *v.t.*, to realize (to cause to materialize)
réalité [realite], *n.f.*, reality
récepteur [resɛptœ:r], *n.m.*, receiver
____ de télévision, television set
recette ([rəsɛt], *n.f.*, recipe
recevoir [rəsəvwa:r], *v.t.*, to receive
recherche [rəʃɛrʃ], *n.f.*, quest, search; *pl.*, research
à la ____ de, looking for
réclame [reklɑ:m], *n.f.*, publicity, advertisement, commercial
faire de la ____, to advertise
recommander [rəkɔmɑ̃de], *v.t.*, to recommend; to register (of mail)

reconnaître [rəkɔnɛ:tr], *v.t.*, to recognize
référence [referɑ̃:s], *n.f.*, reference
réfléchir [refleʃi:r] (à), *v.i.*, to think (about), to give some thought (to)
refuser [rəfyze], *v.t.*, to refuse
régal [regal], *n.m.*, treat
regarder [rəgarde], *v.t.*, to look (at)
régime [reʒim], *n.m.*, diet
  être au ——, to be on a diet
région [reʒjɔ̃], *n.f.*, region
règle [rɛgl], *n.f.*, rule
regretter [rəgrɛte], *v.t.*, to regret, to be sorry
régner [reɲe], *v.i.*, to reign
rejoindre [rəʒwɛ̃:dr], *v.t.*, to rejoin, to reunite
  se ——, to meet (again)
reliure [rəljy:r], *n.f.*, binding
remarquer [rəmarke], *v.t.*, to notice
  faire ——, to show, to point out
remercier [rəmɛrsje], *v.t.*, to thank
remettre [rəmɛ:tr], *v.t.*, to put back, to put again, to hand in, to postpone
  se ——, to recover
  se —— à, to begin again to
remplacer [rɑ̃plase], *v.t.*, to replace
remplir [rɑ̃pli:r], *v.t.*, to fill
rencontre [rɑ̃kɔ̃:tr], *n.f.*, meeting
  aller à la —— de, to go and meet
rencontrer [rɑ̃kɔ̃tre], *v.t.*, to meet
rendre [rɑ̃:dr], *v.t.*, to return, to give back
  se ——, to go, to surrender
renne [rɛn], *n.m.*, reindeer
renommée [rənɔme], *n.f.*, renown, fame
renoncer [rənɔ̃se], *v.i.*, to renounce, to give up (with *à* before the object)
renseigner [rɑ̃sɛɲe], *v.t.*, to teach
  se ——, to find out
rentrer [rɑ̃tre], *v.i.*, to come back, to come in again, to go in again, to re-enter; *v.t.*, to bring in, to take in
répandu, -e [repɑ̃dy], *adj.*, widespread
réparation [reparɑsjɔ̃], *n.f.*, repair
réparer [repare], *v.t.*, to repair
repas [rəpɑ], *n.m.*, meal
repasser [rəpɑse], *v.t.*, to review
repêcher [rəpɛʃe], *v.t.*, to fish out (again)
répondre [repɔ̃:dr], *v.i.*, to answer
  —— à la question, to answer the question
réponse [repɔ̃:s], *n.f.*, answer
reposer [rəpose], *v.t.*, to rest
  se ——, to rest oneself
représenter [rəprezɑ̃te], *v.t.*, to represent
réputation [repytɑsjɔ̃], *n.f.*, reputation
requis, -e [rəki], *adj.*, required
résolu, -e [rezɔly], *adj.*, resolute
ressortir [rɛsɔrti:r], *v.t.*, to bring out again; *v.i.*, to go out again, to come out again
  faire ——, to bring out
restaurant [rɛstɔrɑ̃], *n.m.*, restaurant
reste [rɛst], *n.m.*, rest, remainder
rester [rɛste], *v.i.*, to remain, to stay
retard [rəta:r], *n.m.*, delay, lateness
  en ——, late (for an appointment)
retour [[rətu:r], *n.m.*, return
retourner [rəturne], *v.i.*, to return, to go back
retrouver [rətruve], *v.t.*, to find again, to meet
réunir [reyni:r], *v.t.*, to reunite, to gather
  se ——, to meet
réussir [reysi:r], *v.i.*, to succeed
rêve [rɛ:v], *n.m.*, dream
révélateur [revelatœ:r], révélatrice [revelatris], *adj.*, revealing
révéler [revele], *v.t.*, to reveal
revenir [rəvni:r], *v.i.*, to return, to come back
rêveur [rɛvœ:r], rêveuse [rɛvø:z], *adj.*, dreamy
revoir [rəvwa:r], *v.t.*, to see again
  au ——, good-by, so long
rez-de-chaussée [redʃose], *n.m.*, ground floor
rhume [rym], *n.m.*, cold
riche [riʃ], *adj.*, rich
ridicule [ridikyl], *adj.*, ridiculous
rien [rjɛ̃], *pron.*, nothing, not anything
rigueur [rigœ:r], *n.f.*, rigor, severity
rire [ri:r], *v.i.*, to laugh
robe [rɔb], *n.f.*, dress
roi [rwa], *n.m.*, king
rôle [ro:l], *n.m.*, role
romain [rɔmɛ̃], romaine [rɔmɛn], *adj.*, Roman
roman [rɔmɑ̃], *n.m.*, novel
  —— policier, detective story
rompre [rɔ̃:pr], *v.t.*, to break
rouge [ru:ʒ], *adj.*, red
rougir [ruʒi:r], *v.i.*, to blush

ruine [ryin], *n.f.*, ruin
russe [rys], *adj.*, Russian; *n.m.*, Russian (language)
Russe [rys], *n.m. and f.*, Russian (person)
Russie [rysi], *n.f.*, Russia

S

sa [sa], *poss. adj.*, his, her, its
sac [sak], *n.m.*, bag
 ——— à main, handbag
sain [sɛ̃], saine [sɛn], *adj.*, sound, healthy, wholesome
saisir [sɛzi:r], *v.t.*, to seize
salle [sal], *n.f.*, room
 ——— de bain, bathroom
 ——— de classe, classroom
 ——— d'attente, waiting room
saluer [salɥe], *v.t.*, to greet
samedi [samdi], *n.m.*, Saturday
sandwich [sɑ̃dwitʃ], *n.m.*, sandwich
sans [sɑ̃], *prep.*, without; sans que, *conj.*, without
santé [sɑ̃te], *n.f.*, health
sauter [sote], *v.t.*, to jump, to skip
sauterie [sotri], *n.f.*, dance
sauver [sove], *v.t.*, to save
 se ———, to run along
Savoie [savwa], *n.f.*, Savoy (province in the French Alps)
savoir [savwa:r], *v.t.*, to know
savoyard [savwaja:r], savoyarde [savwajard], *adj.*, of Savoy
Savoyard [savwaja:r], Savoyarde [savwajard], *n.m. and f.*, native of Savoy
scène [sɛ:n], *n.f.*, scene, stage
se [sə], *pron.*, himself, to himself; herself, to herself; themselves, to themselves; oneself, to oneself
sec [sɛk], sèche [sɛʃ], *adj.*, dry
secret [səkrɛ], *n.m.*, secret
secrétaire [səkretɛ:r], *n.m. and f.*, secretary
seize [sɛ:z], *adj.*, sixteen
séjour [seʒu:r], *n.m.*, stay, sojourn
semaine [səmɛn], *n.f.*, week
 par ———, a week, per week
sembler [sɑ̃ble], *v.i.*, to seem, to look, to appear
semestre [səmɛstr], *n.m.*, term, semester
sentir [sɑ̃ti:r], *v.t.*, to feel, to smell
 se ———, to feel (an emotion)
sept [sɛt], *adj.*, seven
septembre [sɛptɑ̃:br], *n.m.*, September
servir [sɛrvi:r], *v.t.*, to serve
 se ——— de, to use
ses [se], *poss. adj.*, his, her, its
seul, -e [sœl], *adj.*, alone
seulement [sœlmɑ̃], *adv.*, only
si [si], *adv.*, so; *conj.*, if
 ——— (adj. or adv.) que, however (adj. or adv.)
sien(s) [sjɛ̃], sienne(s) [sjɛn], *pron.* (used with the *def. art.*), his, hers, its
signe [siɲ], *n.m.*, mark, sign
situation [sitɥɑsjɔ̃], *n.f.*, situation, job
six [sis, si], *adj.*, six
ski [ski], *n.m.*, ski, skiing
skieur [skiœ:r], *n.m.*, skier
sœur [sœ:r], *n.f.*, sister
soi [swa], *pron.*, oneself, themselves
soif [swaf], *n.f.*, thirst
 avoir ———, to be thirsty
soir [swa:r], *n.m.*, evening
soirée [sware], *n.f.*, evening (full evening), party
soixante [swasɑ̃:t], *adj.*, sixty
soixante-dix [swasɑ̃tdis], *adj.*, seventy
sol [sɔl], *n.m.*, soil
soleil [sɔlɛ:j], *n.m.*, sun
solennel, -lle [sɔlanɛl], *adj.*, solemn
solide [sɔlid], *adj.*, solid
solitude [sɔlityd], *n.f.*, solitude
solution (sɔlysjɔ̃], *n.f.*, solution
somme [sɔm], *n.f.*, sum
son [sɔ̃], *poss. adj.*, his, her, its
sonner [sɔne], *v.t. and v.i.*, to ring
sorte [sɔrt], *n.f.*, sort, kind, type
 de ——— que, *conj.*, so that
sortir [sɔrti:r], *v.i.*, to go out, to leave; *v.t.*, to take out
souffrir [sufri:r], *v.t.*, to suffer
 faire ———, to hurt
souhaiter [swɛte], *v.t.*, to wish (for)
soulier [sulje], *n.m.*, shoe
soupe [sup], *n.f.*, soup
 ——— à l'oignon, onion soup
sourire [suri:r], *n.m.*, smile; *v.i.*, to smile
sous [su], *prep.*, under
souvent [suvɑ̃], *adv.*, often
spécial, -e [spesjal], *adj.*, special
spécialiser [spesjalize], se, *v.t.*, to major (in a subject)
spécialité [spesjalite], *n.f.*, specialty

spontané, -e [spɔ̃tane], *adj.*, spontaneous
sport [spɔ:r], *n.m.*, sport
amateur (*m.*) de ——s, sports enthusiast
station [stɑsjɔ̃], *n.f.*, station
—— d'hiver, winter resort
sténographie [stenɔgrafi], *n.f.*, stenography
succès [syksɛ], *n.m.*, success
succomber [sykɔ̃be], *v.i.*, to succumb, to yield, to die
Suisse [sɥis], *n.f.*, Switzerland
suite [sɥit], *n.f.*, continuation
tout de ——, immediately
suivre [sɥi:vr], *v.t.*, to follow
sujet [syʒɛ], *n.m.*, subject
supérieur,-e [syperjœ:r] *adj.*, superior
sur [sy:r], *prep.*, on
sûr, -e [sy:r], *adj.*, sure, certain
bien ——, of course
surmener [syrməne], *v.t.*, to overwork, to overexert
se ——, to overdo it, to overwork
surprise [syrpri:z], *n.f.*, surprise
surtout [syrtu], *adv.*, especially
survoler [syrvɔle], *v.t.*, to fly over
suspendu, -e [syspɑ̃dy], *past part.*, hung

T

table [tabl], *n.f.*, table
tâcher [tɑʃe], *v.i.*, to try
taille-crayon [ta:jkrɛjɔ̃], *n.m.*, pencil sharpener
talent [talɑ̃], *n.m.*, talent
tandis que [tɑ̃diskə], *conj.*, while, whereas
tant [tɑ̃], *adv.*, so much, so many (with de + noun)
tante [tɑ̃:t], *n.f.*, aunt
taper [tape], *v.t.*, to type
taquiner [takine], *v.t.*, to tease
tard [ta:r], *adv.*, late (in the day or night)
tarder [tarde], *v.i.*, to delay
—— à (+ *inf.*), to be long in (+ ——ing)
tarte [tart], *n.f.*, pie
—— aux pommes, apple pie
tas [tɑ], *n.m.*, stack, pile
tasse [ta:s], *n.f.*, cup
te [tə], *pron.*, you, to you
technicien [tɛknisjɛ̃], *n.m.*, technician
tel, -lle [tɛl], *adj.*, such, like
un —— problème, such a problem
téléphone [telefɔn], *n.m.*, telephone
un coup de ——, a ring, a telephone call
téléspectateur [telespɛktatœ:r], téléspectatrice [telespɛktatris], *n.m. and f.*, television viewer
télévision [televizjɔ̃], *n.f.*, television
tellement [tɛlmɑ̃], *adv.*, so, in such a way
tempête [tɑ̃pɛ:t], *n.f.*, storm
temps [tɑ̃], *n.m.*, time, weather
à ——, in time
le —— était à la pluie, it looked like rain
ténacité [tenasite], *n.f.*, tenacity
tenir [təni:r], *v.t.*, to hold, to keep
—— à, to be anxious to
—— de, to take after, to get from
se —— en éveil, to be on the alert
tente [tɑ̃:t], *n.f.*, tent
terme [tɛrm], *n.m.*, term
terminer [tɛrmine], *v.t.*, to finish
terrain [tɛrɛ̃], *n.m.*, land
—— universitaire, campus
tête [tɛ:t], *n.f.*, head
avoir mal à la ——, to have a headache
théâtre [teɑ:tr], *n.m.*, theater
théière [tejɛ:r], *n.f.*, teapot
tien(s) [tjɛ̃], tienne(s) [tjɛn], *pron.* (used with the *def. art.*), yours (fam.)
Tiens! [tjɛ̃], *interj.*, Look! Hold on!
tiers [tjɛ:r], *n.m.*, one third
timbre [tɛ̃:br], *n.m.*, bell, stamp
timbre-poste [tɛ̃brpɔst], *n.m.*, postage stamp
titre [ti:tr], *n.m.*, title
toi [twa], *pron.*, you (familiar)
toit [twɑ], *n.m.*, roof
à —— rayé, with a striped roof
tombeau [tɔ̃bo], *n.m.*, tomb
tomber [tɔ̃be], *v.i.*, to fall
tombola [tɔ̃bɔla], *n.f.*, drawing, raffle
tort [tɔ:r], *n.m.*, wrong
avoir ——, to be wrong
tôt [to], *adv.*, soon
toujours [tuʒu:r], *adv.*, always
touriste [turist], *n.m. and f.*, tourist
tournée [turne], *n.f.*, journey, tour
tous [tu:s], *pron.*, all
tousser [tuse], *v.i.*, to cough

tout [tu], toute [tut], tous [tu], toutes [tut], *adj.*, all, every; *n.*, everything, all; *adv.*, quite
_____ à fait, just, entirely
_____ le monde, everyone, everybody
traditionnel, -le [tradisjɔnɛl], *adj.*, traditional
train [trɛ̃], *n.m.*, train
tranquille [trɑ̃kil], *adj.*, quiet
transporté, -e [trɑ̃spɔrte], *adj.*, transported
travail [travɑ:j], *n.m.*, work, term paper
travailler [travɑje], *v.i.*, to work
travers, [travɛ:r], *n.m.*, breadth, failing
à _____, across, through
de _____, awry, crooked
traverser [travɛrse], *v.t.*, to cross
treize [trɛ:z], *adj.*, thirteen
trente [trɑ̃:t], *adj.*, thirty
très [trɛ], *adv.*, very
tricot [triko], *n.m.*, sweater
triste [trist], *adj.*, sad
trois [trwɑ], *adj.*, three
troisième [trwɑzjɛ:m], *adj.*, third
trombone [trɔ̃bɔn], *n.m.*, paper clip
trop [tro], *adv.*, too, too much, too many (de + noun)
troupe [trup], *n.f.*, troupe, company
trouver [truve], *v.t.*, to find
se _____, to be, to be found
tu [ty], *pron.*, you (familiar form)
tube [tyb], *n.m.*, tube
_____ cathodique, picture tube
type [tip], *n.m.*, type, model

U

un [œ̃], une [yn], *indef. art.*, a; *adj.*, one
unanimité [ynanimite], *n.f.*, unanimity
à l'_____, unanimously
urgent [yrʒɑ̃], urgente [yrʒɑ̃:t], *adj.*, urgent
utile [ytil], *adj.*, useful
utiliser [ytilize], *v.t.*, to use, to utilize

V

vacances [vakɑ̃:s], *n.f.pl.*, holidays, vacation
vallée [vale], *n.f.*, valley
valoir [valwa:r], *v.t.*, to be worth
Ça vaut la peine. That's worth it.
Il vaut mieux que . . . It is better that . . .
vaporisateur [vapɔrizatœ:r], *n.m.*, atomizer
varié, -e [varje], *adj.*, varied
veille [vɛ:j], *n.f.*, eve
la _____ de Noël, Christmas Eve
vendre [vɑ̃:dr], *v.t.*, to sell
vendredi [vɑ̃drədi], *n.m.*, Friday
venir [vəni:r], *v.i.*, to come
vérifier [verifje], *v.t.*, to check, to verify
véritable [veritabl], *adj.*, real
vérité [verite], *n.f.*, truth
verre [vɛ:r], *n.m.*, glass
vers [vɛ:r], *prep.*, toward
verser [vɛrse], *v.t.*, to pour
vert [vɛ:r], verte [vɛrt], *adj.*, green
viande [vjɑ̃:d], *n.f.*, meat
vie [vi], *n.f.*, life
vieiller [vjeji:r], *v.i.*, to grow old
vieux [vjø], vieille [vjɛ:j], *adj.*, old
vif [vif], vive [viv], *adj.*, lively
vilain [vilɛ̃], vilaine [vilɛn], *adj.*, ugly
village [vila:ʒ], *n.m.*, village
ville [vil], *n.f.*, city
villégiature [vileʒjaty:r], *n.f.*, sojourn in the country
en _____, staying in the country
vin [vɛ̃], *n.m.*, wine
vingt [vɛ̃], *adj.*, twenty
violence [vjɔlɑ̃:s], *n.f.*, violence
visiter [vizite], *v.t.*, to visit
visiteur [vizitœ:r], *n.m.*, visitor
vite [vit], *adv.*, quickly
vitesse [vitɛs], *n.f.*, speed
à toute _____, at full speed
vitrail [vitrɑ:j], *n.m.*, stained-glass window
vivre [vi:vr], *v.i.*, to live
voici [vwasi], *adv.*, here is, here are
Me _____. Here I am.
Le _____ qui vient. Here he comes.
voilà [vwala], *adv.*, there is, there are
Le _____. There he is.
voir [vwa:r], *v.t.*, to see
voiture [vwaty:r], *n.f.*, car, automobile
voix [vwa], *n.f.*, voice
vol [vɔl], *n.m.*, flight, robbery
voler [vɔle], *v.t.*, to steal; *v.i.*,to fly
vos [vo], *poss. adj.*, your
votre [vɔtr], *poss. adj.*, your
vôtre(s) [vo:tr] *poss. pron.* (used with the *def. art.*), yours
vouloir [vulwa:r], *v.t.*, to want
_____ bien, to be willing

en ——— à, to have a grudge against
vous [vu], *pron.*, you, to you
voyage [vwaja:ʒ], *n.m.*, trip, voyage
Bon ———. Pleasant journey.
voyager [vwajaʒe], *v.i.*, to travel
voyageur [vwajaʒœ:r], *n.m.*, passenger, traveler
voyelle [vwajɛl], *n.f.*, vowel
vrai, -e [vrɛ], *adj.*, true
à ——— dire, to tell the truth
vraiment [vrɛmɑ̃], *adv.*, really, truly

W

wagon [vagɔ̃], *n.m.*, coach, car (of a train)
le ——— fumoir, the smoking car
le ——— restaurant, the dining car
le ——— lit, the Pullman car

Y

y [i], *adv.*, there, in it, in them, to it, to them
il ——— a, there is, there are

ANSWERS TO THE EXERCISES

CHAPTER ONE

Exercise 1

1. au
2. au
3. à la
4. à la
5. à l'
6. à l'
7. aux
8. aux
9. aux
10. au
11. à la
12. au
13. du
14. du
15. de la
16. de la
17. de l'
18. de l'
19. de l'
20. des
21. des
22. des
23. du
24. de la

Exercise 2

1. le français le lundi
2. le jeudi, le professeur Duval
3. le cours
4. les cours obligatoires, l'histoire
5. Les cours facultatifs
6. la France, l'Allemagne, le Canada
7. à la papeterie
8. la rame
9. dans la poche
10. à la librairie

Exercise 3

1. en mathématiques
2. en français
3. français
4. le français
5. en classe, Allemands, Italiens, Espagnols

Exercise 4

1. un cours obligatoire, ou un cours facultatif
2. un cours facultatif, des cours facultatifs
3. ingénieur, interprète
4. professeur du département de français, un interprète expérimenté
5. Français, un Français qui parle russe et allemand

Exercise 5

1. en France, en Espagne, au Portugal, dans l'Amérique du Sud
2. en France. À Paris, dans la France méridionale
3. à Rome, à Berlin, à Moscou, à Londres, aux États-Unis
4. en Asie, au Japon et en Chine
5. du Mexique, du Brésil, du Canada, et d'Angleterre

Review Exercise

1. La vie universitaire est très agréable cette année.
2. J'ai cinq cours obligatoires et deux cours facultatifs: l'un est la classe d'histoire européenne avec le professeur Roberts et l'autre est l'histoire ancienne avec M. Anderson.
3. Je me spécialise en histoire. Nous avons la classe de littérature anglaise le mardi et le jeudi.
4. Le professeur, auteur bien connu, écrit un livre sur Shakespeare.
5. Les professeurs sont des gens très affairés, je crois.
6. Te spécialises-tu en anglais?
7. Non, en mathématiques. Je veux être ingénieur.
8. Dans notre classe d'algèbre, nous avons pas mal de garçons de France, d'Allemagne et d'Angleterre, deux du Japon et un de l'Amérique du Sud.

9. Trois vont au Canada cette année. Ils ont l'intention de retourner en Europe.
10. La géométrie et l'algèbre doivent être difficiles. Non, elles sont passionnantes.

CHAPTER TWO

Exercise 1

1. la
2. l' (m.)
3. le
4. le or la
5. le
6. le
7. la
8. le
9. le
10. la
11. le
12. la
13. l' (m.)
14. la
15. le
16. la
17. la
18. l' (m.)
19. la
20. le
21. le
22. la
23. le
24. la
25. le
26. la
27. l' (m.)

Exercise 2

1. les héros
2. les gaz
3. les hors-d'œuvre
4. les coupe-papiers
5. les gâteaux
6. les marteaux
7. les clous
8. les taille-crayons
9. les choux-fleurs
10. les beaux-pères
11. les arcs-en-ciel
12. les yeux

Exercise 3

1. du papier carbone
2. de la poésie
3. des romans
4. de la craie
5. des exemplaires d'occasion
6. des cahiers
7. de l'argent
8. de la monnaie
9. des stylos chers
10. des histoires intéressantes

1. des chemises
2. des trombones
3. du papier pour machine à écrire
4. des exemplaires
5. de l'encre
6. de la prose
7. de l'encre bleue
8. des livres brochés
9. du ruban
10. de la monnaie

Exercise 4

1. pas d'exemplaires
2. plus de papier carbone
3. une douzaine de chemises
4. beaucoup de trombones
5. de bons stylos
6. de vieux romans
7. de beaux étalages
8. assez de monnaie
9. de jeunes employés
10. la plupart des journaux
11. beaucoup d'exemplaires or bien des exemplaires
12. quelquechose de bon à lire

Exercise 5

1. en
2. j'en ai
3. en a
4. nous en avons
5. n'en vend

Review Exercise

le, le, le, la, le . . . journaux, gâteaux, taille-crayons, reliures, chefs-d'œuvre . . . J'ai besoin de quelquechose d'important . . . du papier pour machine à écrire, du papier carbone et des chemises . . . assez de papier carbone . . . une anthologie de la poésie française . . . la poésie . . . des exemplaires d'occasion . . . de très beaux livres . . . combien de papier pour machine à écrire . . . une rame de papier . . . des livres brochés, des revues . . . des cahiers . . . d'argent . . . des livres coûteux.

CHAPTER THREE

Exercise 1

1. recommande, choisis, vends
2. apporte, maigrit, attend
3. désirez, remplissez, perdez
4. commandent, salissent, répondent
5. renverses, rougis, entends
6. aimons, finissons, rendons
7. recommande, remplit, répond
8. admirent, choisissent, rendent

Exercise 2

1. commandons
2. attends
3. finit
4. aimez
5. remplissent
6. admires
7. désire
8. choisis
9. recommande
10. perdent
11. salissons
12. rend
13. renverse
14. commandent

Exercise 3

1. Je recommande
2. J'aime
3. J'admire
4. J'admire
5. Nous salissons
6. Il rend
7. Vous attendez depuis dix minutes
8. Ils commandent
9. Nous renversons
10. Vous remplissez
11. Elle aime
12. Il maigrit
13. Tu perds
14. Vous recommandez
15. Je vends

Exercise 4

1. Nous n'aimons pas
2. Je n'attends jamais
3. Vous ne maigrissez point
4. n'aime plus
5. Ils ne finissent guère . . . le garçon apporte
6. Elle ne répond guère
7. Je n'attends pas
8. Il ne recommande jamais
9. Nous rougissons . . . nous renversons . . . nous salissons
10. Elle ne prend jamais

Exercise 5

1. Est-ce que vous aimez
   Aimez-vous
   Vous aimez
2. Est-ce que ces messieurs attendent
   Ces messieurs attendent-ils
   Ces messieurs attendent
3. Est-ce que vous commandez
   Commandez-vous
   Vous commandez
4. Est-ce qu'elle maigrit?
   Maigrit-elle?
   Elle maigrit?
5. Est-ce qu'il choisit
   Choisit-il
   Il choisit

Exercise 6

1. Est-ce que vous n'aimez pas
   N'aimez-vous pas
   Vous n'aimez pas
2. Est-ce que le garçon ne recommande pas
   Le garçon ne recommande-t-il pas
   Le garçon ne recommande pas
3. Est-ce qu'ils ne remplissent pas
   Ne remplissent-ils pas
   Ils ne remplissent pas
4. Est-ce qu'elle n'admire pas
   N'admire-t-elle pas
   Elle n'admire pas
5. Est-ce que je ne commande pas
   Je ne commande pas

Exercise 7

1. Apportez
2. Commandez
3. Ne choisissez pas
4. Répondez

5. Ne salissez pas
6. Attendons
7. Remplissons
8. Ne commandons pas
9. Finissons
10. Vendons
11. Attendez
12. Apportez
13. Rendez
14. Ne commandez pas
15. Finis

Exercise 8

1. J'achète
2. Nous achetons
3. Commençons
4. Nous mangeons
5. Ils préfèrent
6. Vous préférez
7. Elle appelle
8. Nous appelons
9. Il jette
10. Vous jetez
11. Ils commencent
12. Il mange
13. J'essaie
14. Nous nettoyens
15. Ils sèchent

Exercise 9

JE	NOUS	ELLE	VOUS	ILS
vais	allons	va	allez	vont
dors	dormons	dort	dormez	dorment
viens	venons	vient	venez	viennent
connais	connaissons	connaît	connaissez	connaissent
veux	voulons	veut	voulez	veulent
crains	craignons	craint	craignez	craignent
crois	croyons	croit	croyez	croient
dis	disons	dit	dites	disent
mets	mettons	met	mettez	mettent
fais	faisons	fait	faites	font
écris	écrivons	écrit	écrivez	écrivent
lis	lisons	lit	lisez	lisent
sais	savons	sait	savez	savent
dois	devons	doit	devez	doivent
peux	pouvons	peut	pouvez	peuvent
reçois	recevons	reçoit	recevez	reçoivent
vois	voyons	voit	voyez	voient
prends	prenons	prend	prenez	prennent
suis	suivons	suit	suivez	suivent
vis	vivons	vit	vivez	vivent

Review Exercise

1. N'attendons pas plus longtemps. J'appelle le garçon.
2. Garçon, la carte, s'il vous plaît. Commandons la bouillabaisse.
3. Je prends le bifteck. Qu'est-ce que vous commandez?
4. Je choisis les côtelettes d'agneau, avec des carottes, des épinards et du chou-fleur.
5. Garçon, apportez-nous le bifteck et les côtelettes d'agneau, s'il vous plaît.
6. Ah! Le garçon revient. . . . Merci. Commençons, voulez-vous? Nous mangeons toujours bien dans ce petit restaurant.
7. Ne voulez-vous pas de pain? (Est-ce que vous ne voulez pas de pain? Vous ne voulez pas de pain?) Merci, je suis au régime.
8. Vous maigrissez. Depuis quand êtes-vous au régime?
9. Je suis au régime depuis trois semaines.
10. Est-ce que les dames désirent commander le dessert maintenant? (Les

dames désirent-elles commander...? Les dames désirent commander...?) Je recommande la tarte aux pommes ou le flan.

11. Merci, je ne veux pas de dessert. Ne commandez-vous pas de dessert, Jeanne? (Est-ce que vous ne commandez pas...? Vous ne commandez pas de dessert...?)
12. Non, je prends du café.

CHAPTER FOUR

Exercise 1

1. vous le
   les lui
   le lui
   vous en
   leur en
2. nous le
   me les
   m'en
   vous y
   le leur
3. Le leur
   Vous en
   Les lui
   Lui en
   Vous le
4. m'en
   le lui
   nous en
   la leur
   lui en
5. Vous le
   Nous les
   M'en
   Les lui
   Les leur

Exercise 2

1. Ils se racontent
2. Ne vous levez pas!
3. Nous nous parlons
4. Je ne me lève pas
5. Vous demandez-vous?

Exercise 3

1. les — moi
   le — lui
   nous — en
   le — nous
   les — lui
2. les — moi
   les — lui
   nous — en
   les — leur
   les — lui

Exercise 4

1. moi
2. pour eux
3. Présentez-moi à eux
4. Moi je... lui
5. Lui? Présentez-vous à lui

Review Exercise

1. Où est le journal français? Ah, le voilà. Donne-le-moi, veux-tu, Paul?
2. Voici l'annonce. Je te la lis.
3. Grande chambre à deux personnes chez famille française. Rendons-nous-y!
4. Vous avez une grande chambre, madame? Est-ce que nous pourrions la voir?
5. J'en ai deux, messieurs. Je vous les fais voir tout de suite.
6. C'est très tranquille. Serait-il possible d'y mettre un bureau et une lampe?
7. Certainement. Je n'ai qu'à les demander à mon mari.
8. Est-ce qu'il a ces meubles? Oui, il les a dans le grenier.
9. Ne les lui demandez pas aujourd'hui, madame.
10. Nous avons deux autres locataires et il est maintenant chez eux.
11. Moi j'aime la chambre en arrière mais eux préfèrent une chambre à côté de la salle de bain.
12. Avez-vous beaucoup de chambres? Nous en avons six.

CHAPTER FIVE

Exercise 1

1. excellente
2. chère
3. difficile
4. fraîche

5. coûteuse
6. révélatrice
7. ancienne
8. heureuse
9. fausse
10. bonne
11. première
12. nouvelle
13. douce
14. flatteuse
15. exceptionnelle
16. belle
17. vieille
18. candide

Exercise 2

1. une grande cabine
2. de vieilles bandes
3. des disques et des bandes coûteux
4. une bonne prononciation
5. des bibliothèques et des salles de classe excellentes

Exercise 3

1. un grand laboratoire
2. un nouvel exercice
3. un professeur exigeant
4. une prononciation excellente
5. un long devoir
6. un bel enregistrement
7. des théâtres français
8. une diction honteuse
9. un exercice facile
10. une magnifique bibliothèque
11. le pauvre étudiant travaille dur
12. la difficile voyelle *u*
13. un jeune homme intelligent
14. chaque misérable fois
15. les longues voyelles et les courtes voyelles

Exercise 4

1. complètement
2. sèchement
3. infiniment
4. franchement
5. galamment
6. résolument
7. différemment
8. cruellement
9. vivement
10. facilement

Exercise 5

1. toutes grandes . . . plus grandes que
2. plus rapidement que
3. beaucoup plus utile que vous ne le croyez
4. aussi fidèles que
5. moins difficiles que

Review Exercise

1. Nous avons un beau laboratoire nouveau.
2. J'y vais chaque après-midi corriger ma misérable prononciation.
3. J'enregistre deux courts exercices sur le disque magnétique et, si je fais de mauvaises fautes, j'efface l'enregistrement.
4. Je prononce aussi soigneusement que possible parce que je veux avoir une prononciation aussi parfaite que possible.
5. François a une prononciation excellente, mais la prononciation d'Henri est pire que la mienne.
6. C'est un travail plus dur que vous ne le croyez, mais il en vaut la peine.
7. Quand mes précieux enregistrements ont été faits, j'emprunte des bandes intéressantes des grands classiques français.
8. J'écoute les belles voix des fameux acteurs de la Comédie Française.
9. Le temps passe si agréablement.
10. Un jour moi aussi j'aurai une diction distincte et parfaite.

CHAPTER SIX

Exercise 1

1. raccrochais, choisissais, attendais
2. écoutait, remplissait, perdait
3. essayiez, finissiez, entendiez
4. commençaient, réussissaient, répondaient
5. appelais, rougissais, vendais
6. enragions, finissions, perdions
7. sonnait, réussissait, attendait
8. sonnaient, réussissaient, attendaient
9. mangeait, mangions, mangiez
10. plaçais, placions, plaçaient

Exercise 2

allait	faisais
avions	fallait
connaissaient	lisiez
couriez	mettais
croyais	pouvions
devait	prenais
disaient	recevais
dormicz	savaient
écrivions	venaient
envoyais	voyiez
était	voulais

Exercise 3

1. Je composais.
2. Elle finissait.
3. Nous entendions.
4. Ils attendaient depuis dix minutes.
5. Le téléphone sonnait.
6. Répondiez-vous?
7. Il n'écoutait pas.
8. Je n'étais pas libre.
9. Choisissiez-vous?
10. Ils enrageaient.
11. Nous commencions.
12. Elle appelait depuis quinze minutes.
13. Si vous entendiez la question vous y répondriez.
14. Vous réussissiez.
15. Il raccrochait.

Review Exercise

Nous attendions . . . si vous saviez . . . il avait . . . il était libre . . . il allait à la cabine téléphonique . . . il n'avait jamais . . . il composait précisément le numéro . . . il voulait nous appeler . . . étaient toutes prises . . . il voyait . . . était libre . . . il croyait qu'il avait de la chance . . . la ligne était occupée! Il allait . . .

CHAPTER SEVEN

Exercise 1

1. accompagnerai, finirai, vendrai
2. inviterez, remplirez, attendrez
3. passeront, puniront, répondront
4. préparerons, divertirons, entendrons
5. écoutera, rougira, rendra
6. porteras, bâtiras, perdras
7. tâcheront, vieilliront, répondront
8. lancera, divertira, attendra
9. attrapera, finira, attendra
10. attraperont, finiront, attendront

Exercise 2

1. Il lancera
2. J'inviterai
3. Quand vous irez avec Henri
4. Ils finiront
5. expliquera
6. Quand le joueur attrape le ballon
7. Nous porterons
8. Lancerez-vous le ballon?
9. je préparerai une tarte aux pommes
10. je vous l'expliquerai

Exercise 3

1. Il inviterait
2. Ils accompagneraient
3. Je me divertirais
4. Vous finiriez
5. Vous devriez finir
6. Attendriez-vous . . .
7. Voudriez-vous m'expliquer le jeu?
8. Paul ne lui expliquerait pas le football.
9. Serait-il inutile de courir . . .
10. arriverait?

Exercise 4

1. acquerrez, acquerriez
2. irai, irais
3. aura, aurait
4. courrez, courriez
5. cueilleront, cueilleraient
6. devrai, devrais
7. enverrons, enverrions
8. seront, seraient
9. feras, ferais
10. faudra, faudrait
11. mourra, mourrait
12. pleuvra, pleuvrait
13. pourrai, pourrais
14. recevrez, recevriez
15. sauront, sauraient
16. vaudront, vaudraient
17. viendrons, viendrions
18. verrai, verrais
19. voudrez, voudriez

Review Exercise

Marianne accompagnera Henri à la partie de football . . . elle n'y comprenda rien ... Mais il le lui expliquera ... L'expliquerait-il à sa sœur ... Oui, il le ferait ... il lui fera un petit dessin ... Quand tu iras au jeu, voici ce que tu verras! ... Il y aura naturellement deux équipes ... On lancera le ballon ... qui l'attrapera courra ... Dès qu'il se mettra (commencera) à courir . . . tâcheront de l'empêcher ... pourra ... peut-être qu'il faudra ... Courra-t-il ... il serait inutile ... Tu apprendras ... lorsque tu verras ... Tu te divertiras ... Tu ne devrais pas avoir.

CHAPTER EIGHT

Exercise 1

1. J'ai attrapé
2. Vous avez fini
3. Elle a attendu
4. Ils ont recommandé
5. Nous n'avons pas choisi
6. Tu n'as pas perdu
7. Je n'ai pas appelé
8. Vous avez taquiné
9. Avons-nous essayé?
10. A-t-il parlé?
11. N'êtes-vous pas parti?
12. N'est-elle pas venue?
13. Il est resté
14. Vous êtes allé
15. Il n'est pas tombé
16. Êtes-vous arrivé?
17. Je suis entré
18. Tu es descendu
19. Il s'est reposé
20. Je me suis gargarisé
21. Vous vous êtes remis
22. Se sont-ils reposé la voix?
23. Il ne s'est pas remis
24. Vous vous êtes plaint

Exercise 2

qu'elle a attrapée ... elle a complètement perdu la voix ... a-t-il recommandée? Il lui a fait une injection ...

Exercise 3

1. est arrivée ... elle n'est pas entrée
2. elle est allée ... Ta sœur est-elle restée à la maison aujourd'hui?
3. n'est pas venue. Elle n'est pas sortie
4. sont descendus

Exercise 4

... s'est plainte ... qu'elle s'est reposé la voix et s'est complètement remise ... se sont parlé ... lui a dit ... s'est dit ...

Exercise 5

Nous avons attendu ... elle n'est pas venue ... qu'elle a attrapée ... elle est restée à la maison. Le médecin lui a donné ... elle s'est gargarisée. L'injection qu'il lui a faite ... Elle s'est presque complètement remise ... Je l'ai appelée et je l'ai entendue parler ... qu'elle s'est reposé la voix ... Son frère l'a-t-il taquinée? ... Ah, la paix qui est descendue sur notre maison! Jeannine n'est pas allée

j'ai eu
vous avez connu
ils ont couru
nous avons cru
elle a dû
elles ont dit
vous avez écrit
il a été
j'ai fait
il a fallu
nous avons lu
ils ont mis
vous avez ouvert
j'ai pris
il a reçu
elles ont su
nous sommes venus
vous avez vécu
j'ai vu
elles ont voulu

CHAPTER NINE

Exercise 1

A. The Future Perfect

1. J'aurai gardé
2. Vous aurez choisi
3. Il aura entendu
4. Elle aura préparé
5. Nous serons arrivés
6. Ils seront sortis

B. The Pluperfect

1. J'avais gardé
2. Vous aviez choisi

3. Il avait entendu
4. Elle avait préparé
5. Nous étions arrivés
6. Ils étaient sortis

C. The Conditional Perfect

1. J'aurais gardé
2. Vous auriez choisi
3. Il aurait entendu
4. Elle aurait préparé
5. Nous serions arrivés
6. Ils seraient sortis

Exercise 2

. . . aurait découvert . . . elle aurait consulté . . . Si elle avait seulement gardé . . . elle n'aurait pas rencontré . . . avait-elle choisi . . . s'était-elle décidée . . . Est-ce que son travail aurait mieux marché si elle avait gardé . . . Si seulement elle s'était servie d' . . . aurait été . . . Si Marianne n'avait pas laissé . . . elle aurait pu sortir . . . Lorsqu'elle aura vérifié . . . Aussistôt que le travail aura été tapé . . . Lorsque vous aurez fini . . . Si je n'avais pas passé . . . J'aurais déjà fini mon travail.

CHAPTER TEN

Exercise 1

1. Si vous aimez . . . vous la trouverez
2. Si nous n'avons pas . . . nous n'allumerons pas
3. Si Mme Desjardins donne . . . il pourra l'envoyer

Exercise 2

1. Laurent priserait . . . s'il savait
2. avait . . . serait-ce
3. La dinde serait-elle . . . si nous n'avions pas

Exercise 3

1. Si Mme Desjardins n'avait pas invité . . . il aurait passé
2. n'était pas allée . . . n'aurait pu
3. Si Laurent n'était pas venu . . . n'auraient pas fait

Exercise 4

1. . . . nous trouverions que nous avons bien des bénédictions.
2. . . . nous ne pourrons pas voir la belle flamme bleue.
3. . . . elle n'aurait pas pu l'allumer.
4. . . . ce ne serait plus un régal.
5. . . . Mme Desjardins n'aurait jamais trouvé cette belle recette.

Review Exercise

Si Laurent n'avait pas fait la connaissance de Marianne et Paul . . . aurait été . . . Comment aurait-il passé le Jour d'Actions de grâces . . . ne l'avaient pas invité à prendre le dîner . . . Où serait-il allé? Comment se serait-il diverti? S'il n'avait pas ces bons amis, il serait certainement . . . Si Marianne et Paul et leurs parents vont . . . Laurent et sa mère les recevront . . .

CHAPTER ELEVEN

Exercise 1

1. ce
2. ces
3. cette
4. cet
5. ce
6. ce
7. cet
8. ce
9. ces
10. cette
11. cette
12. cette
13. ce
14. ces
15. cette
16. ce vol-ci, ce vol-là
17. ces avions-ci, ces avions-là
18. ce décollage-ci, ces décollages-là
19. ces hélices-ci, ces hélices-là
20. cet atterrissage-ci, cet atterrissage-là

Exercise 2

1. celui
2. ceux
3. celle-là
4. ceux-là
5. celui
6. ceux
7. celui-ci, celui-là

8. celles-ci, celles-là
9. celle-ci, celle-là
10. celui-ci, ceux-là
11. ceci
12. cela or ça

Exercise 3

1. each plane
2. some of the pilots
3. you can ask anyone
4. each of the take-offs
5. anyone will tell you
6. whoever takes a jet
7. some plane or other
8. some runways
9. I would fly anywhere
10. several hours

Exercise 4

1. Je dois
2. Ils devaient
3. Vous avez dû attendre.
4. Vous auriez dû arriver.
5. Il devrait voler.
6. Est-ce que je dois remettre?
7. Devait-elle atterrir?
8. Avez-vous dû voler? or Deviez-vous voler?
9. Je ne devrai pas attendre.
10. L'avion n'aurait pas dû décoller.
11. Le jet ne devrait-il pas arriver?
12. Nous n'aurions pas dû attendre.

Review Exercise

. . . devait . . . Il a dû . . . il aurait dû . . . doit . . . Il devrait . . . ce doit être celui de Georges . . . celui-ci ou celui-là. Celui-là, celui . . . cela (ça) . . . quelques-uns . . . plusieurs différences . . . Ceux qui ont . . . ceux qui ont celles . . . Ce jet atterrit . . . Ce . . . Chaque fois . . . quelques voyageurs . . .

CHAPTER TWELVE

Exercise 1

son	leur	mon
sa	vos	ses
notre	son	votre
ses	ton	ses
		leurs

Exercise 2

1.	mon	ma	mon
	ma	mes	mes
	mon	mon	mon
	mes	mon	mes
			mes
2.	son	sa	son
	sa	ses	ses
	son	son	son
	ses	son	ses
			ses
3.	votre	votre	votre
	votre	vos	vos
	votre	votre	votre
	vos	votre	vos
			vos
4.	Same as 2.		
5.	notre	notre	notre
	notre	nos	nos
	notre	notre	notre
	nos	notre	nos
			nos
6.	leur	leur	leur
	leur	leurs	leurs
	leur	leur	leur
	leurs	leur	leurs
			leurs

Exercise 3

1. le sien
2. le nôtre
3. la mienne
4. les vôtres
5. la sienne
6. le mien
7. la vôtre
8. les leurs
9. le leur
10. les miennes

Exercise 4

le mien, la mienne, les miens, les miennes
le sien, la sienne, les siens, les siennes
le nôtre, la nôtre, les nôtres, les nôtres
le sien, la sienne, les siens, les siennes
le leur, la leur, les leurs, les leurs
le vôtre, la vôtre, les vôtres, les vôtres

Exercise 5

. . . ma liste . . . mon amie . . . sa liste. ses étrennes . . . les miennes . . . les vôtres? Mon frère . . . les siennes . . . les leurs . . . mon père . . . la sienne . . . ma mère . . . le sien . . . sa . . . ma . . . mon . . . la vôtre

. . . son . . . nos . . . les nôtres . . . vos amis . . . les leurs . . . nos

Exercise 6

quatre	soixante-cinq
quinze	soixante-douze
vingt	quatre-vingt-sept
vingt-six	quatre-vingt-treize
quarante-neuf	cent trente-six
cinquante-huit	un million trois mille

troisième
cinquième
vingt-neuvième
trente-septième
cinquante-deuxième
quatre-vingt-treizième

1. Il est onze heures. Il est onze heures cinq. Il est onze heures et quart. Il est onze heures et demie. Il est midi moins le (or un) quart. Il est midi.
2. C'est aujourd'hui le quatorze décembre, dix-neuf cent soixante-cinq (or mil neuf cent soixante-cinq).
3. une cinquantaine
4. est longue de deux pieds et large d'un pied (or a deux pieds de long sur un pied de large)
5. Il a cinq ans.
6. Oui, il est d'un an plus âgé.
7. Louis Neuf, Henri Quatre, Louis Quatorze, François Premier.
8. à dix heures.
9. quatre-vingts . . . cinquante . . . soixante

CHAPTER THIRTEEN

Exercise 1

1. que
2. qui
3. que
4. qui
5. que

Exercise 2

1. dans laquelle or où
2. devant lequel
3. ce qui . . . ce sont
4. quoi
5. tout ce qu'
6. dont
7. pour l'agilité de qui
8. ce dont . . . c'est
9. qui
10. que
11. à qui
12. ce dont

Review Exercise

. . . dont la beauté naturelle . . . parmi les pics neigeux desquelles, où (or dans lequel) . . . qui . . . lesquels . . . dans lesquels (or où) . . . tout ce qu'il a écrit . . . qui . . . ce qui attire . . . sur lesquelles . . . qui (or lesquels).

CHAPTER FOURTEEN

Exercise 1

1. Qu'est-ce que c'est qu'
2. Que
3. Quels
4. Qui or qui est-ce qui
5. Laquelle
6. Qui est-ce que
7. quoi
8. Qu'est-ce que
9. Qu'est-ce qui
10. Qu'

Review Exercise

. . . quelle . . . Que . . . Quoi? . . . qu'est-ce que c'est qu' . . quelle est . . . à qui . . . qu'est-ce qu' . . . Que . . . Qui or qui est-ce qui . . . Qu'est-ce qui . . . Laquelle . . . De quoi . . .

CHAPTER FIFTEEN

Exercise 1

1. C'est
2. Elle est
3. Il est
4. C'est
5. C'était lui
6. qu'elles étaient saines . . . ce n'était pas vrai
7. elles sont
8. sera-t-il possible
9. ce sera
10. c'est . . . ce doit être

Exercise 2

1. Le dentiste fait radiographier la dent.
   Le dentiste la fait radiographier.
   Le dentiste la fait radiographier par l'infirmière.
   Le dentiste la lui fait radiographier.
   Faites radiographier la dent par le dentiste.
   Faites-lui radiographier la dent.
   Faites-la-lui radiographier.
2. Le dentiste a fait radiographier la dent.
   Le dentiste l'a fait radiographier.
   Le dentiste l'a fait radiographier par l'infirmière.
   Le dentiste la lui a fait radiographier.
3. Le dentiste fera radiographier la dent.
   Le dentiste la fera radiographier.
   Le dentiste la fera radiographier par l'infirmière.
   Le dentiste la lui fera radiographier.

Exercise 3

1. Faites-les examiner par le dentiste.
2. que j'ai fait plomber
3. il nous fera attendre
4. Faites-lui examiner
5. Je le lui ai fait examiner
6. Il vous fera entrer
7. Il le leur fait écrire
8. Il le lui fait toujours écrire
9. il me la fera voir
10. faire arracher la dent . . . la faire creuser

Review Exercise

C'est une molaire . . . faire arracher. L'as-tu fait radiographier . . . ? . . . elle est . . . qu'il est impossible . . . faire arracher une dent . . . la faire creuser . . . Il est mon dentiste . . . Ils sont . . . C'est le guignon . . . C'est embêtant . . . c'est de la patience.

CHAPTER SIXTEEN

Exercise 1

1. trouvai, finis, rendis
2. attirâtes, enrichîtes, attendîtes
3. observa, réussit, vendit
4. étudiâmes, punîmes, entendîmes
5. fondèrent, réunirent, perdirent
6. succombas, accueillis, répandis
7. se surmenèrent, se réunirent, s'attendirent
8. pria, finit, rendit

Exercise 2

1. fonda
2. ne réussit pas
3. se réfugièrent
4. enrichirent
5. Il y trouva
6. Les acteurs établirent
7. revinrent . . . accueillit
8. Il accorda
9. Il donna
10. se répandit

Exercise 3

1. acquîtes
2. alla
3. eûmes
4. coururent
5. cueillis
6. dut
7. envoyèrent
8. fûmes
9. fit
10. . . .
11. moururent
12. . . .
13. pûtes
14. reçut
15. surent
16. valus
17. vinrent
18. vîmes
19. voulut

Exercise 4

j'eus inspiré	je fus allé
vous eûtes enrichi	vous fûtes venu
elle eut répondu	elle fut arrivée
nous eûmes protégé	nous fûmes rentrés
tu eus établi	tu fus resté
ils eurent perdu	ils furent partis

Exercise 5

1. À peine Molière eut-il obtenu . . . qu'il abandonna
2. Après que Molière et sa troupe furent allés . . . il trouva

3. Aussitôt que l'Illustre Théâtre eut attiré . . . une pension fut accordée
4. Quand la troupe eut établi . . . Molière et les acteurs retournèrent
5. Après qu'il fut parvenu . . . Molière succomba

Exercise 6

Notre conférencier est-il arrivé . . .? Oui, Marguerite, lui et un autre professeur sont venus il y a une demi-heure. Ils bavardaient avec notre directeur dans son bureau. Il faisait des cours . . . naquit . . . Il entreprit . . . il l'abandonna . . . établit . . . Molière et ses acteurs ne trouvèrent pas . . . ils décidèrent . . . il observait . . . Il passait . . . C'était . . . établit sa réputation . . . trouva . . .

CHAPTER SEVENTEEN

Exercise 1

1. répare, remplisse, perde
2. monte, choisisse, entende
3. manquiez, punissiez, vendiez
4. doutent, se divertissent, attendent
5. fermes, finisses, vendes
6. regardions, nous réunissions, rendions
7. desserre, réussisse, descende
8. coûtent, éclaircissent, rendent

Exercise 2

1. prenne, prenions
2. vienne, veniez
3. buviez, boive
4. fassent, fasse
5. voies, voyions
6. disions, dise
7. sache, sachiez
8. aillent, allions
9. doive, deviez
10. ouvre
11. puissent
12. craigne

Exercise 3

1. aie manqué
   aie choisi
   aie répondu
2. soit arrivée
   se soit divertie
   soit descendue
3. ayez fermé
   ayez fini
   ayez perdu
4. soient montés
   se soient réunis
   aient attendu
5. aies écouté
   aies réussi
   aies entendu
6. ayons regardé
   soyons partis
   ayons vendu
7. ait desserré
   soit sorti
   ait rendu
8. aient coûté
   aient éclairci
   aient répandu

Exercise 4

1. Je voudrais que vous puissiez voir
2. Paul veut examiner . . . qu'il mette la main sur l'appareil.
3. nous changions de programme . . . voulez-vous attendre
4. cela n'empêchera pas que mon père voie
5. que les programmes soient interrompus . . . veut voir?

Exercise 5

1. qu'il y ait
2. le dépanneur vienne avant cinq heures.
3. que la tempête de la semaine passée ait desserré l'antenne.

Exercise 6

1. J'ai peur
2. Je suis content
3. Je m'étonne
4. C'est dommage
5. regrettent

Exercise 7

1. que nous fassions venir le dépanneur.
2. que le tube cathodique soit garanti?
3. que nous ne soyons pas obligés de le remplacer nous-mêmes.
4. que le dépanneur examine immédiatement l'antenne.
5. que nous puissions avoir notre programme après tout.

Exercise 8

1. prennent plaisir à
2. que ce soit
3. qu'on puisse
4. devraient être plus variés
5. n'ont pas

Exercise 9

1. Si intéressante que soit l'émission
2. si bon que soit le jeu
3. Qui que nous soyons
4. Si longues qu'aient été les réclames
5. Quoi que cet acteur ait dit et quoi qu'il ait fait

Review Exercise

Je doute que vous puissiez deviner . . . C'est dommage que vous n'ayez pas été avec nous, mais il a été impossible de vous le faire savoir . . . Je crois qu'il est impossible que les téléspectateurs s'imaginent . . . Si simple (or peu compliquée) que soit la scène, il semble qu'on se serve . . . Il est étonnant qu'on ait besoin de . . . Il se peut que ce ne soit qu'une réclame . . . on est étonné de voir . . . On défend que les invités fassent signe de la main . . . il est important qu'ils applaudissent . . . qu'ils répondent . . . il convient que les invités obéissent à . . . Je suis bien content que Paul ait pu avoir . . . je regrette que nous les ayons obtenus si tard et que nous soyons allés sans vous . . . quelque interruption que ce soit . . . Mais, je ne crois pas que le téléspectateur se rende compte de . . . Je doute que la plupart d'entre nous désirions être . . .

CHAPTER EIGHTEEN

Exercise 1

1. de sorte que le détective puisse être plus admiré.
2. sans être prête à le saisir avant qu'il soit entré dans la banque.
3. Pourvu que le candidat ait une connaissance de la dactylographie
4. de sorte qu'elle aussi peut être une secrétaire bilingue
5. À moins que le candidat puisse offrir le français et l'espagnol

Exercise 2

1. ne veut pas de candidats qui ne puissent offrir
2. Il n'y a pas de roman policier où la police soit plus intelligente
3. Il n'y a personne qui lise plus de romans policiers
4. Ce n'est pas que Laurent n'ait pu trouver un poste
5. Nous n'avons jamais eu de candidat qui soit venu ici

Exercise 3

1. des promesses qui soient
2. une maison française qui ait besoin d'un comptable
3. une maison américaine qui soit bien connue et qui puisse offrir un bon salaire
4. un poste qui me permette d'employer . . . que vous avez trouvé pour moi
5. une jeune fille qui lise les petites annonces plus attentivement

Exercise 4

1. le jeune homme le plus ambitieux qu'on puisse trouver.
2. la plus grande collection de romans policiers que j'aie jamais vue.
3. Le seul roman policier que Laurent ait jamais lu
4. la lecture la plus intéressante qu'on puisse faire.
5. La meilleure chose que vous puissiez étudier

Exercise 5

1.	demandasse	saisisse
2.	glissât	finît
3.	annonçassiez	remplissiez
4.	encourageassent	salissent
5.	découpasses	embellisses
6.	nous moquassions	choisissions
7.	désirât	choisît
8.	utilisissent	finissent

perdisse
attendît
entendissiez
rendissent
répondisses
vendissions
attendît
répondissent

Review Exercise

1. Avant que Laurent fût entré (soit entré), Marianne et Paul lisaient.
2. Marianne avait acheté un nouveau roman policier qu'elle espérait terminer ce soir-là.
3. "C'est l'intrigue la plus passionnante que j'aie jamais lue," dit-elle à Paul, "et j'en cherchais précisément un qui ait un dénouement différent.
4. Je n'aime pas une intrigue qui soit facile à deviner.
5. Le meilleur roman policier qui ait jamais été écrit c'en était un que j'ai lu il y a quelques années.
6. Une froide journée d'hiver en janvier, une femme fut tuée.
7. Les seules choses qu'on ait trouvées c'étaient un verre renversé qui avait contenu de l'eau, un livre et une tache sur le tapis.
8. Elle avait été poignardée, mais il n'y avait pas d'arme que la police pût (ait pu) voir, de sorte qu'il était vraiment difficile de savoir par où commencer.
9. On s'est mis en contact avec tous les parents et les amis et même les connaissances qui pussent (puissent) les aider.
10. Mais il n'y avait personne qui connût (ait connu) un mobile qui expliquât (explique) le meurtre.
11. On attendit que l'analyse revînt (soit revenue) du laboratoire.
12. A moins qu'on y trouvât (trouve) quelqu'indication qui leur donnât (donne) une idée, le cas ne pourrait pas être résolu.
13. Mais quand on reçut le rapport on apprit que la tache était — de l'eau!
14. Tout à coup, un des détectives de la police eut une idée. De l'eau! L'hiver!
15. La seule solution qui fût (ait été) possible c'était que l'arme était un glaçon.
16. Et en effet c'était la piste qui leur a donné la solution.
17. La femme avait été poignardée par un glaçon.
18. "Je ne l'aurais jamais deviné!" s'écria Marianne. "C'est l'intrigue la plus originale que j'aie jamais entendue!"

CHAPTER NINETEEN

Exercise 1

1. seront faits par les garçons.
2. ont été préparés par les jeunes filles.
3. ont été commandées.
4. était offerte
5. est aimé des étudiants et des professeurs.

Exercise 2

1. On mettra de jolies petites tables
2. On tirera les prix
3. On a construit une grande tente
4. on donne une belle voiture
5. Bien qu'on n'ait pas encore commencé

Exercise 3

1. s'illumine
2. La couleur de l'eau se change en rouge
3. Une jolie Citroën se voit
4. des billets se vendaient
5. s'ajouteront

Review Exercise

1. À cette université, le carnaval est une institution qui est aimée de tous.
2. Il est promu par les professeurs, les étudiants, les amis, et même les marchands du voisinage.
3. Des prix y sont contribués par quelques-unes des grandes maisons.
4. Les décors sont fournis par les garçons, et les rafraîchissements sont préparés par les jeunes filles.
5. Pour l'occasion, on donne d'habitude aux étudiants des gâteaux et des boissons non-alcooliques et de la glace.
6. L'année passée, les fontaines ont été illuminées et des lanternes ont été suspendues à travers la promenade (Or, L'année passée, on a illuminé les fontaines et on a suspendu des lanternes . . .)

7. Toutes les belles couleurs de l'arc-en-ciel étaient reflétées (or, se reflétaient) dans le ciel comme les feux d'artifice éclataient dans l'obscurité de la nuit.
8. C'était si beau!

CHAPTER TWENTY

Exercise 1

1. Aller en France, après y avoir songé si longtemps
2. Passer deux mois à Paris et voir
3. Aimez-vous visiter les musées?... j'aime visiter les musées et voyager
4. Après être restés à Saint-Jean-de-Maurienne... sans voir nos amis.
5. Voir c'est croire!

Exercise 2

1. Marianne et sa mère tâchent de trouver
2. Elles ont oublié de s'orienter
3. Elle n'est pas facile à trouver
4. qui peut les aider à arriver au
5. Si elles lui demandent de leur montrer le chemin, il leur dira de retourner
6. Il est intéressant de voir
7. Et il est saisissant de se trouver à bord
8. j'espère visiter
9. je compte passer l'été entier à visiter
10. La mère de mon ami m'a invité à passer l'été
11. je réussirai à économiser ... pour pouvoir faire le voyage
12. Je voudrais pouvoir aller voir tous les endroits

Exercise 3

1. C'est en voyageant
2. Ayant vu ... tout en appréciant
3. En passant ... on finit par parler
4. Et tout en se divertissant
5. En économisant votre argent

Review Exercise

1. En traversant la passerelle, Marianne s'est rendu compte que son plus doux rêve allait se réaliser.
2. Avec sa mère, elle espérait passer l'été à voir Paris et à voyager à tous les endroits que son père leur avait dit de voir.
3. Aller visiter son village natal dans la Savoie serait un des moments les plus saisissants du voyage.
4. Mais elle et sa mère oubliaient qu'elles devraient se dépêcher car elles avaient invité des amis à venir célébrer l'occasion.
5. Étant montées jusqu'au Pont A, elles ont tâché de trouver leur cabine mais elles n'ont pas pu réussir à y arriver.
6. Il valait mieux demander au mousse de les aider à la trouver.
7. Elles venaient de passer par la piscine quand elles ont vu Paul et il a commencé (or, s'est mis) à crier: "Bon voyage, Maman! Bon voyage, Marianne!"

INDEX